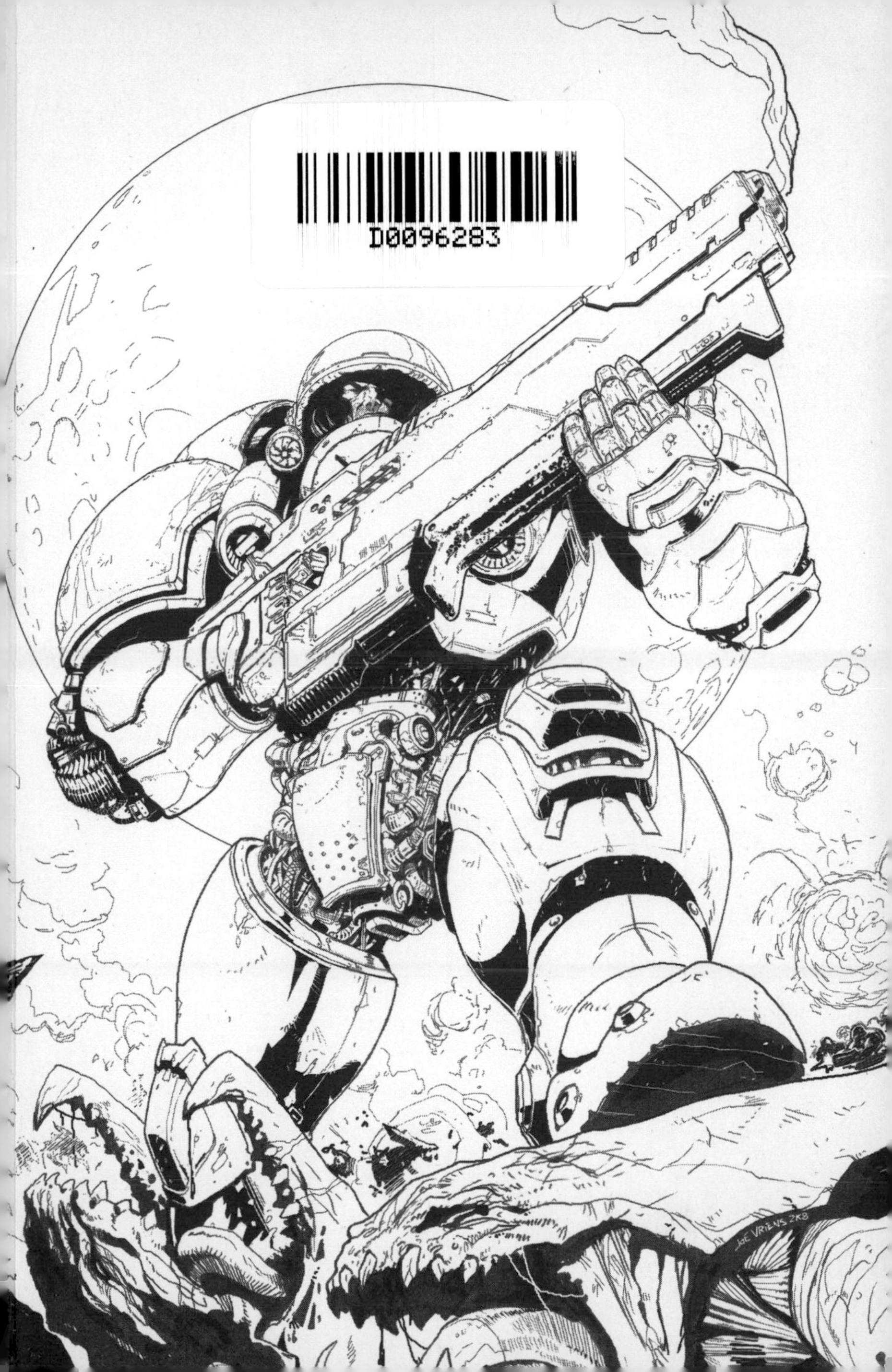
JOE VRIENS 2K8

Copy Editor - Jessica Chavez
Layout and Lettering - Michael Paolilli and Lucas Rivera
Creative Consultant - Michael Paolilli
Graphic Designer - Louis Csontos
Cover Artist - UDON with Saejin Oh and Joe Vriens

Editor - Paul Morrissey
Digital Imaging Manager - Chris Buford
Pre-Production Supervisor - Vince Rivera
Art Director - Al-Insan Lashley
Managing Editor - Vy Nguyen
Editor-in-Chief - Rob Tokar
Publisher - Mike Kiley
President and C.O.O. - John Parker
C.E.O. and Chief Creative Officer - Stu Levy

BLIZZARD ENTERTAINMENT

Senior Vice President, Creative Development - Chris Metzen
Manager, Creative Development - Shawn Carnes
Story Consultation and Development - Micky Neilson
Art Director - Glenn Rane
Director, Global Business
Development and Licensing - Cory Jones
Associate Licensing Manager - Jason Bischoff
Additional Development - Samwise Didier, Evelyn Fredericksen,
Ben Brode, Sean Wang
Blizzard Special Thanks - Brian Hsieh, Gina Pippin

A **TOKYOPOP** Manga

TOKYOPOP and ⊙ are trademarks or registered trademarks of TOKYOPOP Inc.

TOKYOPOP Inc.
5900 Wilshire Blvd. Suite 2000
Los Angeles, CA 90036

E-mail: info@TOKYOPOP.com
Come visit us online at www.TOKYOPOP.com

ISBN: 978-1-4278-0721-2

First TOKYOPOP printing: August 2008

10 9 8 7 6 5 4 3 2 1

Printed in the USA

STARCRAFT

FRONTLINE

VOLUME 1

TOKYOPOP®

HAMBURG // LONDON // LOS ANGELES // TOKYO

STARCRAFT

FRONTLINE
VOLUME 1

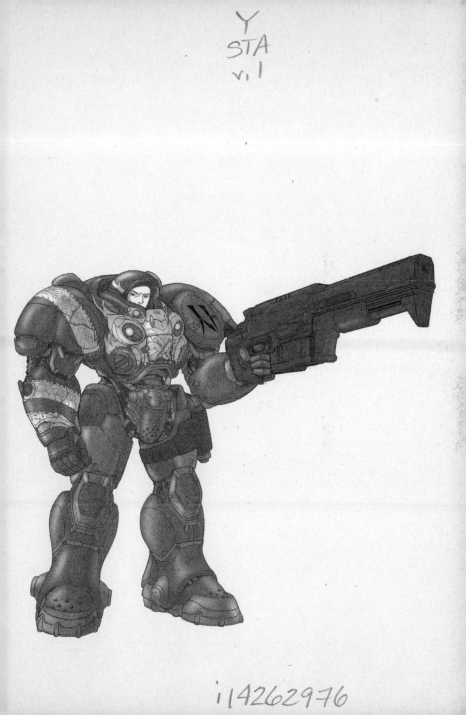

Y
STA
v.1

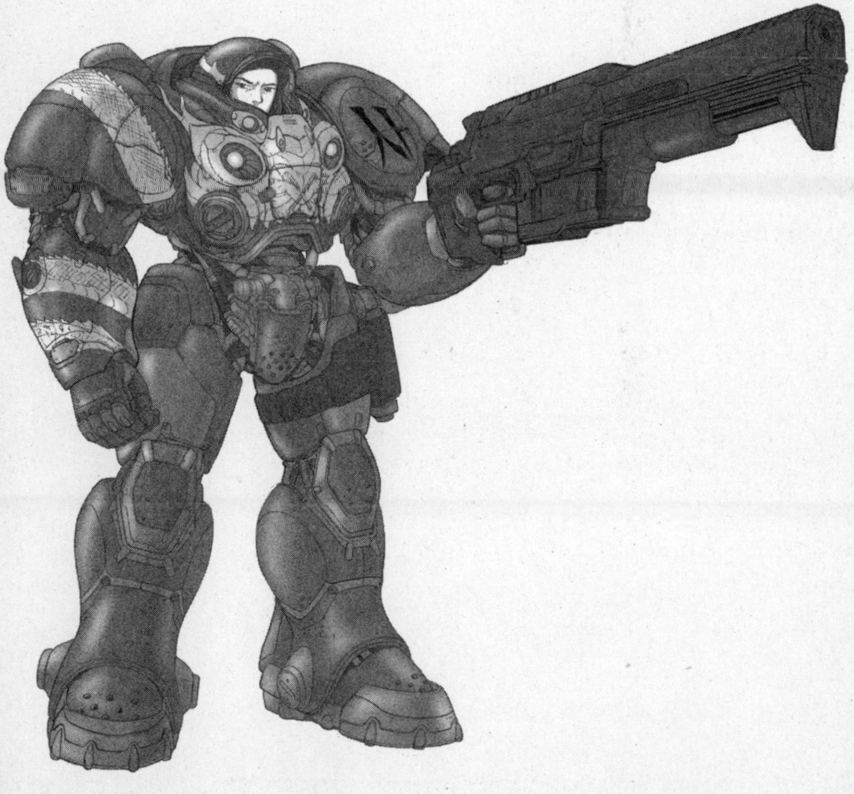

i14262976

STARCRAFT

FRONTLINE
VOLUME 1

WHY WE FIGHT

Written by Josh Elder

Pencils by Ramanda Kamarga

Inks by Erfian Asafat, Chris Lie and Lius Lasahido
of CARAVAN STUDIO

Tones by Erfian Asafat of CARAVAN STUDIO

Associate Editor: Jessica Chavez
Letterer: Michael Paolilli

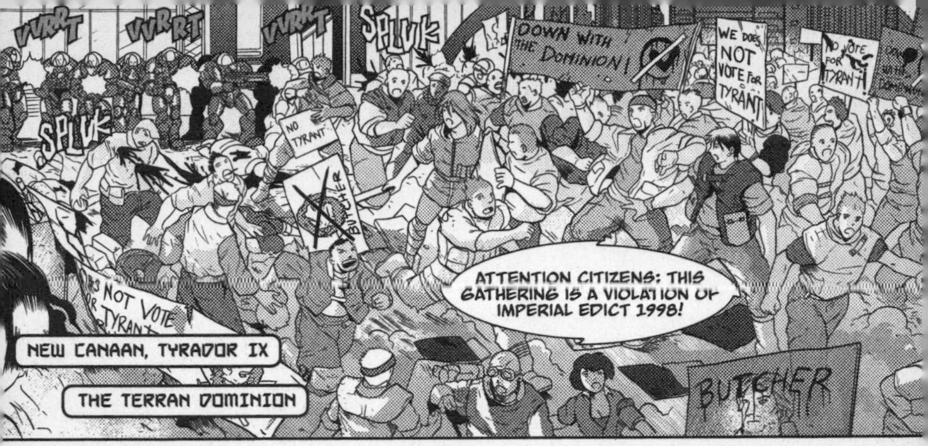
VVRRT
VVRRT
VVRKT
SPLUK
DOWN WITH THE DOMINION!
WE DOES NOT VOTE FOR TYRANT
NO VOTE FOR TYRANT
SPLUK
NO TYRANT
BUTCHER
ATTENTION CITIZENS: THIS GATHERING IS A VIOLATION OF IMPERIAL EDICT 1998!
NEW CANAAN, TYRADOR IX
THE TERRAN DOMINION
BUTCHER

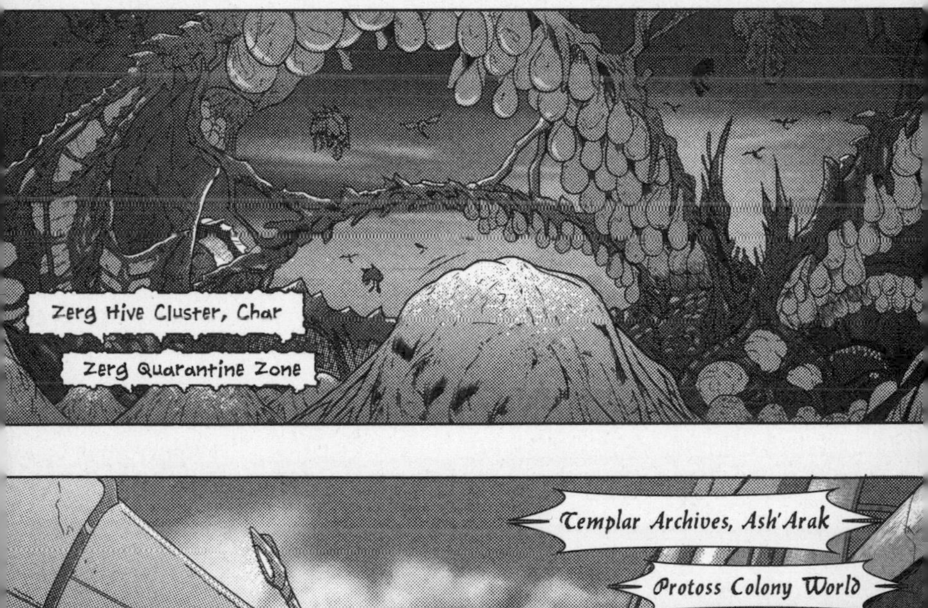
Zerg Hive Cluster, Char
Zerg Quarantine Zone

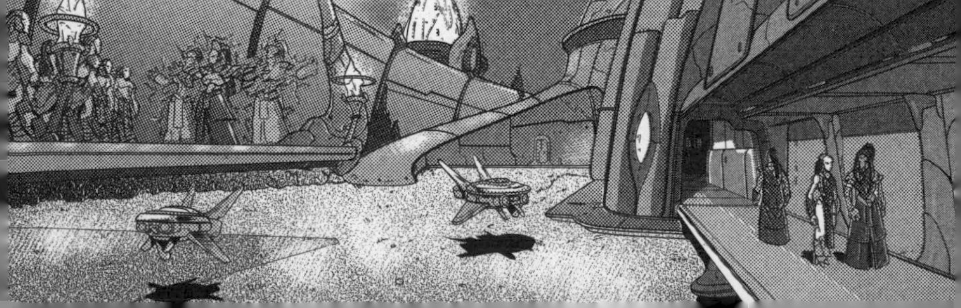
Templar Archives, Ash'Arak
Protoss Colony World

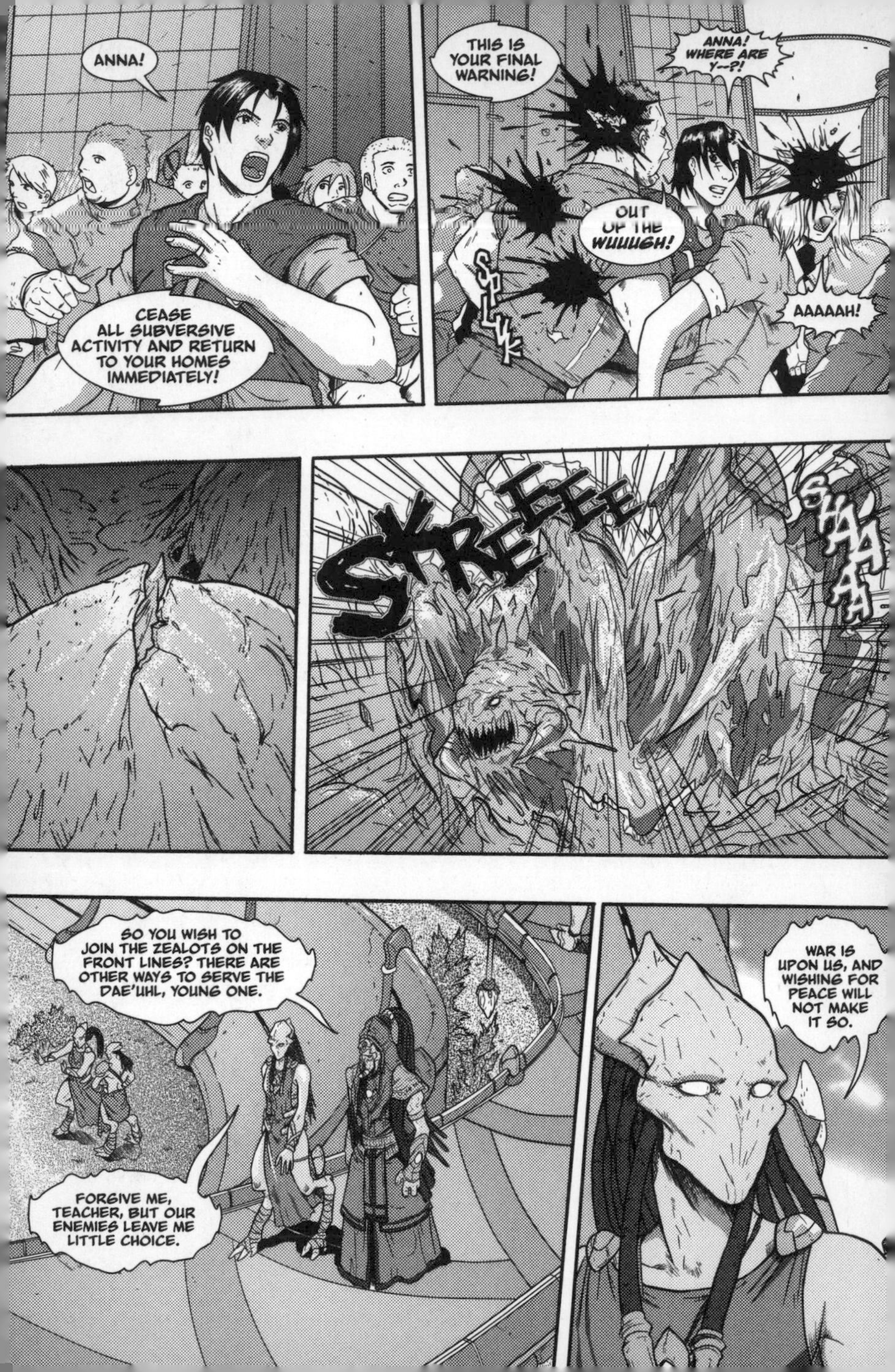
ANNA!
CEASE ALL SUBVERSIVE ACTIVITY AND RETURN TO YOUR HOMES IMMEDIATELY!
THIS IS YOUR FINAL WARNING!
ANNA! WHERE ARE Y--?!
OUT UP THE WUUUGH!
SPLUK
AAAAAH!
SKREEEE
SHAAA
SO YOU WISH TO JOIN THE ZEALOTS ON THE FRONT LINES? THERE ARE OTHER WAYS TO SERVE THE DAE'UHL, YOUNG ONE.
FORGIVE ME, TEACHER, BUT OUR ENEMIES LEAVE ME LITTLE CHOICE.
WAR IS UPON US, AND WISHING FOR PEACE WILL NOT MAKE IT SO.

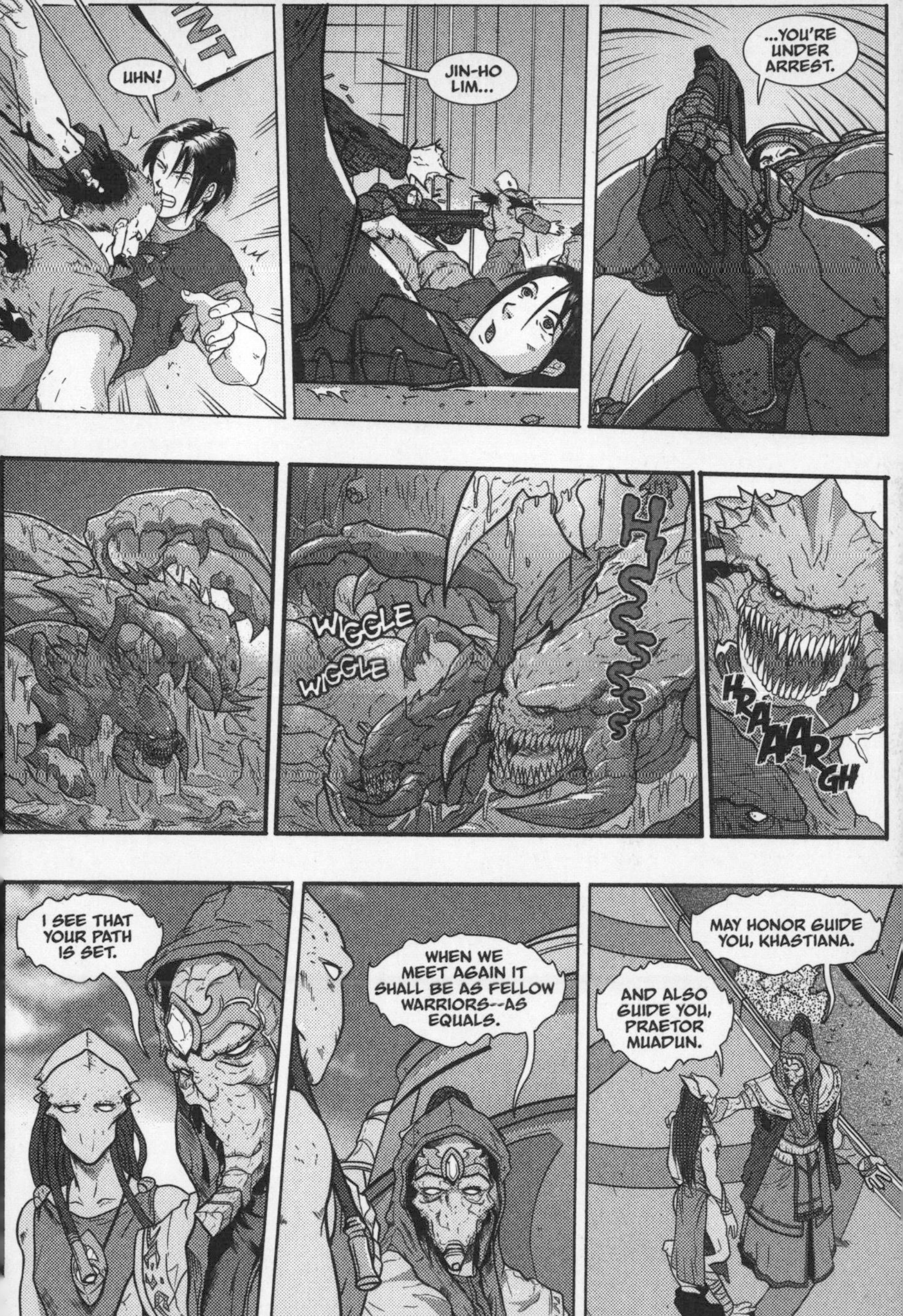
UHN!
JIN-HO LIM...
...YOU'RE UNDER ARREST.
WIGGLE
WIGGLE
HRAAAARGH
I SEE THAT YOUR PATH IS SET.
WHEN WE MEET AGAIN IT SHALL BE AS FELLOW WARRIORS--AS EQUALS.
MAY HONOR GUIDE YOU, KHASTIANA.
AND ALSO GUIDE YOU, PRAETOR MUADUN.

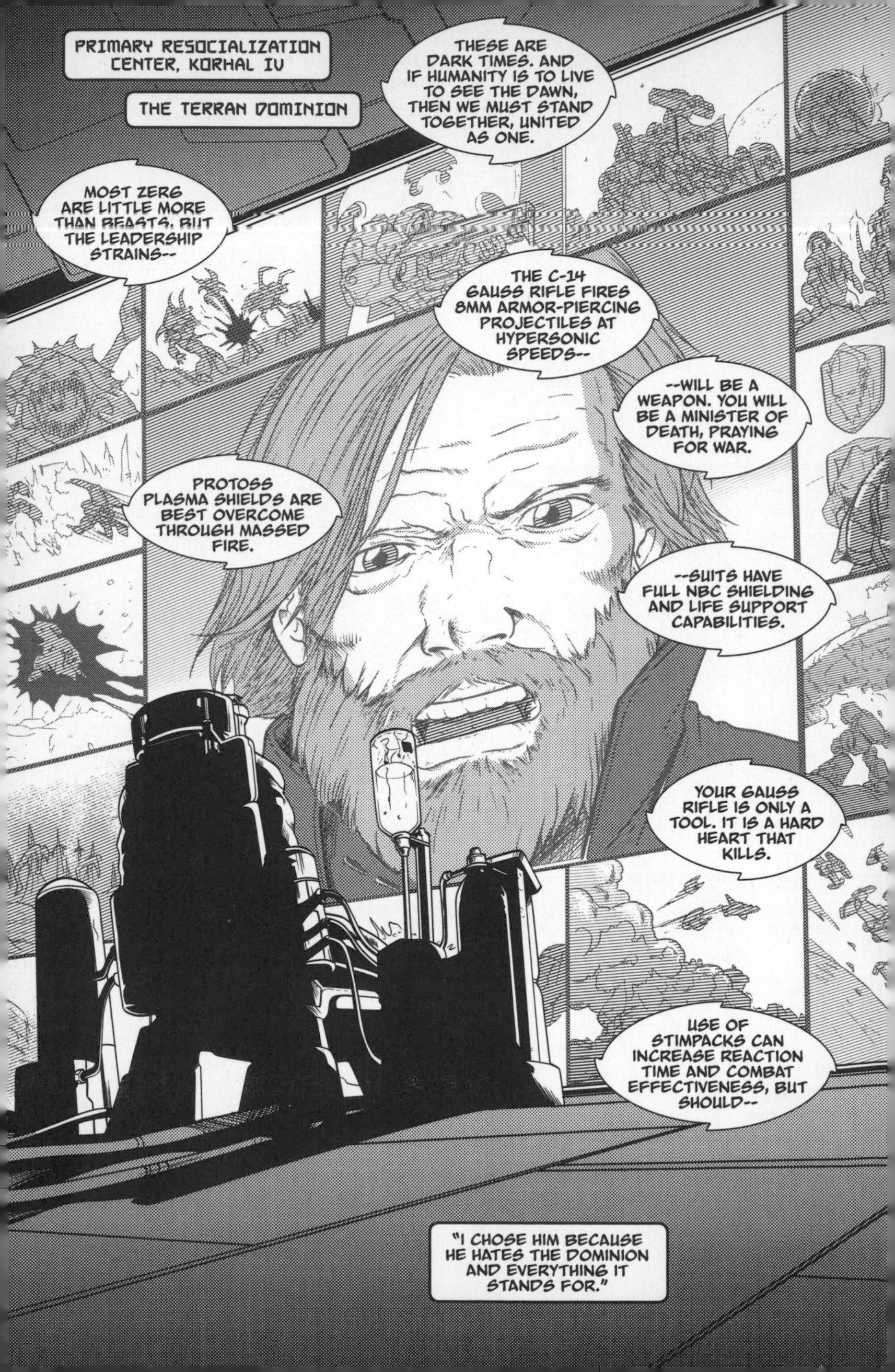

PRIMARY RESOCIALIZATION CENTER, KORHAL IV
THE TERRAN DOMINION
THESE ARE DARK TIMES. AND IF HUMANITY IS TO LIVE TO SEE THE DAWN, THEN WE MUST STAND TOGETHER, UNITED AS ONE.
MOST ZERG ARE LITTLE MORE THAN BEASTS. BUT THE LEADERSHIP STRAINS--
THE C-14 GAUSS RIFLE FIRES 8MM ARMOR-PIERCING PROJECTILES AT HYPERSONIC SPEEDS--
--WILL BE A WEAPON. YOU WILL BE A MINISTER OF DEATH, PRAYING FOR WAR.
PROTOSS PLASMA SHIELDS ARE BEST OVERCOME THROUGH MASSED FIRE.
--SUITS HAVE FULL NBC SHIELDING AND LIFE SUPPORT CAPABILITIES.
YOUR GAUSS RIFLE IS ONLY A TOOL. IT IS A HARD HEART THAT KILLS.
USE OF STIMPACKS CAN INCREASE REACTION TIME AND COMBAT EFFECTIVENESS, BUT SHOULD--
"I CHOSE HIM BECAUSE HE HATES THE DOMINION AND EVERYTHING IT STANDS FOR."

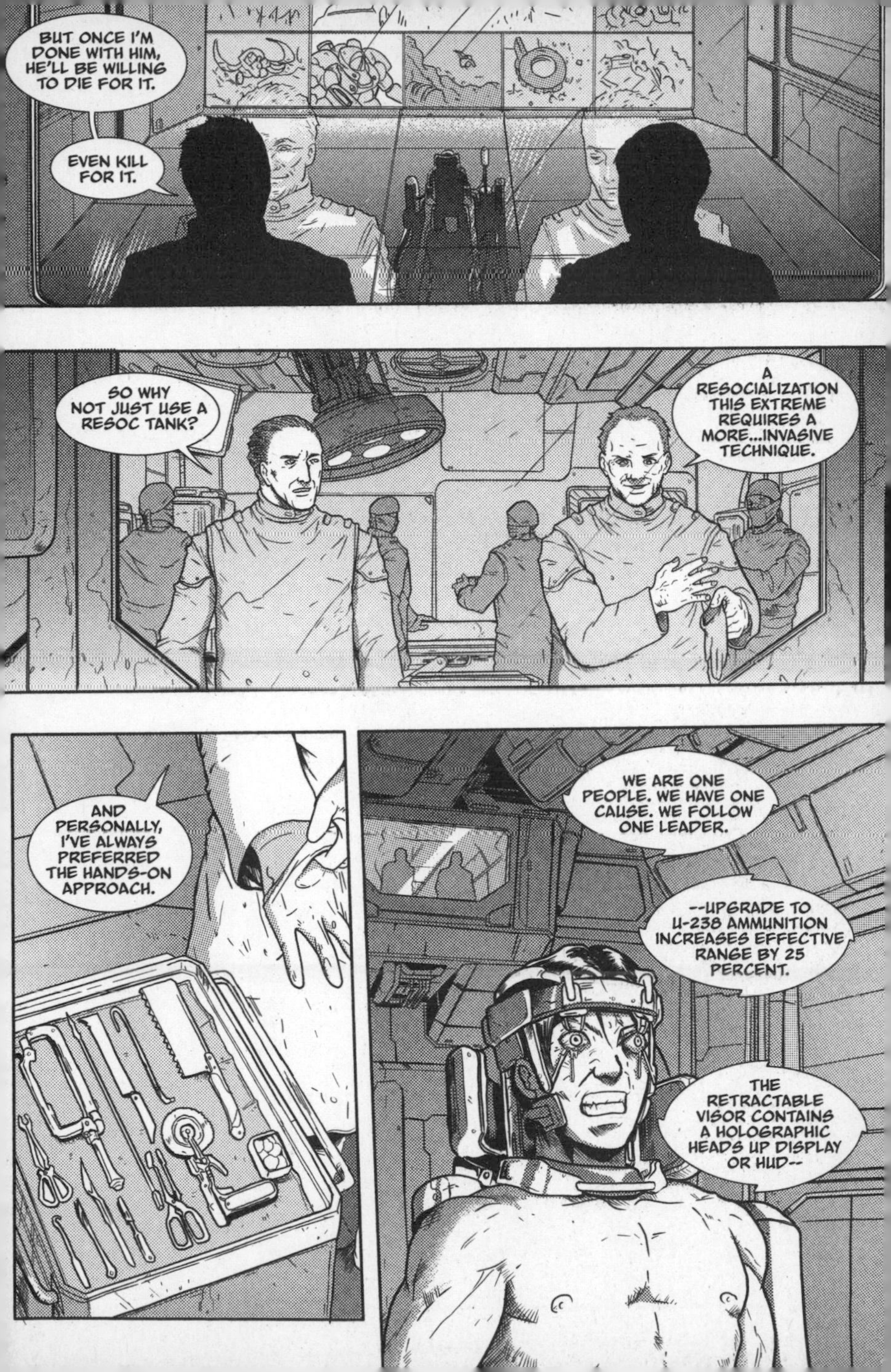

BUT ONCE I'M DONE WITH HIM, HE'LL BE WILLING TO DIE FOR IT.
EVEN KILL FOR IT.
SO WHY NOT JUST USE A RESOC TANK?
A RESOCIALIZATION THIS EXTREME REQUIRES A MORE...INVASIVE TECHNIQUE.
AND PERSONALLY, I'VE ALWAYS PREFERRED THE HANDS-ON APPROACH.
WE ARE ONE PEOPLE. WE HAVE ONE CAUSE. WE FOLLOW ONE LEADER.
--UPGRADE TO U-238 AMMUNITION INCREASES EFFECTIVE RANGE BY 25 PERCENT.
THE RETRACTABLE VISOR CONTAINS A HOLOGRAPHIC HEADS UP DISPLAY OR HUD--

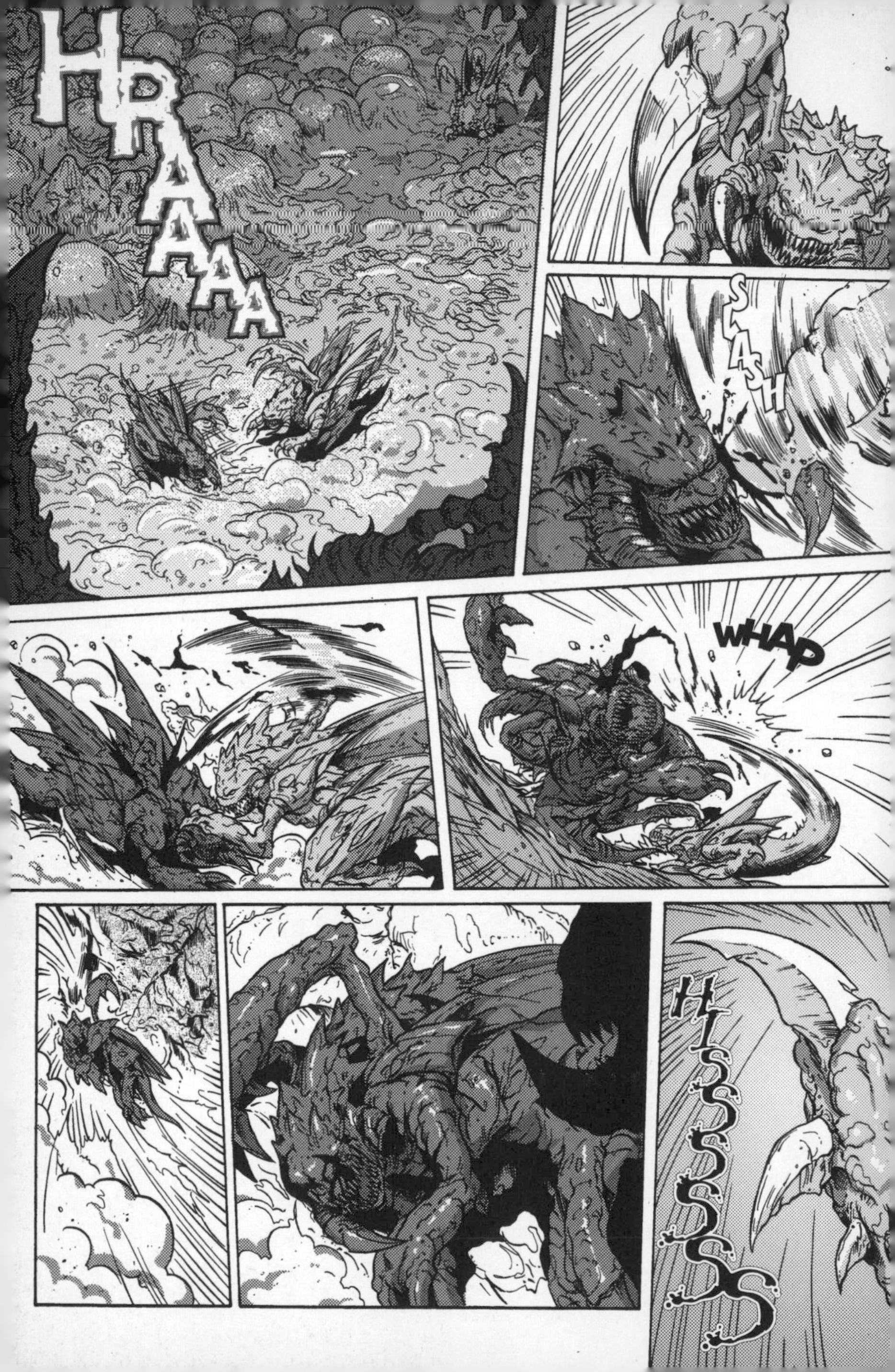
HRAAAA
SLASH
WHAP
HISSSSS

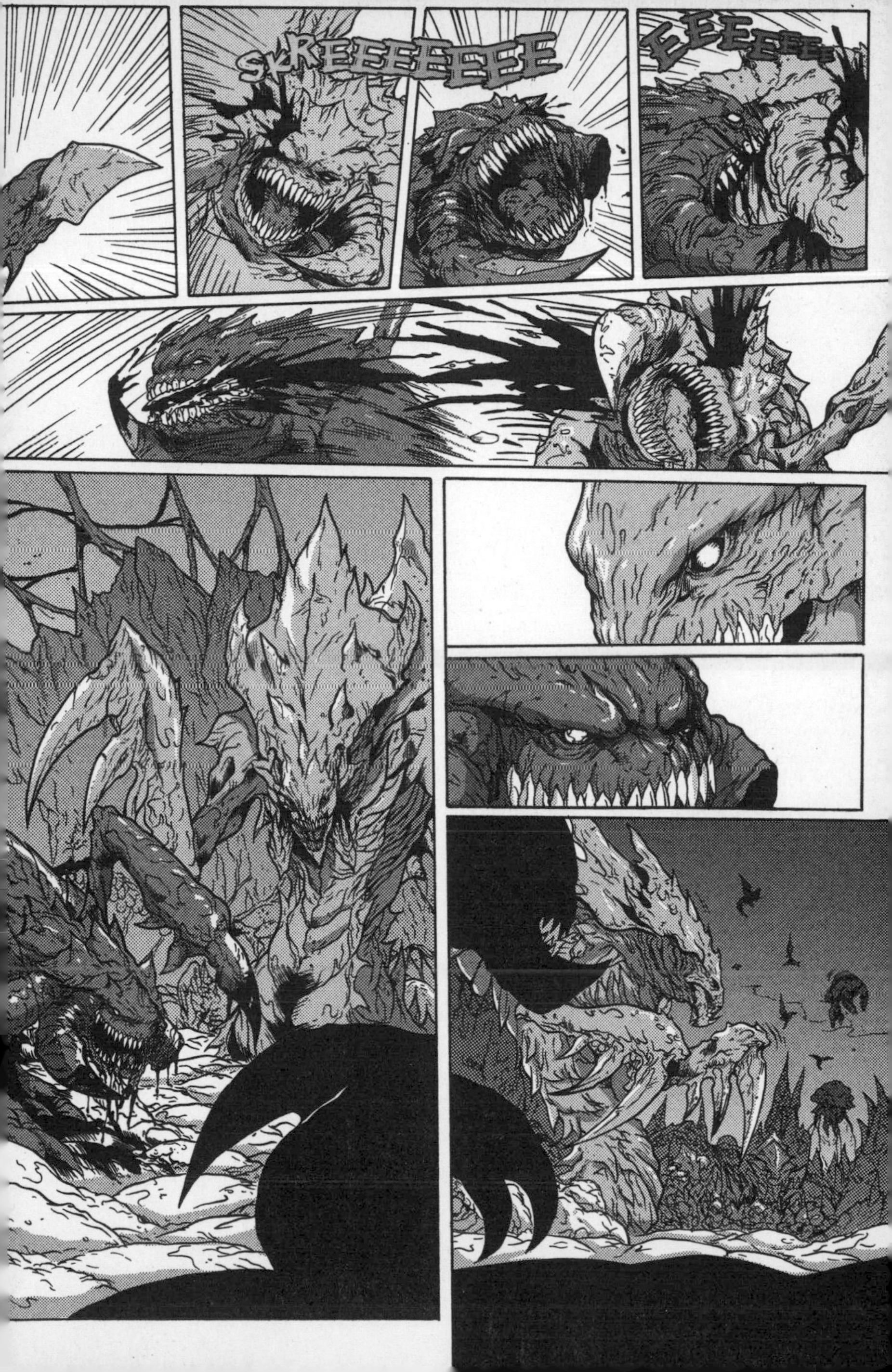
SKREEEEEEEEE
EEEEEEE

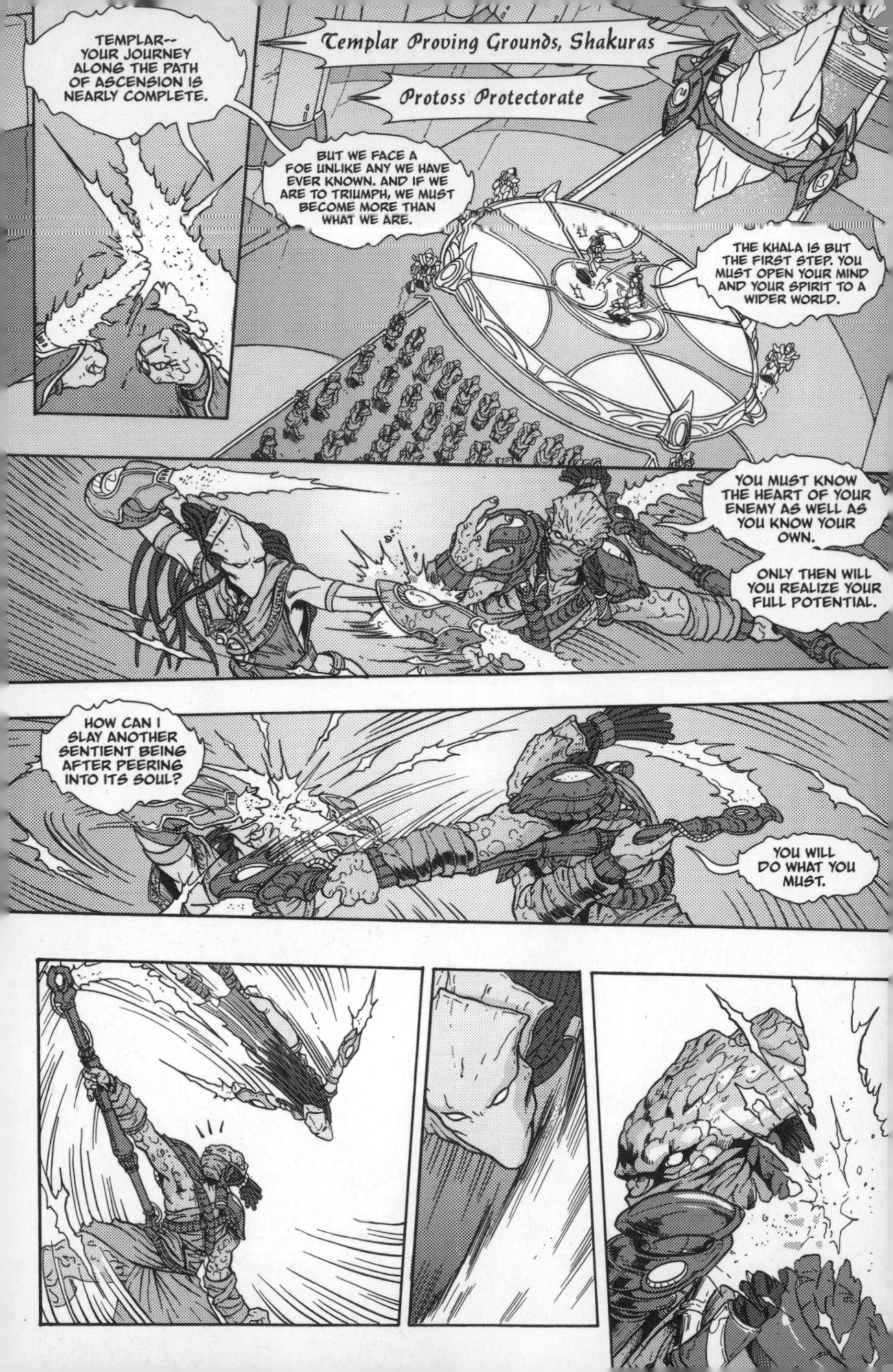

TEMPLAR-- YOUR JOURNEY ALONG THE PATH OF ASCENSION IS NEARLY COMPLETE.
Templar Proving Grounds, Shakuras
Protoss Protectorate
BUT WE FACE A FOE UNLIKE ANY WE HAVE EVER KNOWN. AND IF WE ARE TO TRIUMPH, WE MUST BECOME MORE THAN WHAT WE ARE.
THE KHALA IS BUT THE FIRST STEP. YOU MUST OPEN YOUR MIND AND YOUR SPIRIT TO A WIDER WORLD.
YOU MUST KNOW THE HEART OF YOUR ENEMY AS WELL AS YOU KNOW YOUR OWN.
ONLY THEN WILL YOU REALIZE YOUR FULL POTENTIAL.
HOW CAN I SLAY ANOTHER SENTIENT BEING AFTER PEERING INTO ITS SOUL?
YOU WILL DO WHAT YOU MUST.

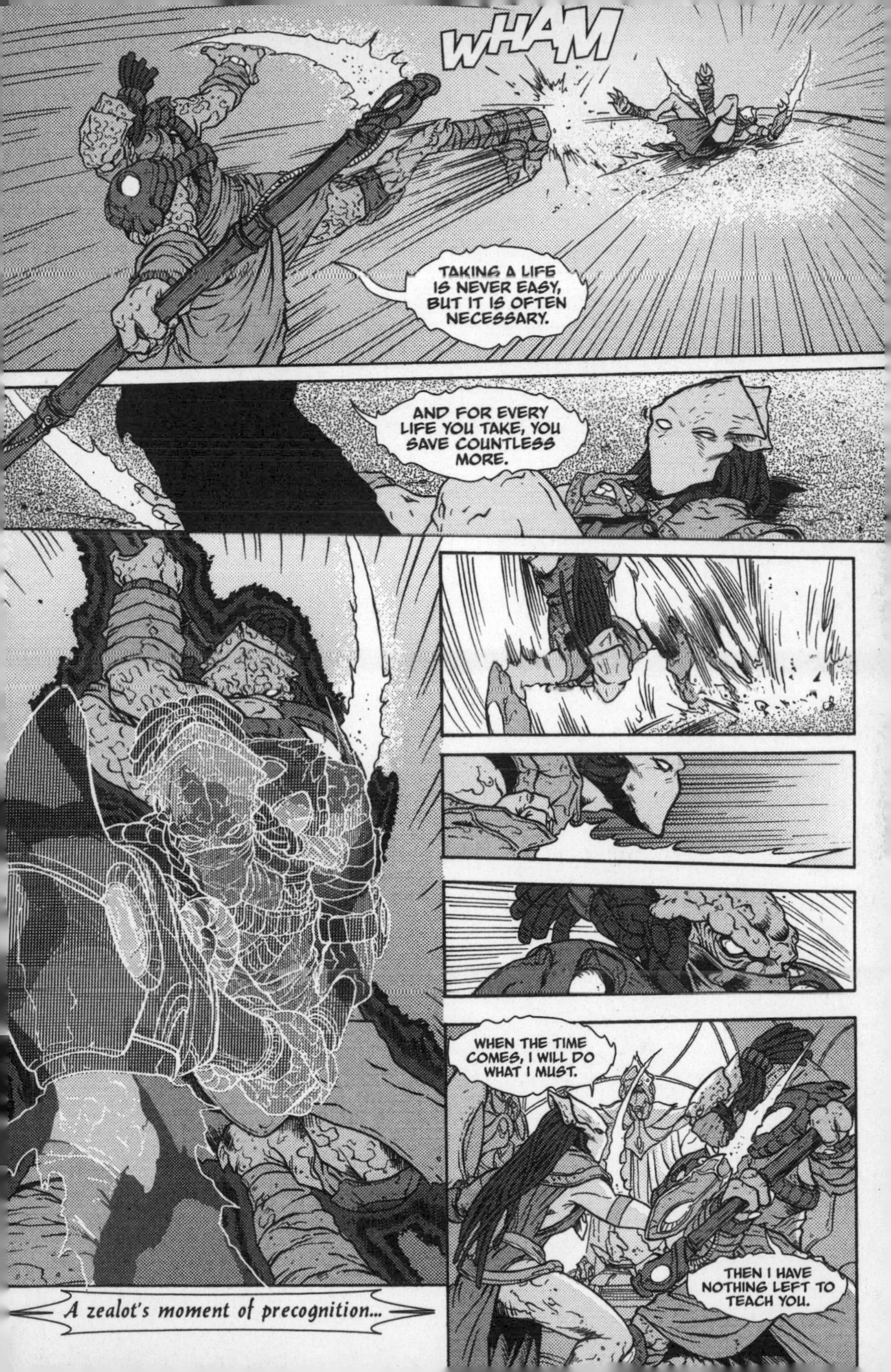
WHAM
TAKING A LIFE IS NEVER EASY, BUT IT IS OFTEN NECESSARY.
AND FOR EVERY LIFE YOU TAKE, YOU SAVE COUNTLESS MORE.
A zealot's moment of precognition...
WHEN THE TIME COMES, I WILL DO WHAT I MUST.
THEN I HAVE NOTHING LEFT TO TEACH YOU.

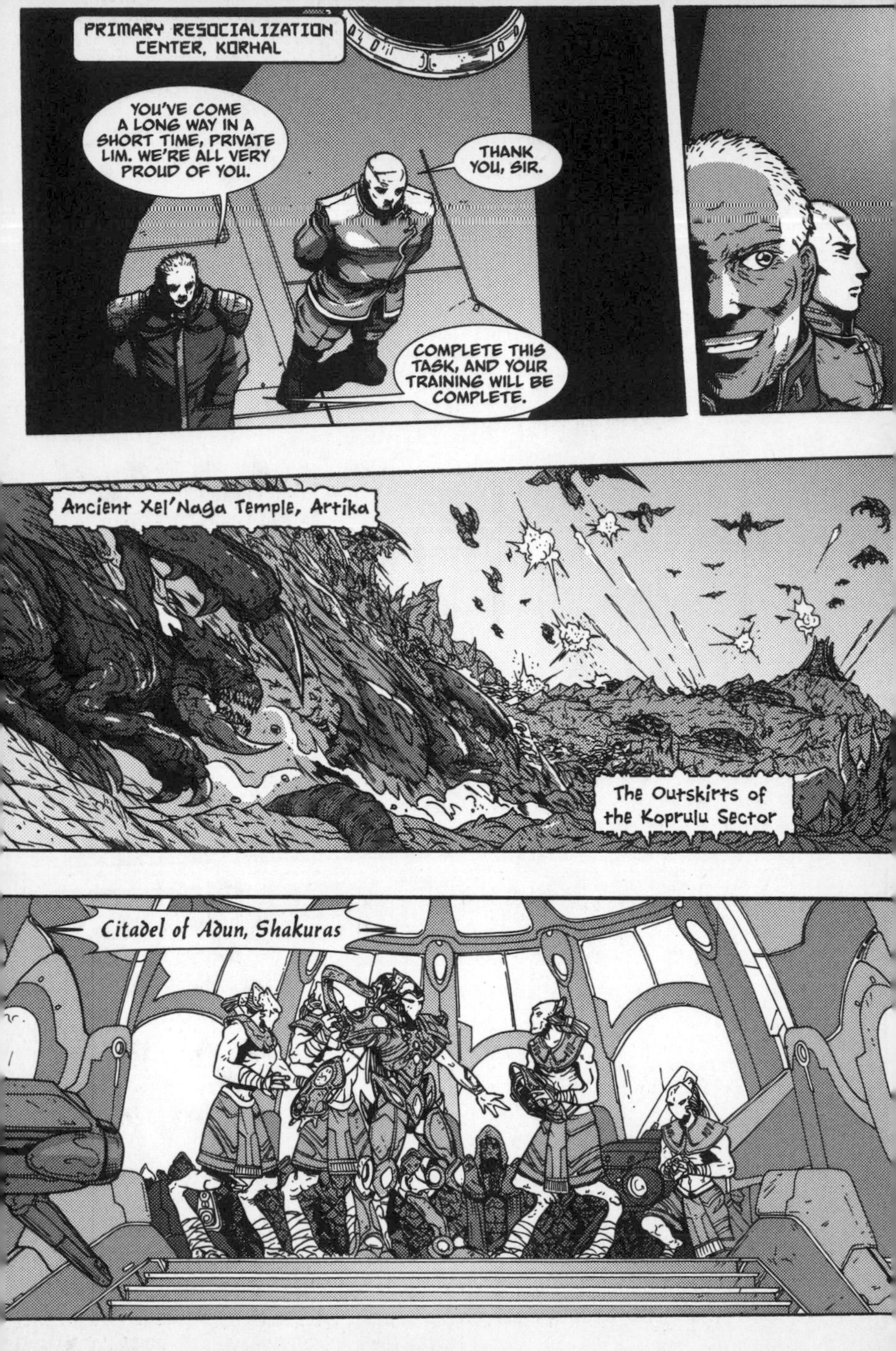
PRIMARY RESOCIALIZATION CENTER, KORHAL
YOU'VE COME A LONG WAY IN A SHORT TIME, PRIVATE LIM. WE'RE ALL VERY PROUD OF YOU.
THANK YOU, SIR.
COMPLETE THIS TASK, AND YOUR TRAINING WILL BE COMPLETE.
Ancient Xel'Naga Temple, Artika
The Outskirts of the Koprulu Sector
Citadel of Adun, Shakuras

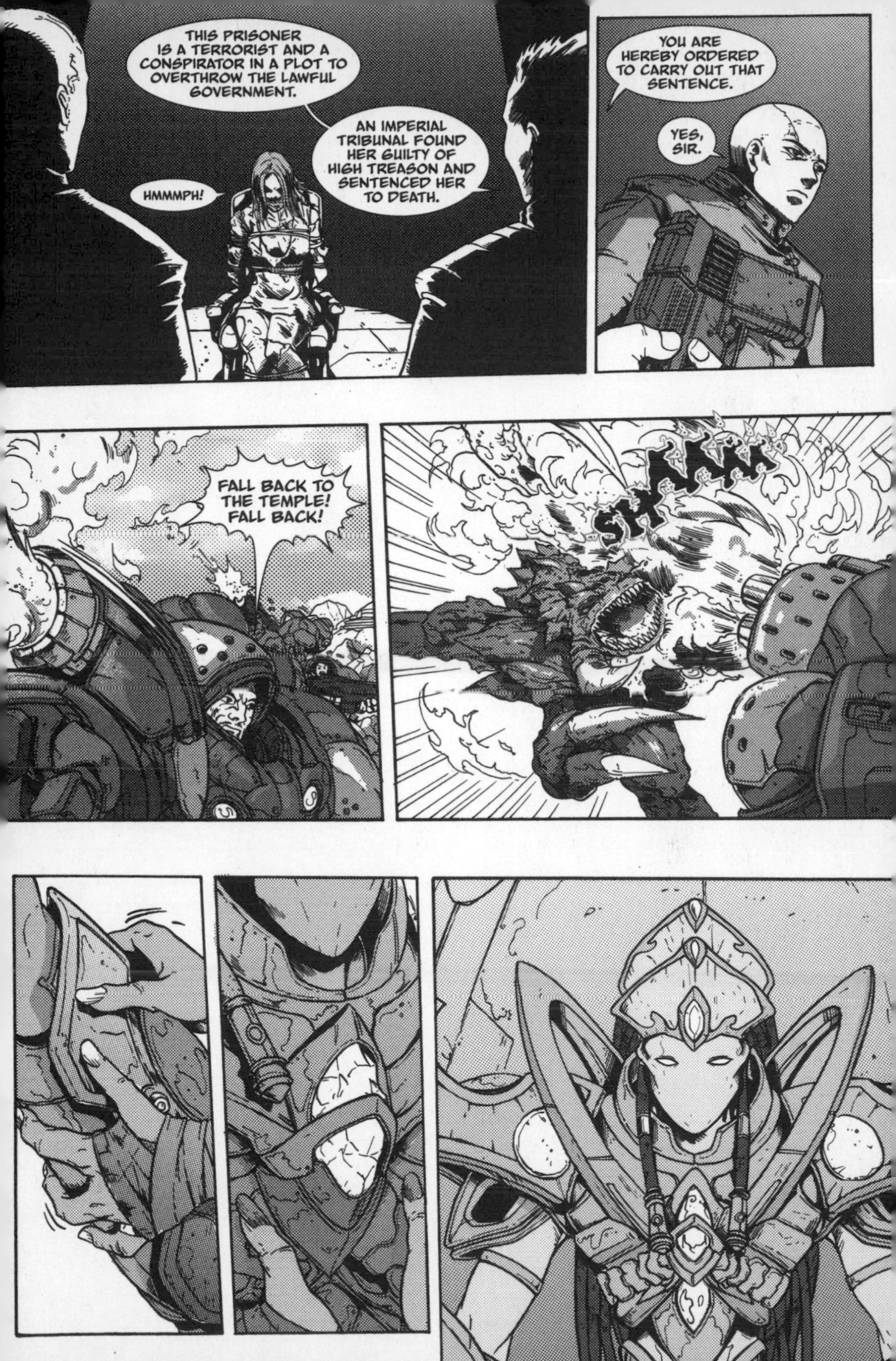
THIS PRISONER IS A TERRORIST AND A CONSPIRATOR IN A PLOT TO OVERTHROW THE LAWFUL GOVERNMENT.
HMMMPH!
AN IMPERIAL TRIBUNAL FOUND HER GUILTY OF HIGH TREASON AND SENTENCED HER TO DEATH.
YOU ARE HEREBY ORDERED TO CARRY OUT THAT SENTENCE.
YES, SIR.
FALL BACK TO THE TEMPLE! FALL BACK!
SHAAM

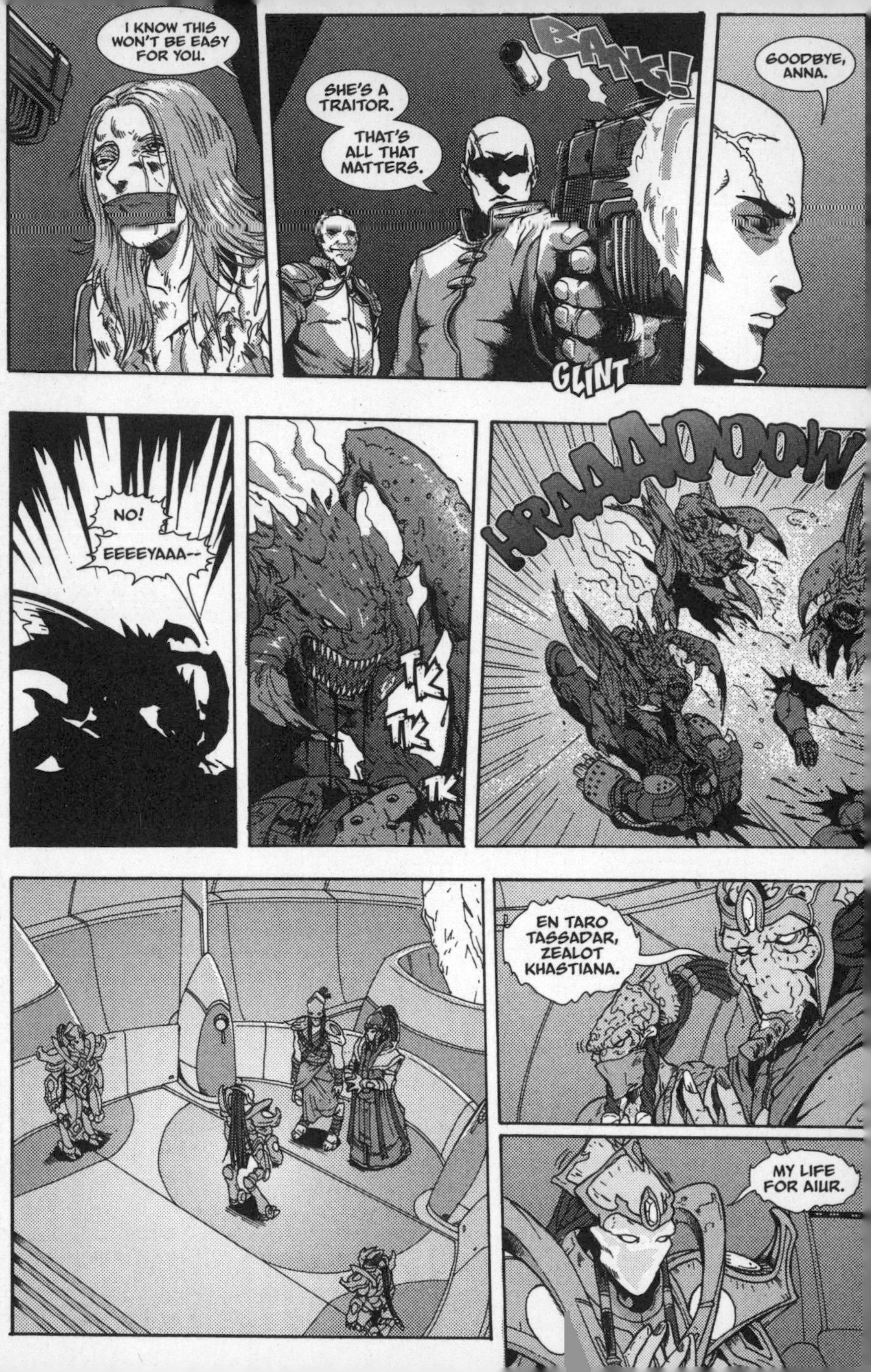
I KNOW THIS WON'T BE EASY FOR YOU.
SHE'S A TRAITOR.
THAT'S ALL THAT MATTERS.
BANG!
CLINT
GOODBYE, ANNA.
NO!
EEEEYAAA--
TK
TK
TK
HRAAAOOOW
EN TARO TASSADAR, ZEALOT KHASTIANA.
MY LIFE FOR AIUR.

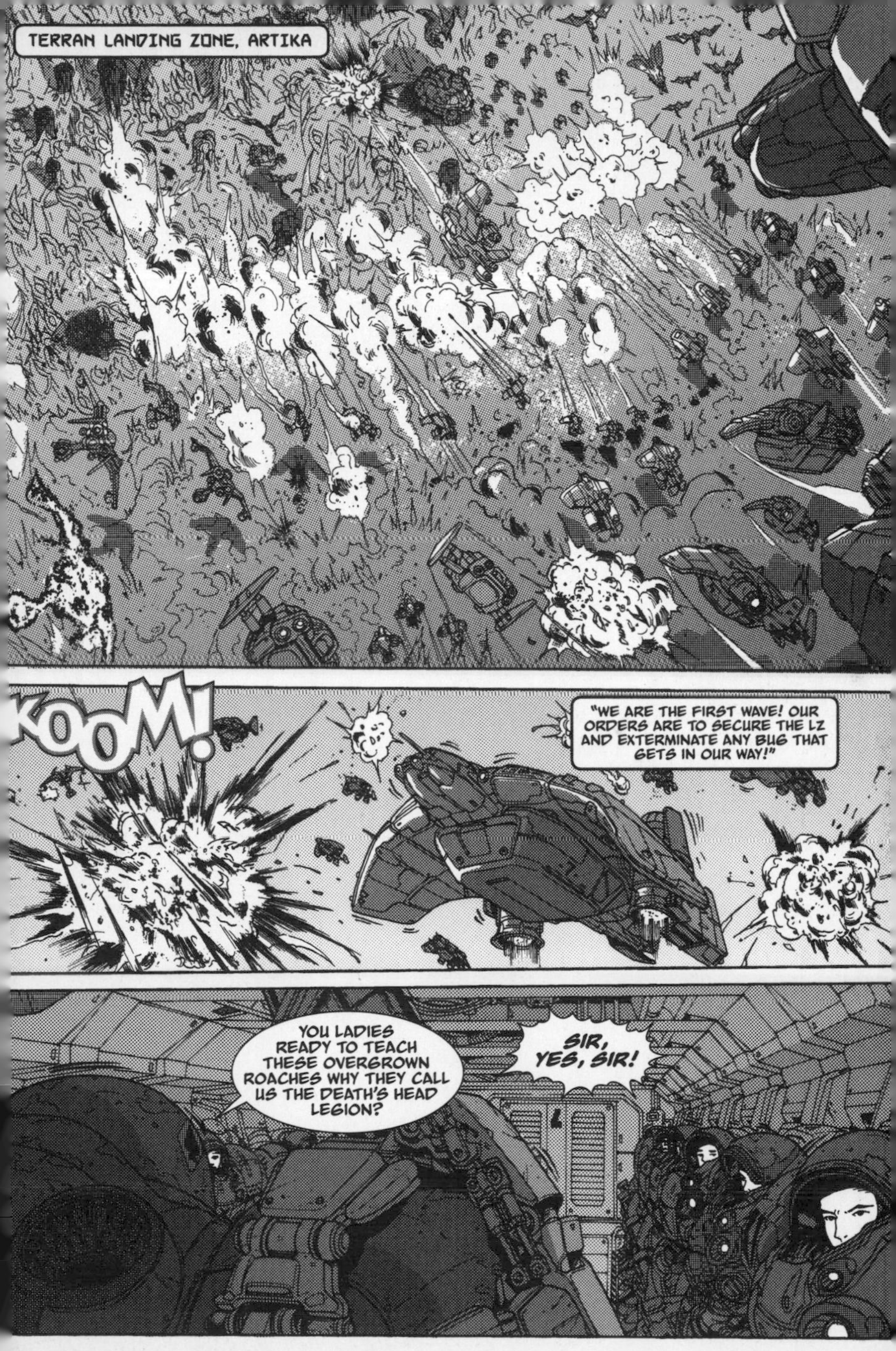
TERRAN LANDING ZONE, ARTIKA
KOOM!
"WE ARE THE FIRST WAVE! OUR ORDERS ARE TO SECURE THE LZ AND EXTERMINATE ANY BUG THAT GETS IN OUR WAY!"
YOU LADIES READY TO TEACH THESE OVERGROWN ROACHES WHY THEY CALL US THE DEATH'S HEAD LEGION?
SIR, YES, SIR!

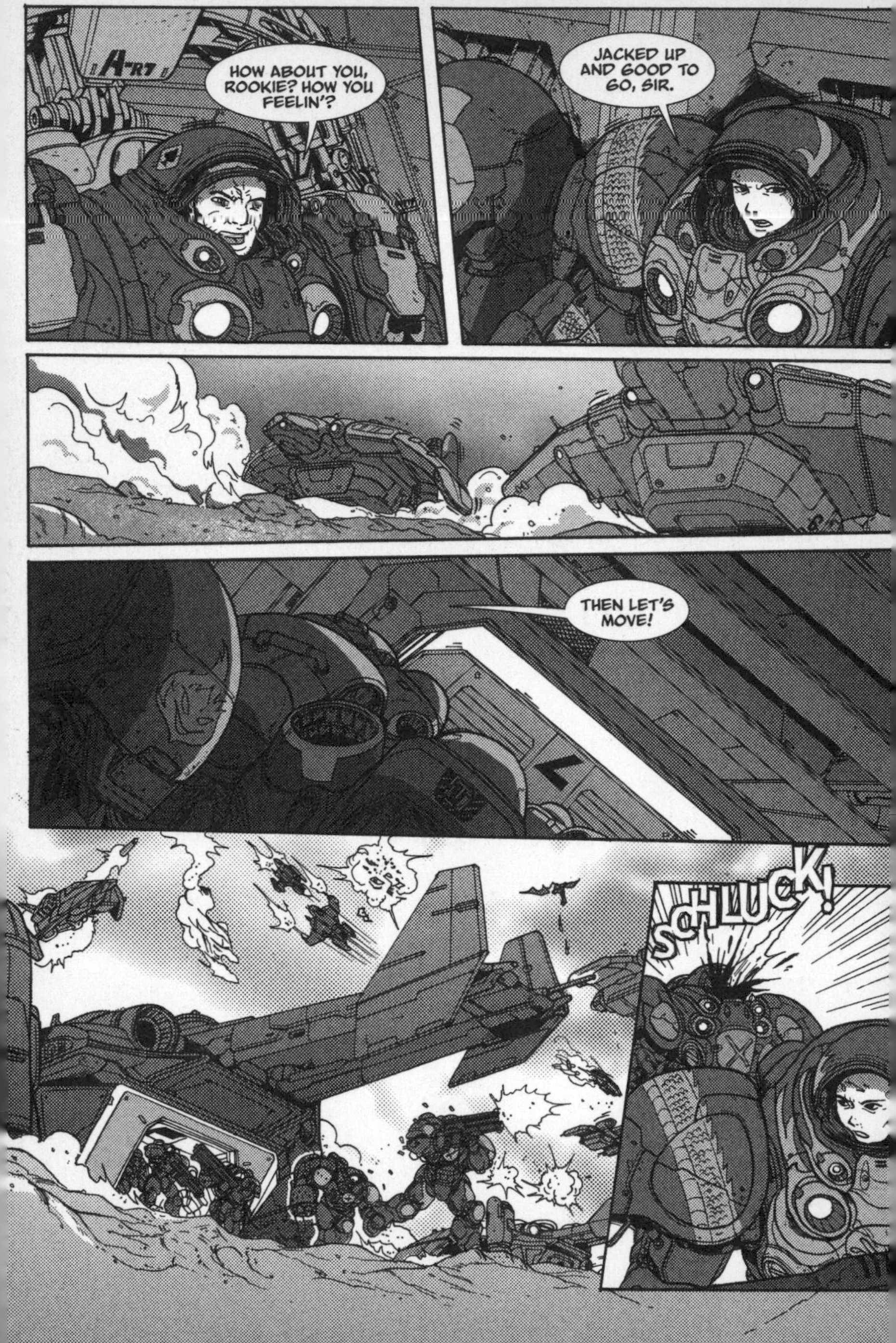
HOW ABOUT YOU, ROOKIE? HOW YOU FEELIN'?
JACKED UP AND GOOD TO GO, SIR.
THEN LET'S MOVE!
SCHLUCK!

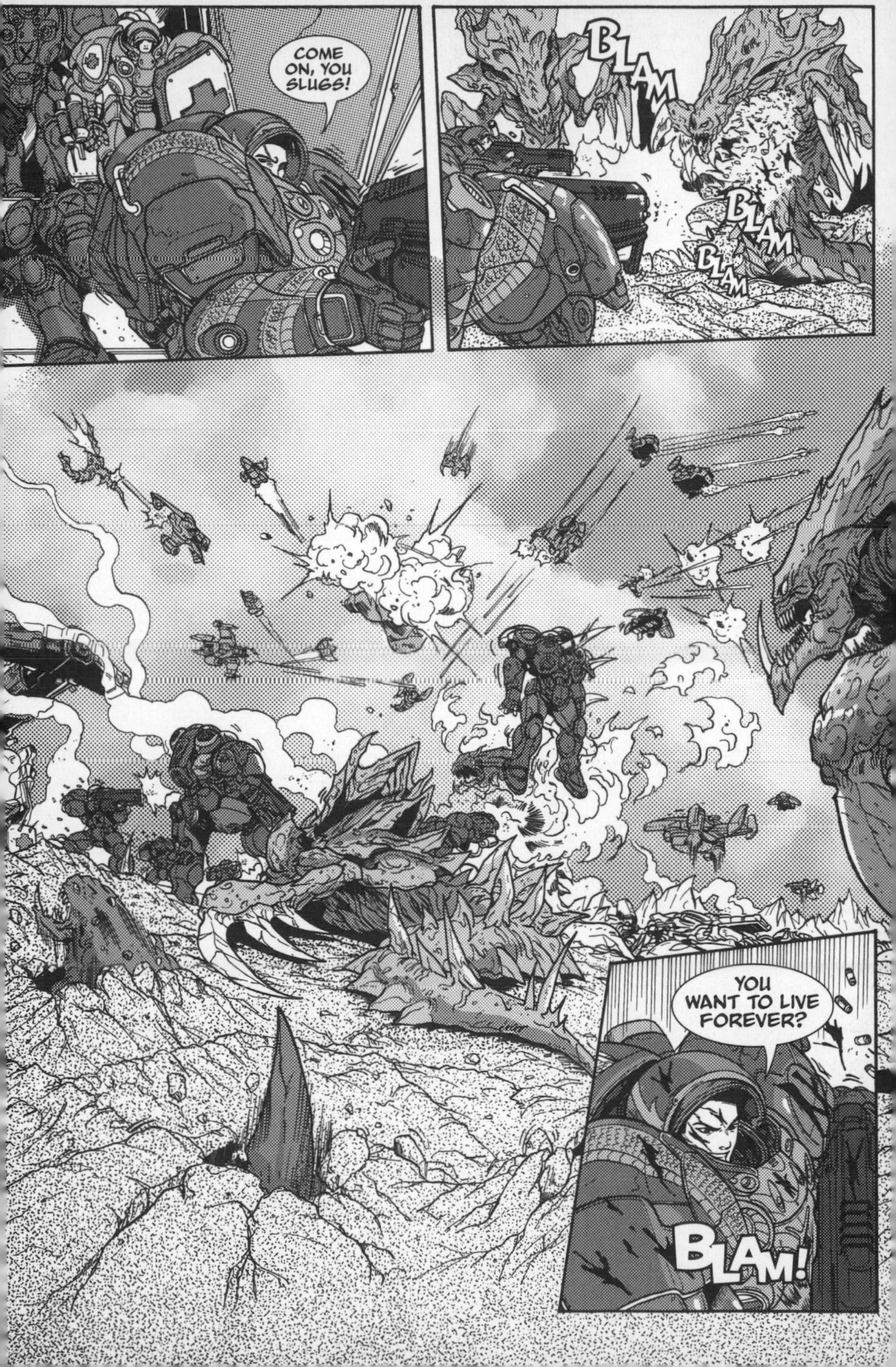

COME ON, YOU SLUGS!
BLAM
BLAM
BLAM
YOU WANT TO LIVE FOREVER?
BLAM!

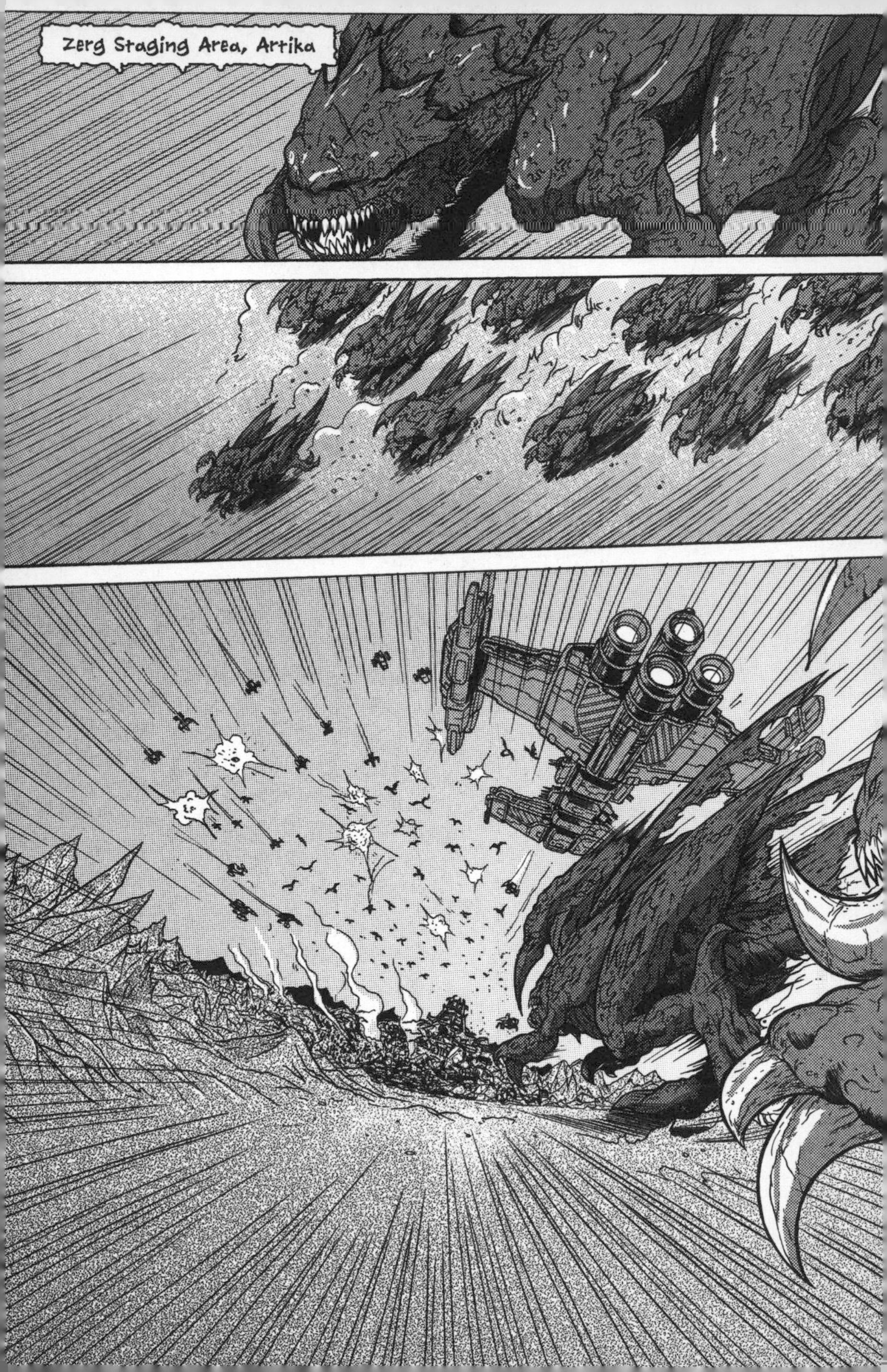
Zerg Staging Area, Artika

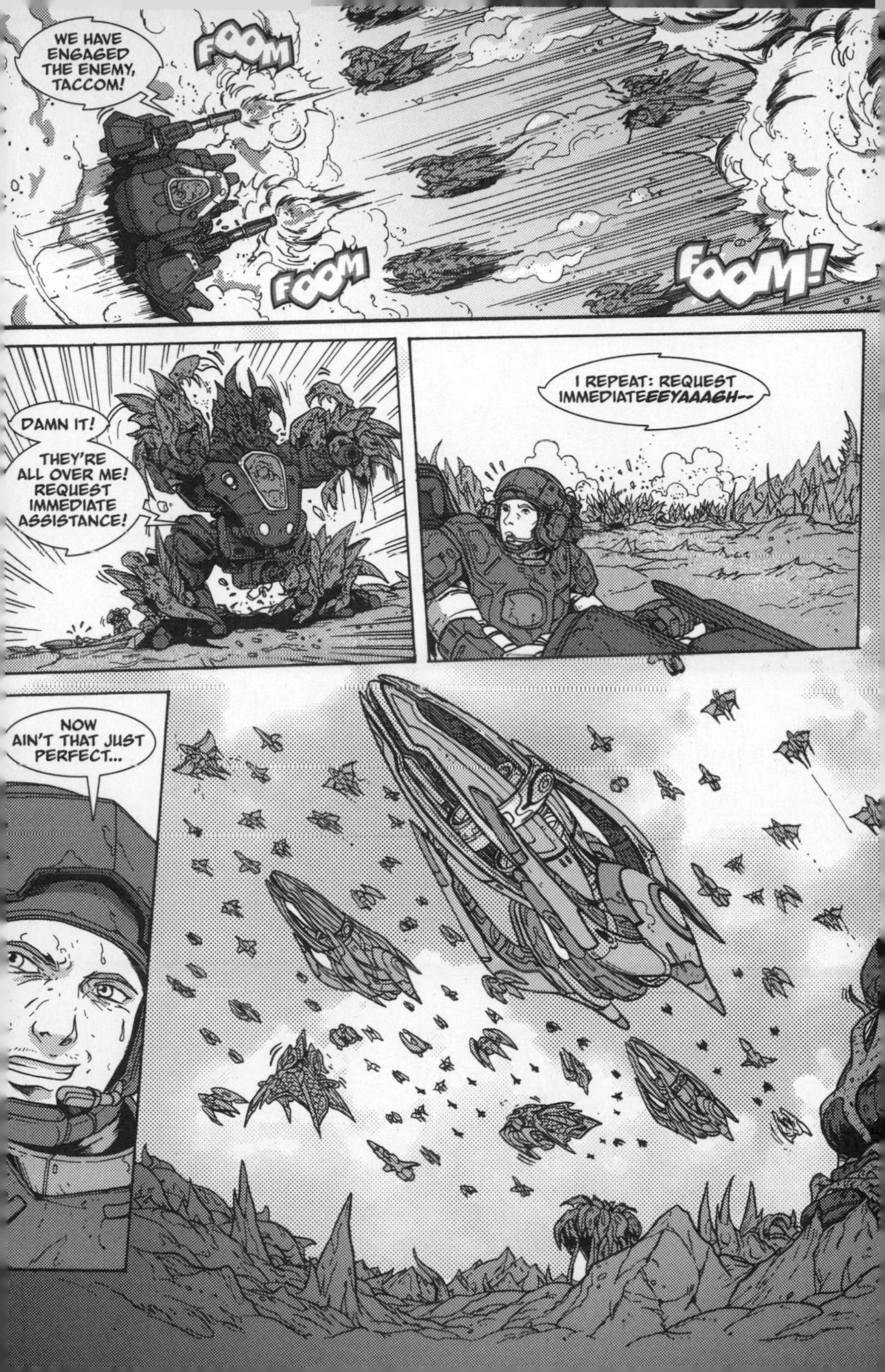
WE HAVE ENGAGED THE ENEMY, TACCOM!
FOOM
FOOM
FOOM!
DAMN IT!
THEY'RE ALL OVER ME! REQUEST IMMEDIATE ASSISTANCE!
I REPEAT: REQUEST IMMEDIATEEEYAAAGH--
NOW AIN'T THAT JUST PERFECT...

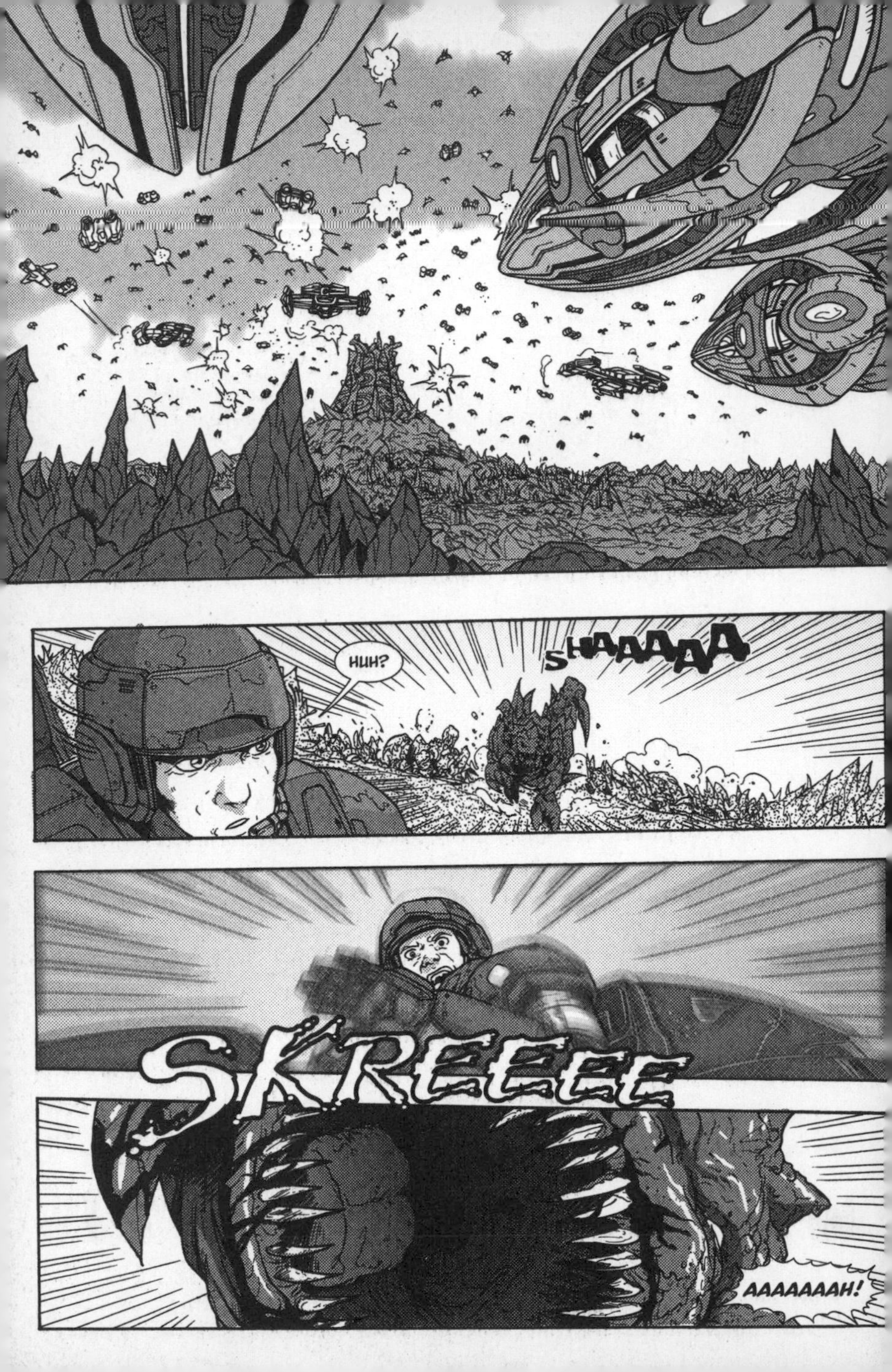
HUH?
SHAAAAAA
SKREEEE
AAAAAAAH!

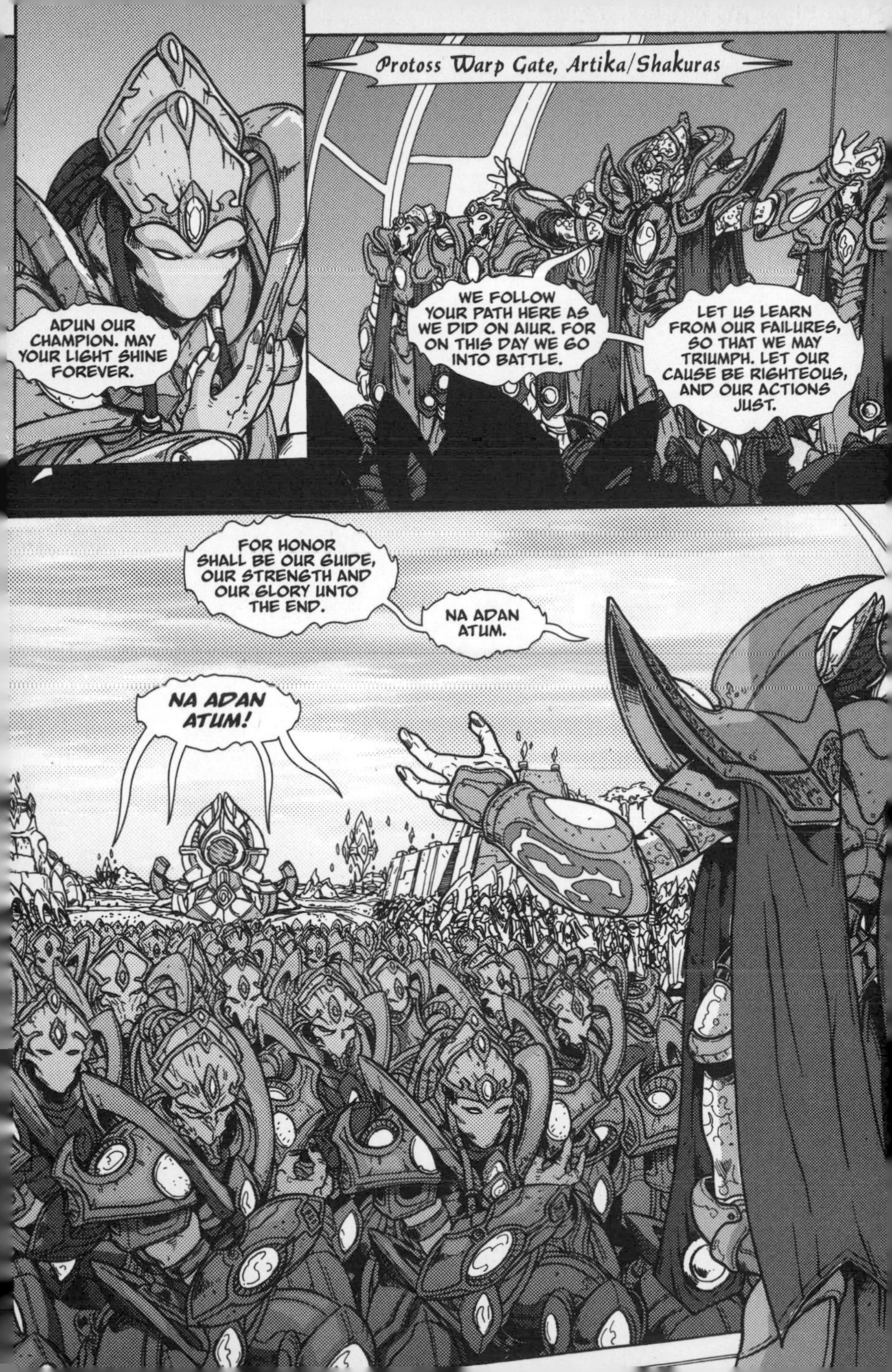
ADUN OUR CHAMPION. MAY YOUR LIGHT SHINE FOREVER.
Protoss Warp Gate, Artika/Shakuras
WE FOLLOW YOUR PATH HERE AS WE DID ON AIUR. FOR ON THIS DAY WE GO INTO BATTLE.
LET US LEARN FROM OUR FAILURES, SO THAT WE MAY TRIUMPH. LET OUR CAUSE BE RIGHTEOUS, AND OUR ACTIONS JUST.
FOR HONOR SHALL BE OUR GUIDE, OUR STRENGTH AND OUR GLORY UNTO THE END.
NA ADAN ATUM.
NA ADAN ATUM!

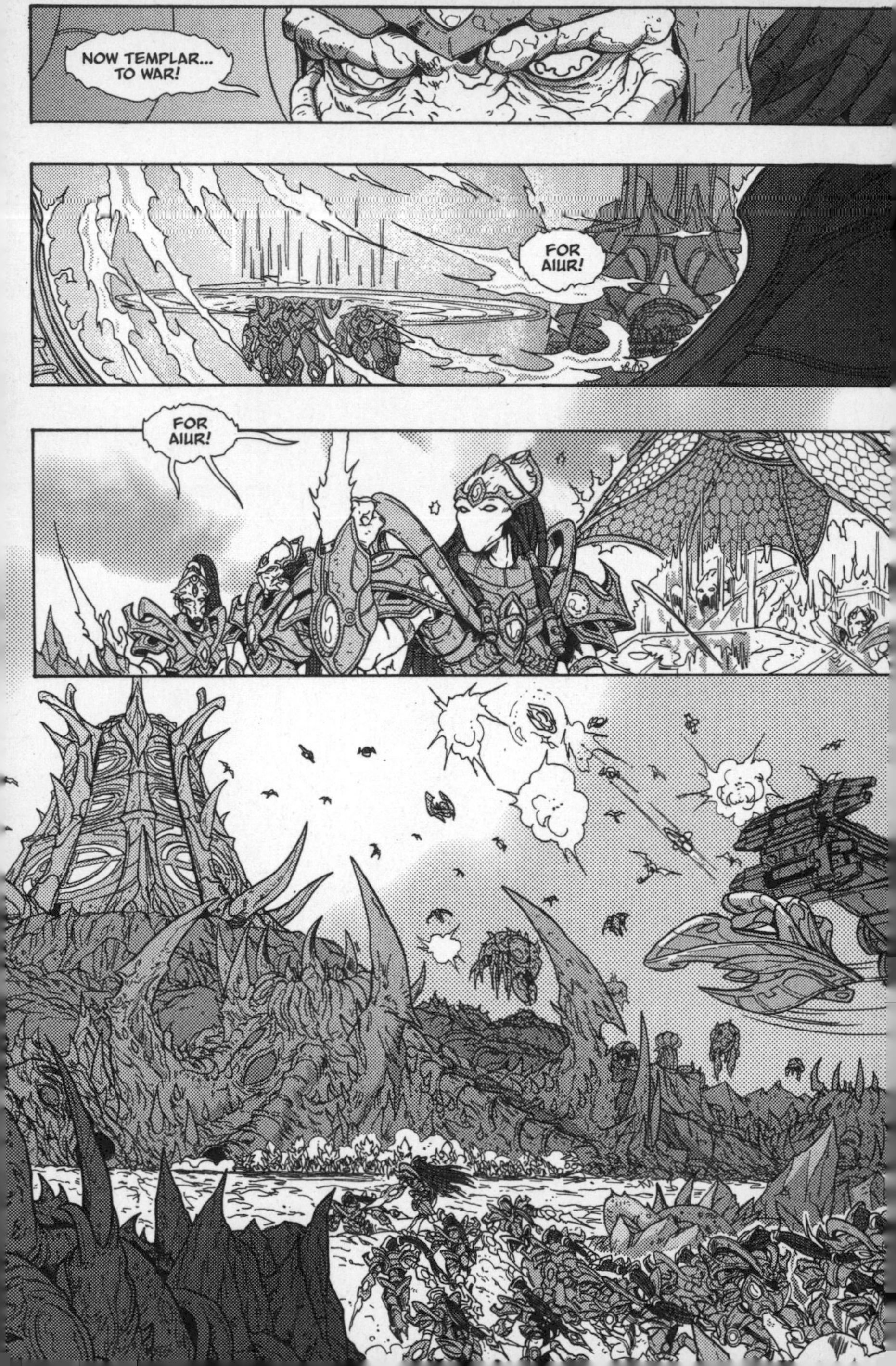
NOW TEMPLAR... TO WAR!
FOR AIUR!
FOR AIUR!

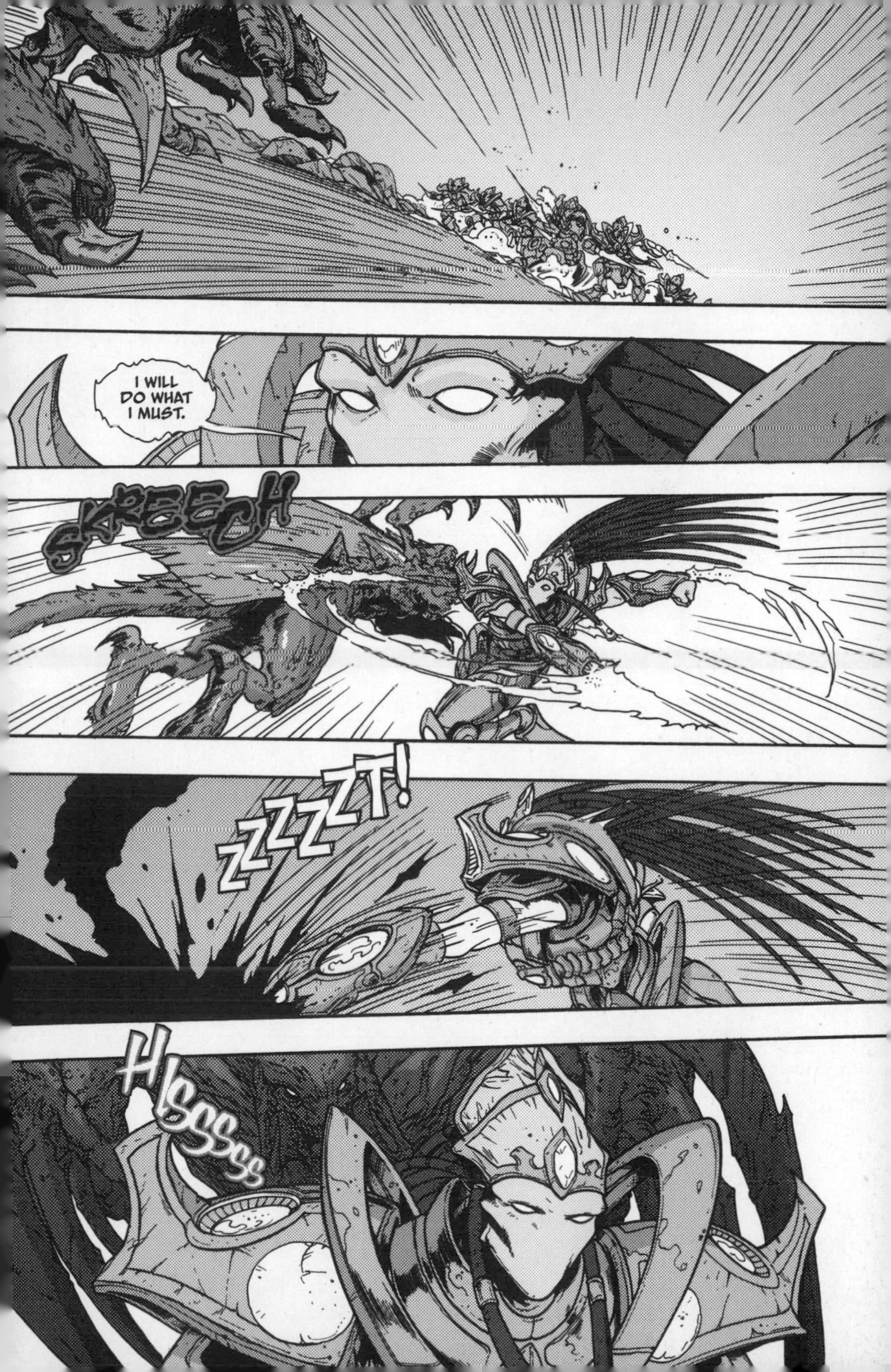

I WILL DO WHAT I MUST.
SKREECH
ZZZZZZT!
HISSSSSS

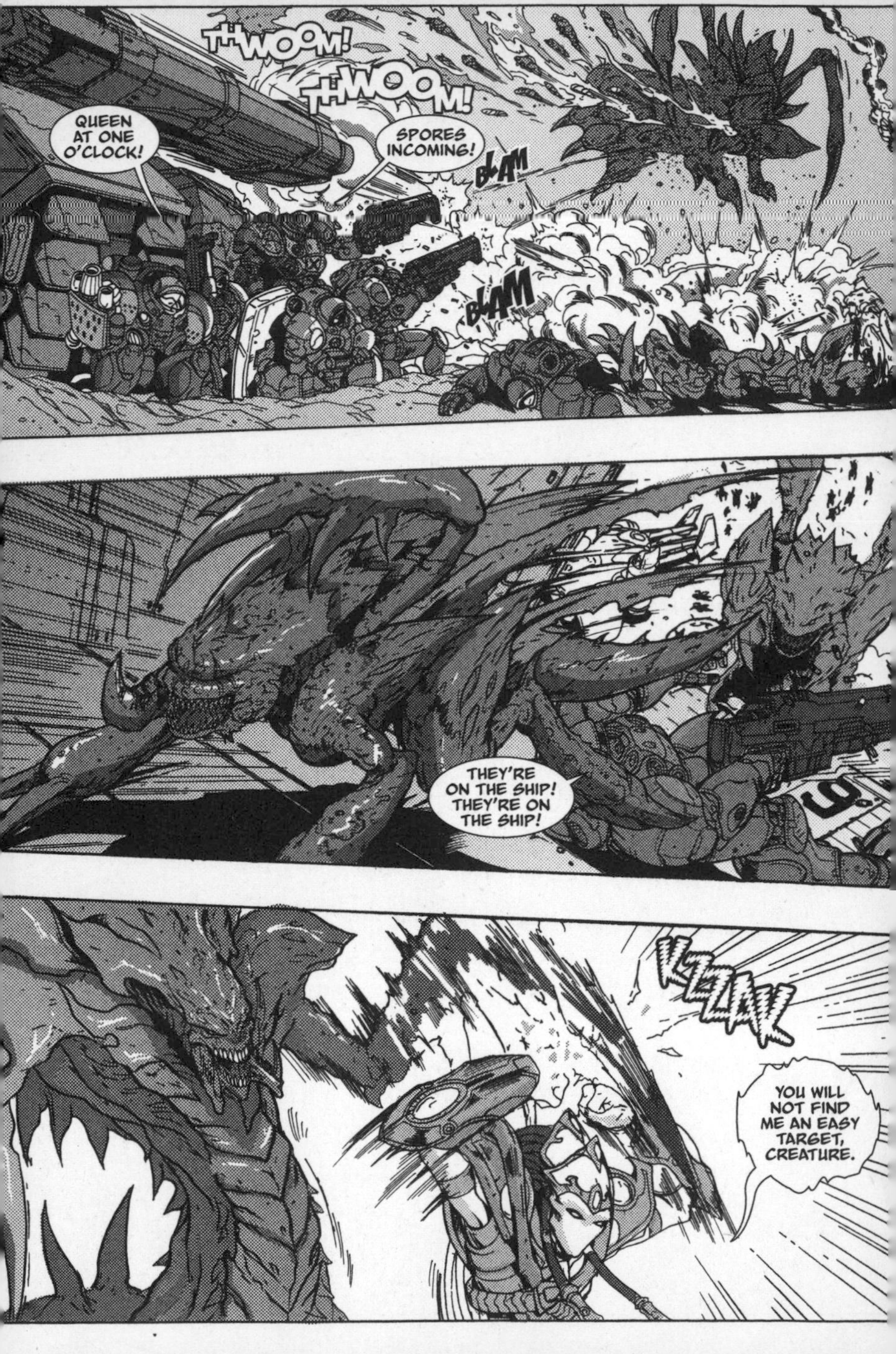
THWOOM!
THWOOM!
QUEEN AT ONE O'CLOCK!
SPORES INCOMING!
BLAM
BLAM
THEY'RE ON THE SHIP! THEY'RE ON THE SHIP!
VZZAK
YOU WILL NOT FIND ME AN EASY TARGET, CREATURE.

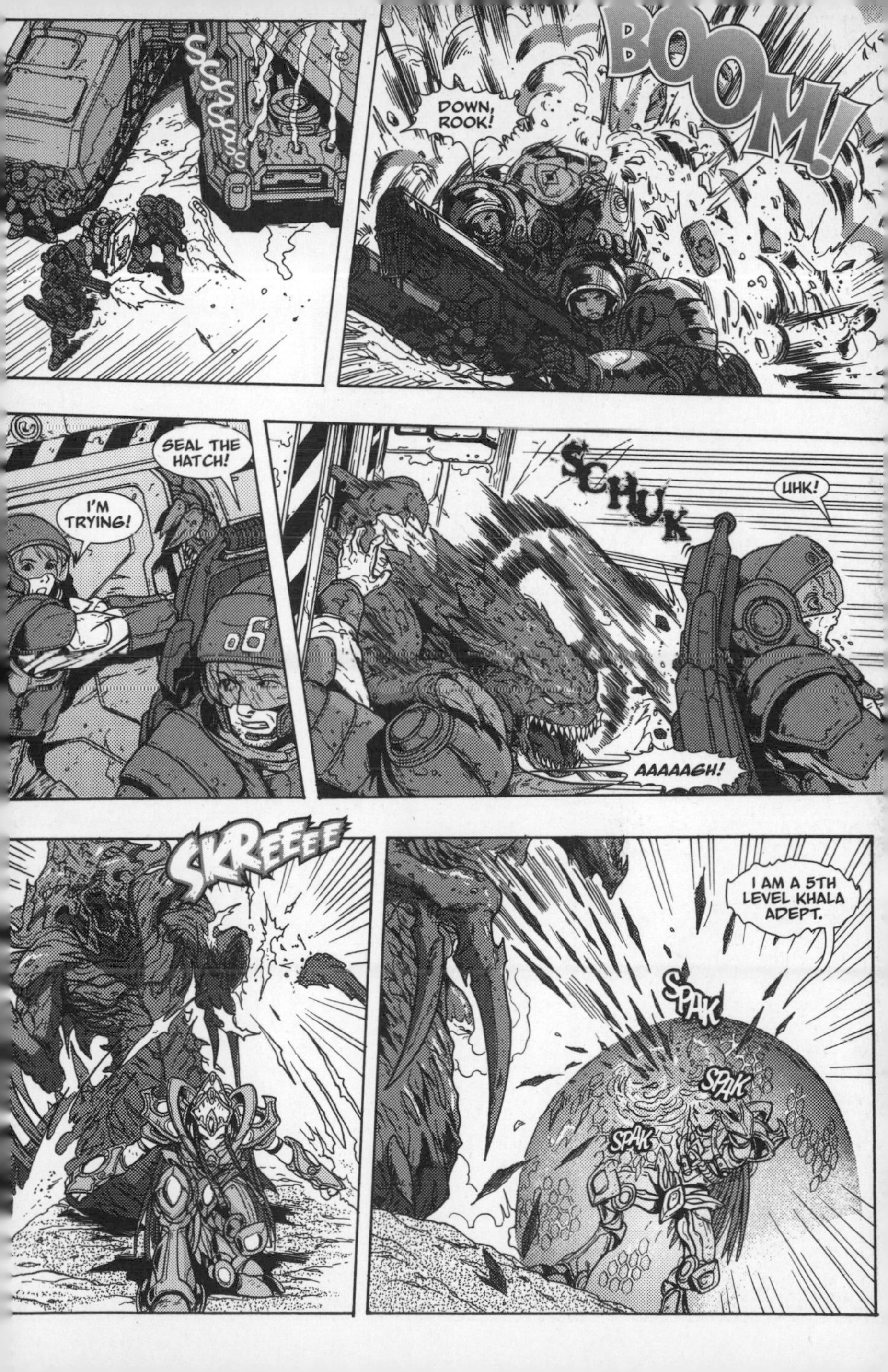
SSSSSSSSS
BOOM!
DOWN, ROOK!
SEAL THE HATCH!
I'M TRYING!
SCHUK
UHK!
AAAAAGH!
SKREEEEE
I AM A 5TH LEVEL KHALA ADEPT.
SPAK
SPAK
SPAK

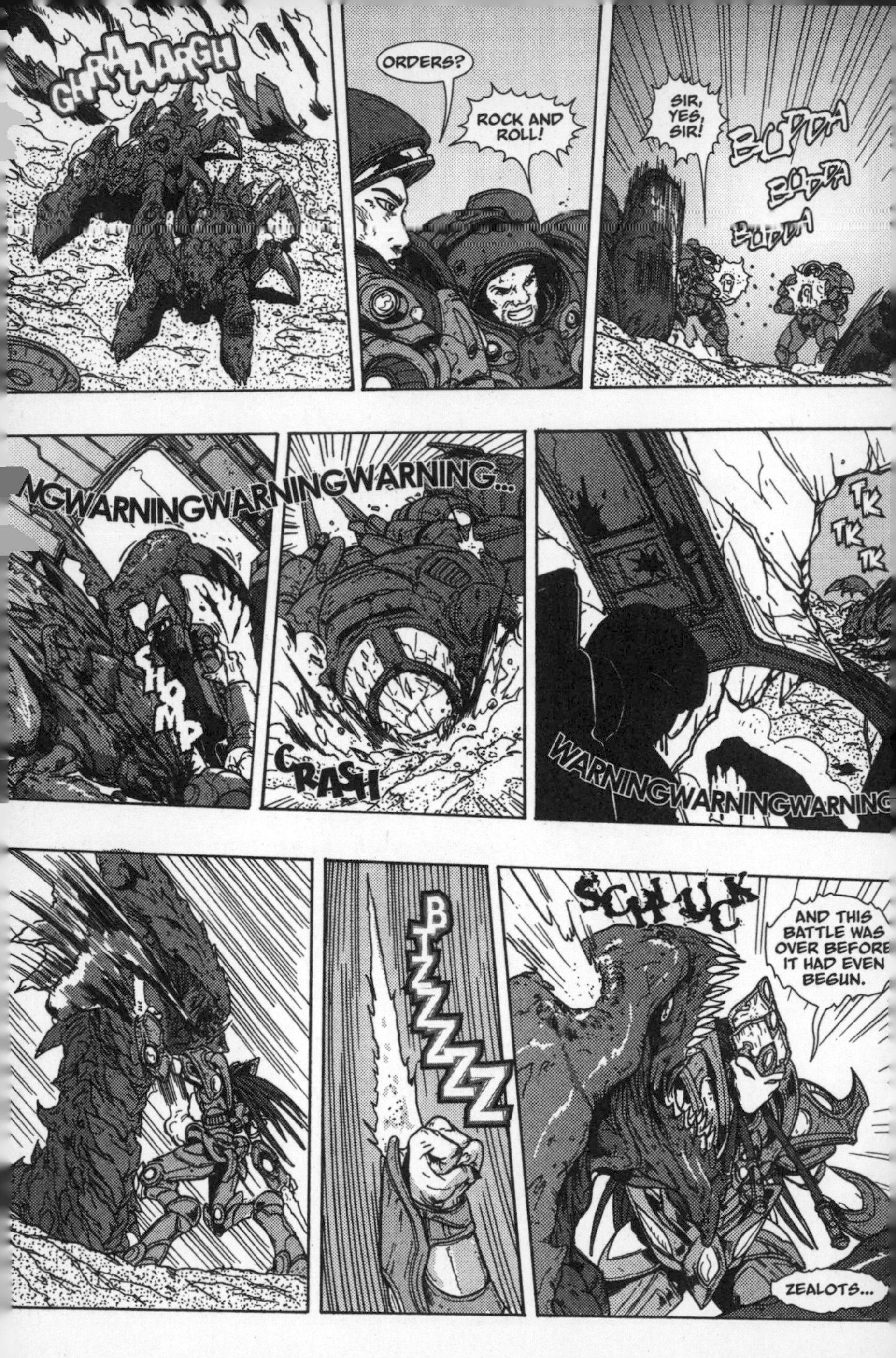

GHRAAAARGH
ORDERS?
ROCK AND ROLL!
SIR, YES, SIR!
BUDDA
BUDDA
BUDDA
NGWARNINGWARNINGWARNING...
CHOMP
CRASH
TK
TK
TK
WARNINGWARNINGWARNING
BIZZZZZ
SCHUCK
AND THIS BATTLE WAS OVER BEFORE IT HAD EVEN BEGUN.
ZEALOTS...

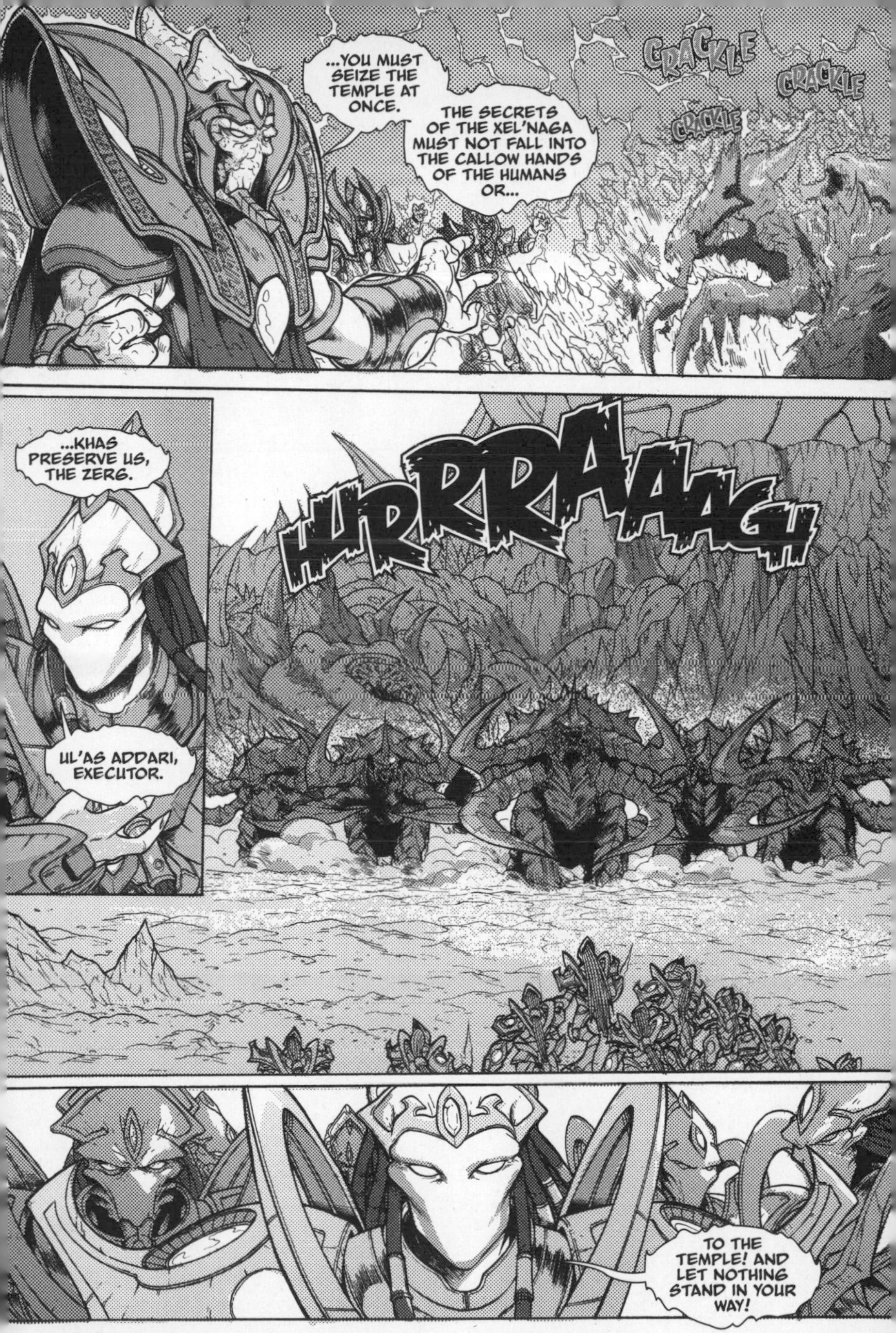
...YOU MUST SEIZE THE TEMPLE AT ONCE.
THE SECRETS OF THE XEL'NAGA MUST NOT FALL INTO THE CALLOW HANDS OF THE HUMANS OR...
CRACKLE
CRACKLE
CRACKLE
...KHAS PRESERVE US, THE ZERG.
UL'AS ADDARI, EXECUTOR.
HURRRAAAGH
TO THE TEMPLE! AND LET NOTHING STAND IN YOUR WAY!

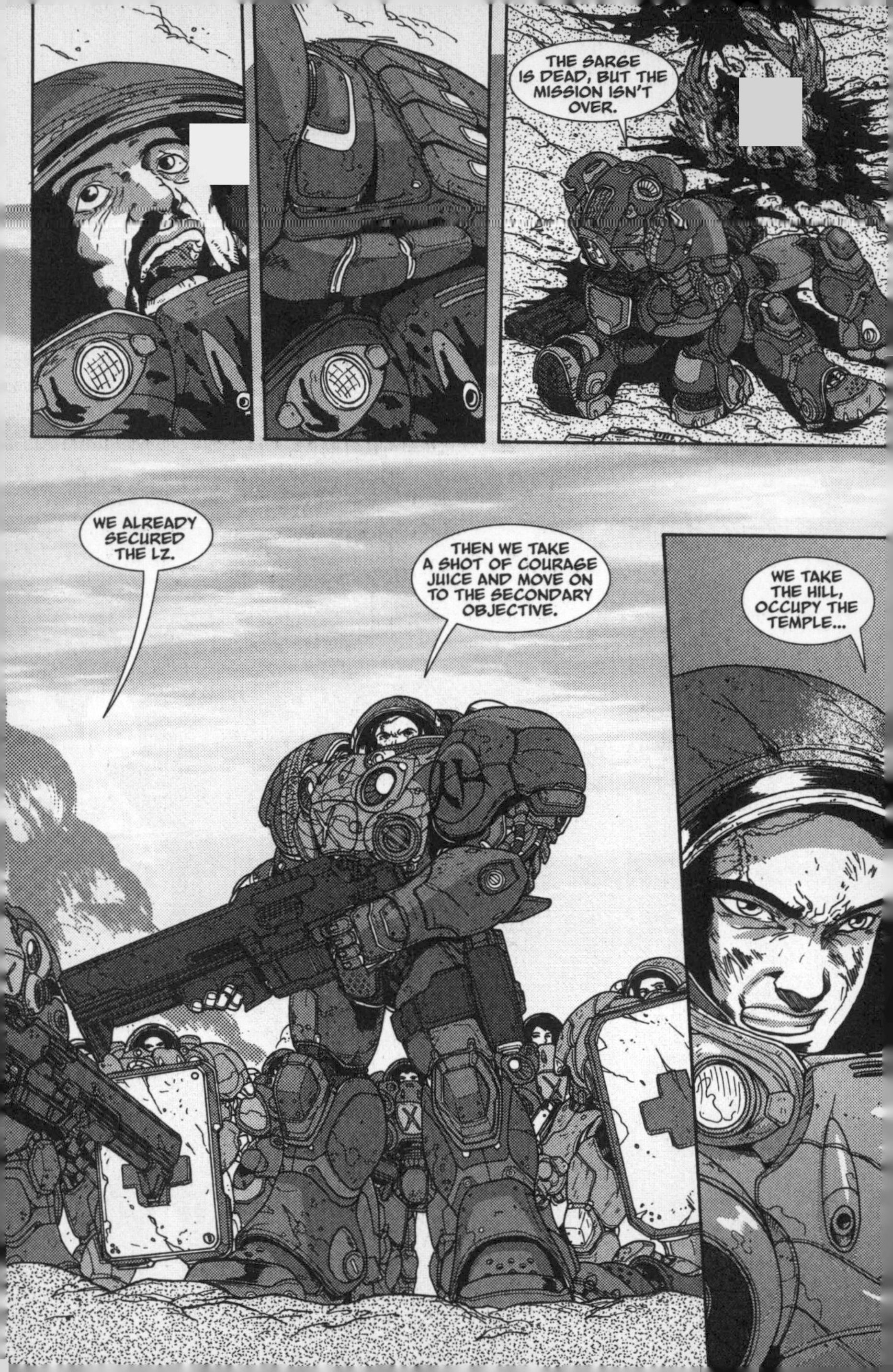
THE SARGE IS DEAD, BUT THE MISSION ISN'T OVER.
WE ALREADY SECURED THE LZ.
THEN WE TAKE A SHOT OF COURAGE JUICE AND MOVE ON TO THE SECONDARY OBJECTIVE.
WE TAKE THE HILL, OCCUPY THE TEMPLE...

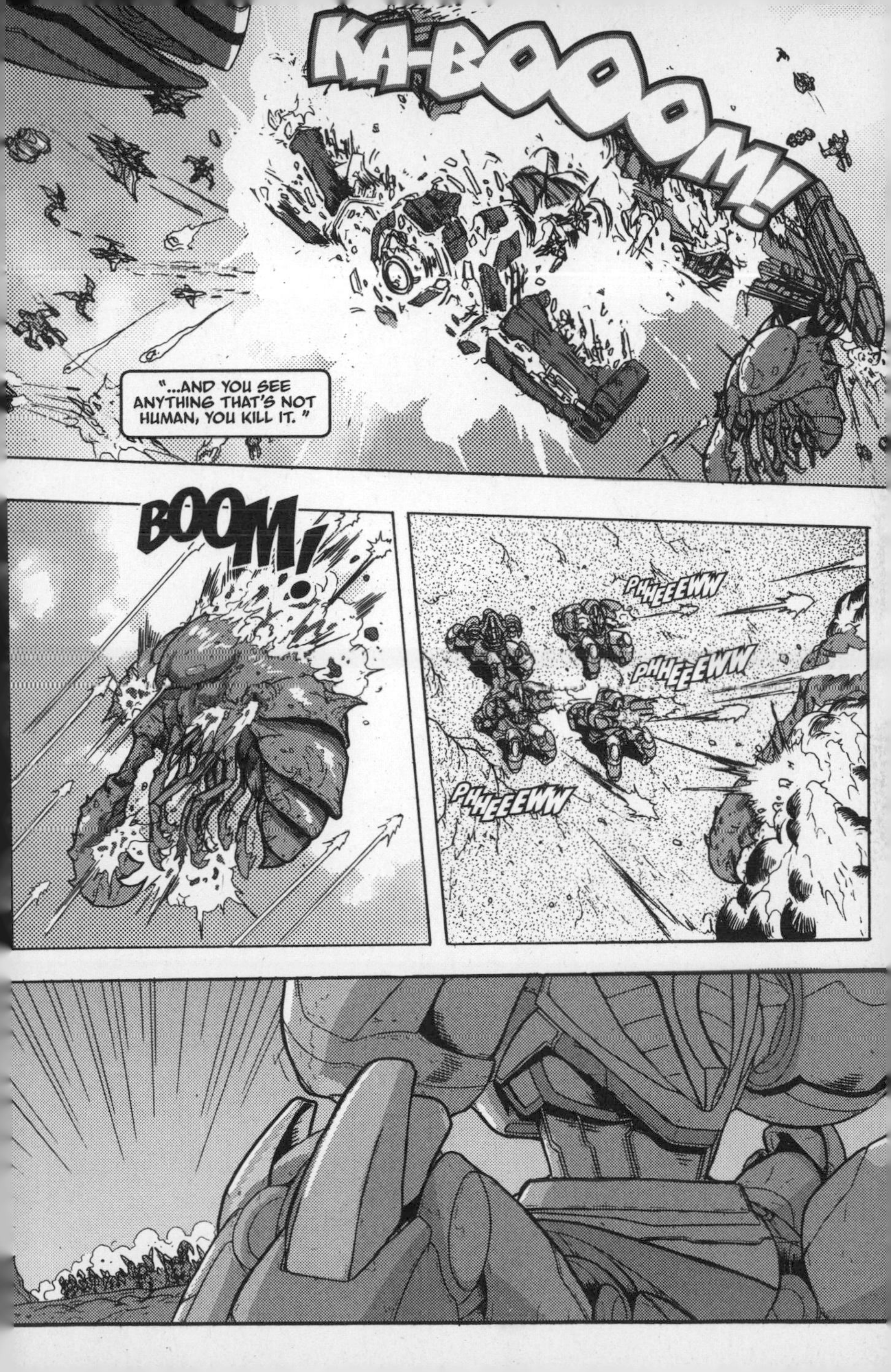

KA-BOOOOM!
"...AND YOU SEE ANYTHING THAT'S NOT HUMAN, YOU KILL IT."
BOOM!
PHHEEEWW
PHHEEEWW
PHHEEEWW

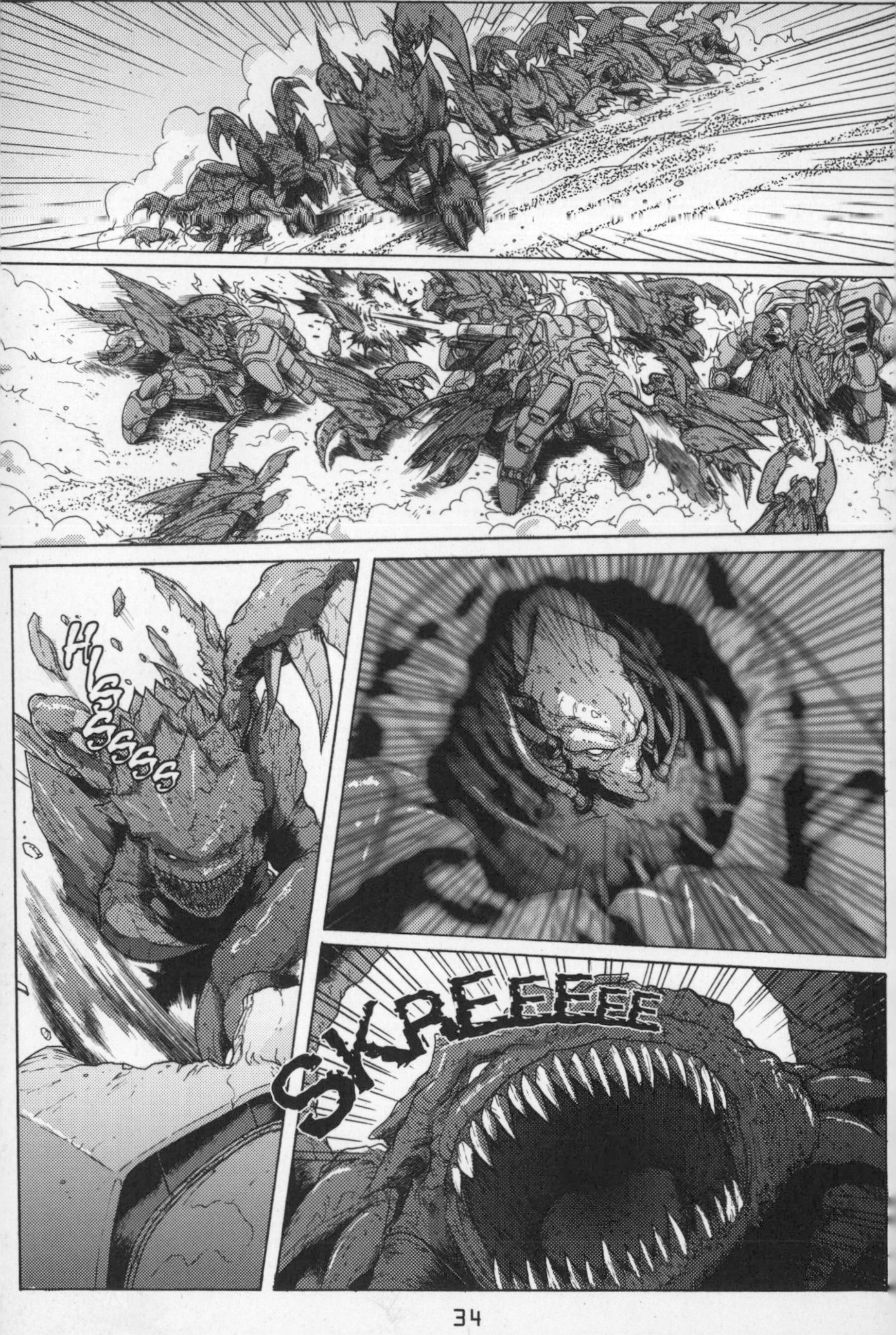
HISSSSS
SKREEEEE

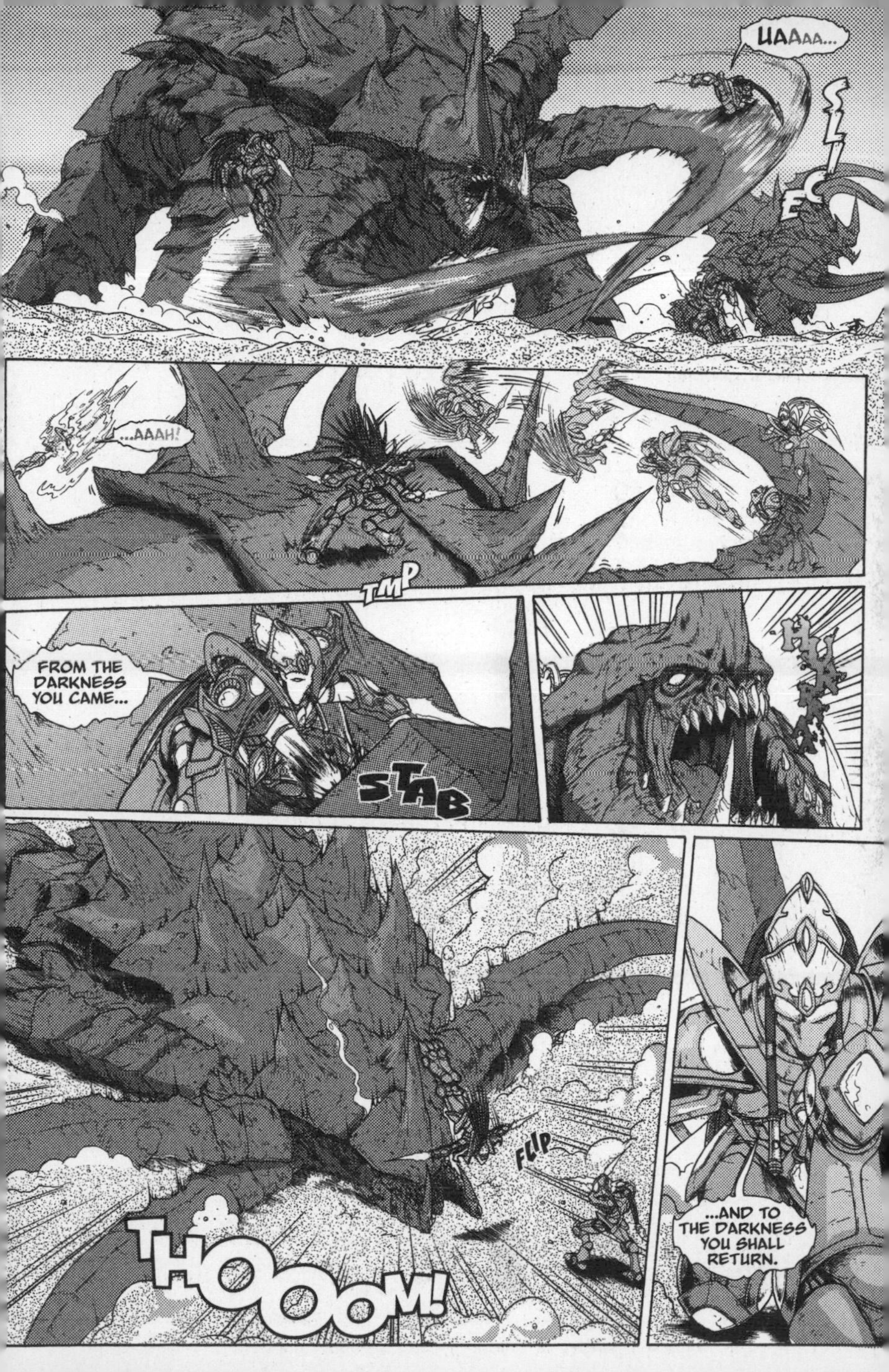
UAAAA...
SLICE
...AAAH!
TMP
FROM THE DARKNESS YOU CAME...
STAB
FLIP
THOOOOM!
...AND TO THE DARKNESS YOU SHALL RETURN.

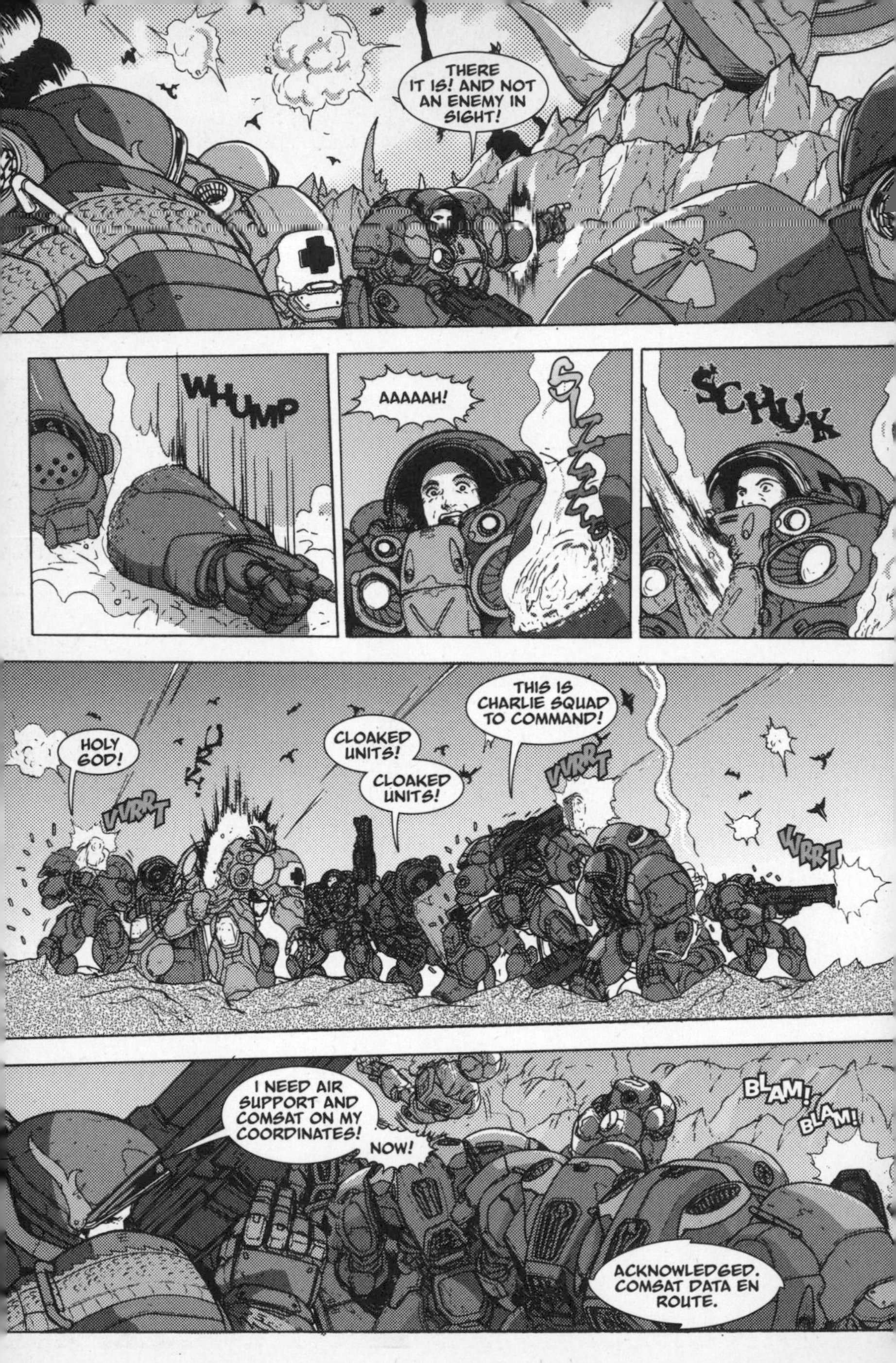
THERE IT IS! AND NOT AN ENEMY IN SIGHT!
WHUMP
AAAAAH!
SIZZZZ
SCHUK
HOLY GOD!
VVRRT
CLOAKED UNITS!
CLOAKED UNITS!
THIS IS CHARLIE SQUAD TO COMMAND!
VVRRT
VVRRT
I NEED AIR SUPPORT AND COMSAT ON MY COORDINATES!
NOW!
BLAM! BLAM!
ACKNOWLEDGED. COMSAT DATA EN ROUTE.

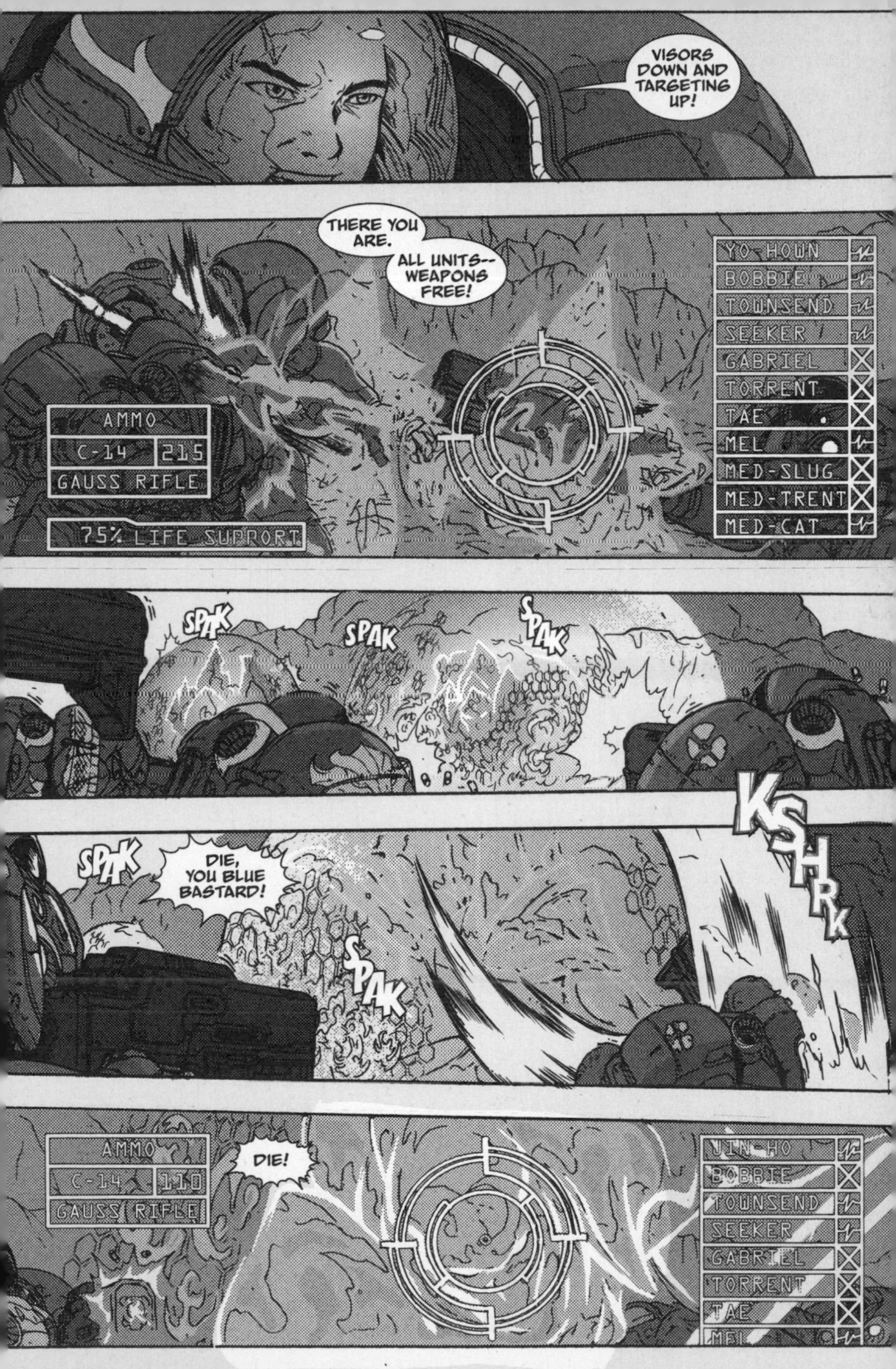
VISORS DOWN AND TARGETING UP!
THERE YOU ARE.
ALL UNITS-- WEAPONS FREE!
AMMO
C-14 215
GAUSS RIFLE
75% LIFE SUPPORT
YO-HOWN
BOBBIE
TOWNSEND
SEEKER
GABRIEL
TORRENT
TAE
MEL
MED-SLUG
MED-TRENT
MED-CAT
SPAK
SPAK
SPAK
SPAK
DIE, YOU BLUE BASTARD!
SPAK
KSHRK
AMMO
C-14 110
GAUSS RIFLE
DIE!
JIN-HO
BOBBIE
TOWNSEND
SEEKER
GABRIEL
TORRENT
TAE

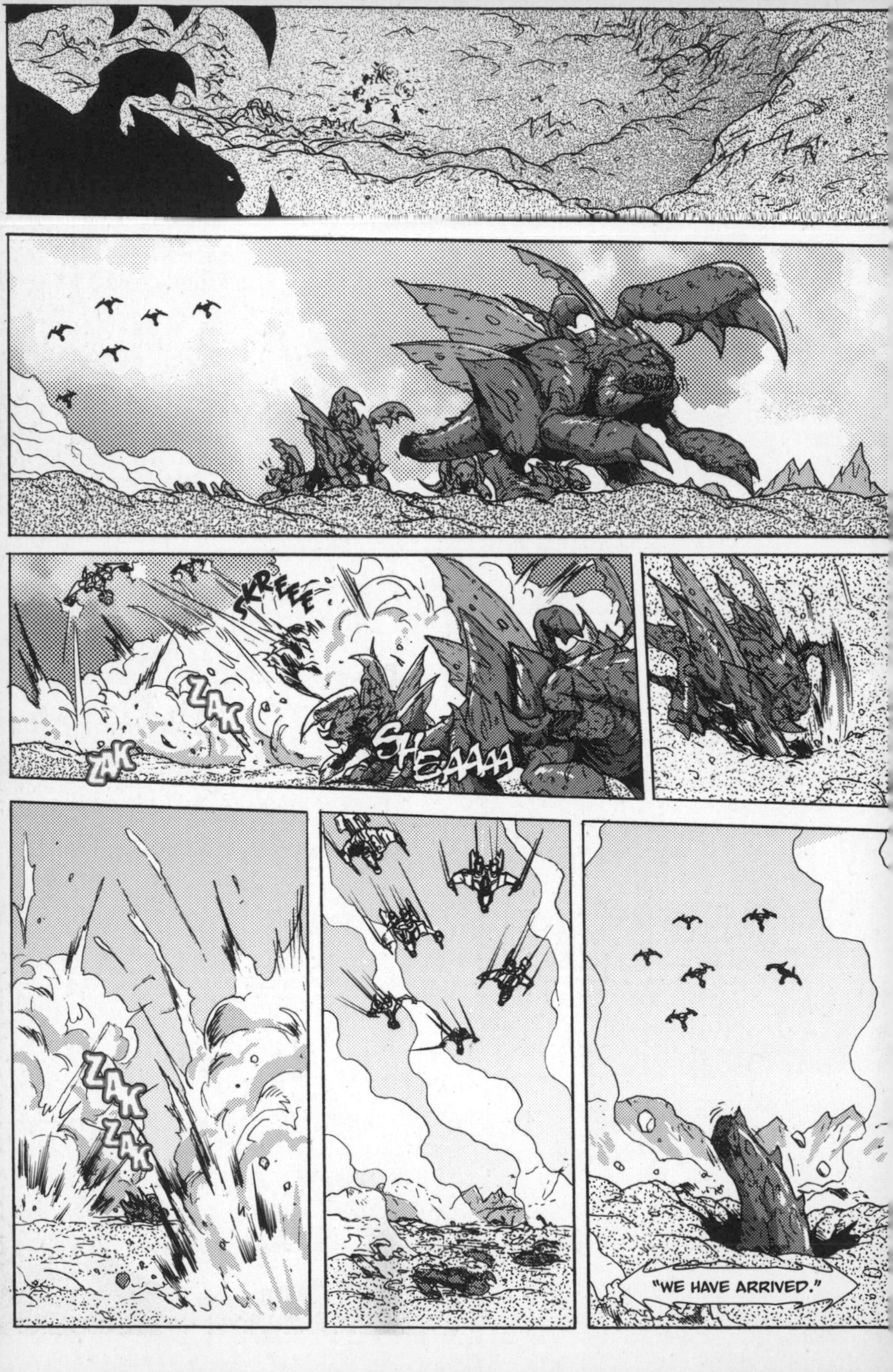
SKREEEE
ZAK
ZAK
SHEAAAA
ZAK
ZAK
"WE HAVE ARRIVED."

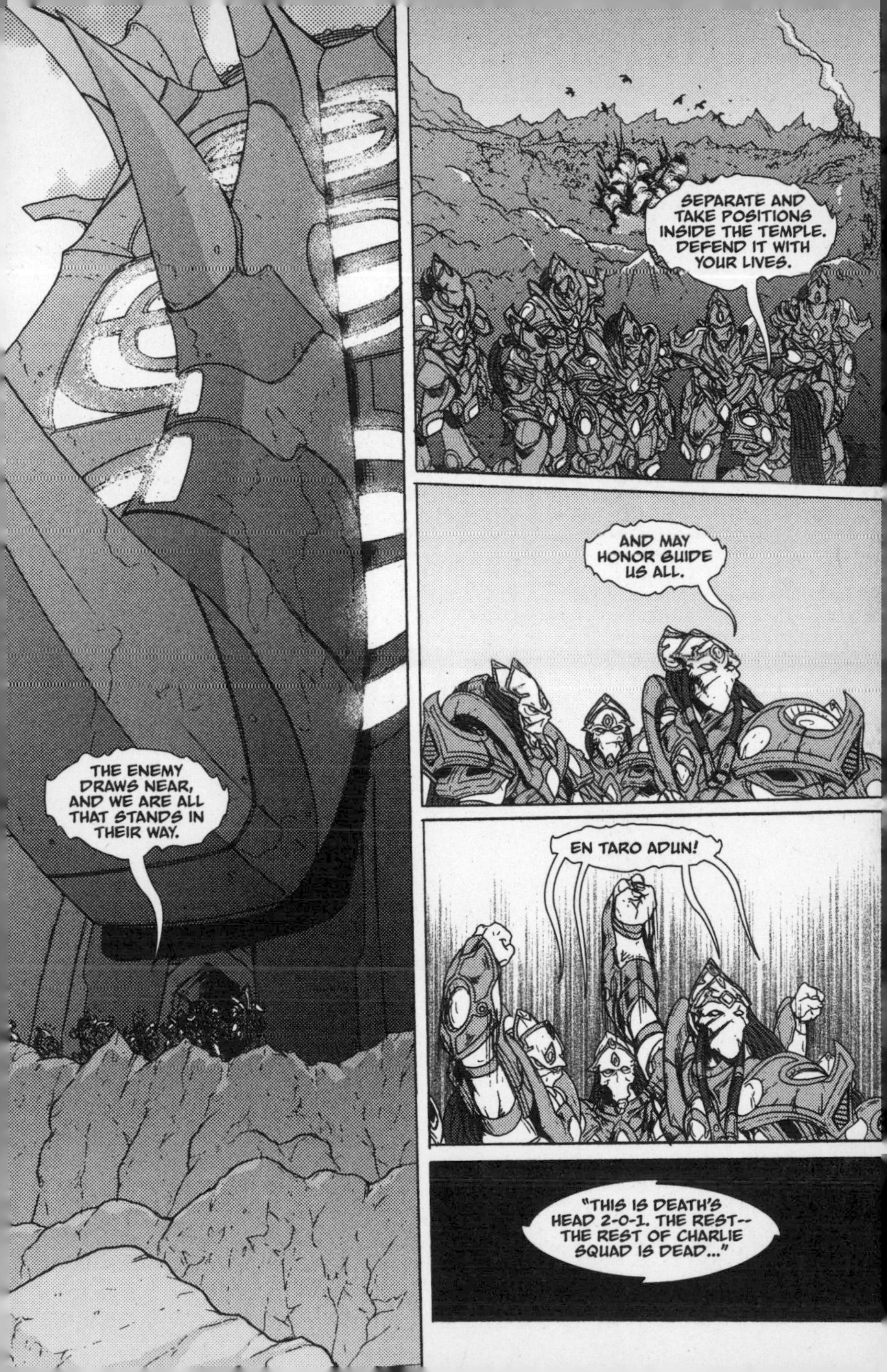
THE ENEMY DRAWS NEAR, AND WE ARE ALL THAT STANDS IN THEIR WAY.
SEPARATE AND TAKE POSITIONS INSIDE THE TEMPLE. DEFEND IT WITH YOUR LIVES.
AND MAY HONOR GUIDE US ALL.
EN TARO ADUN!
"THIS IS DEATH'S HEAD 2-0-1. THE REST-- THE REST OF CHARLIE SQUAD IS DEAD..."

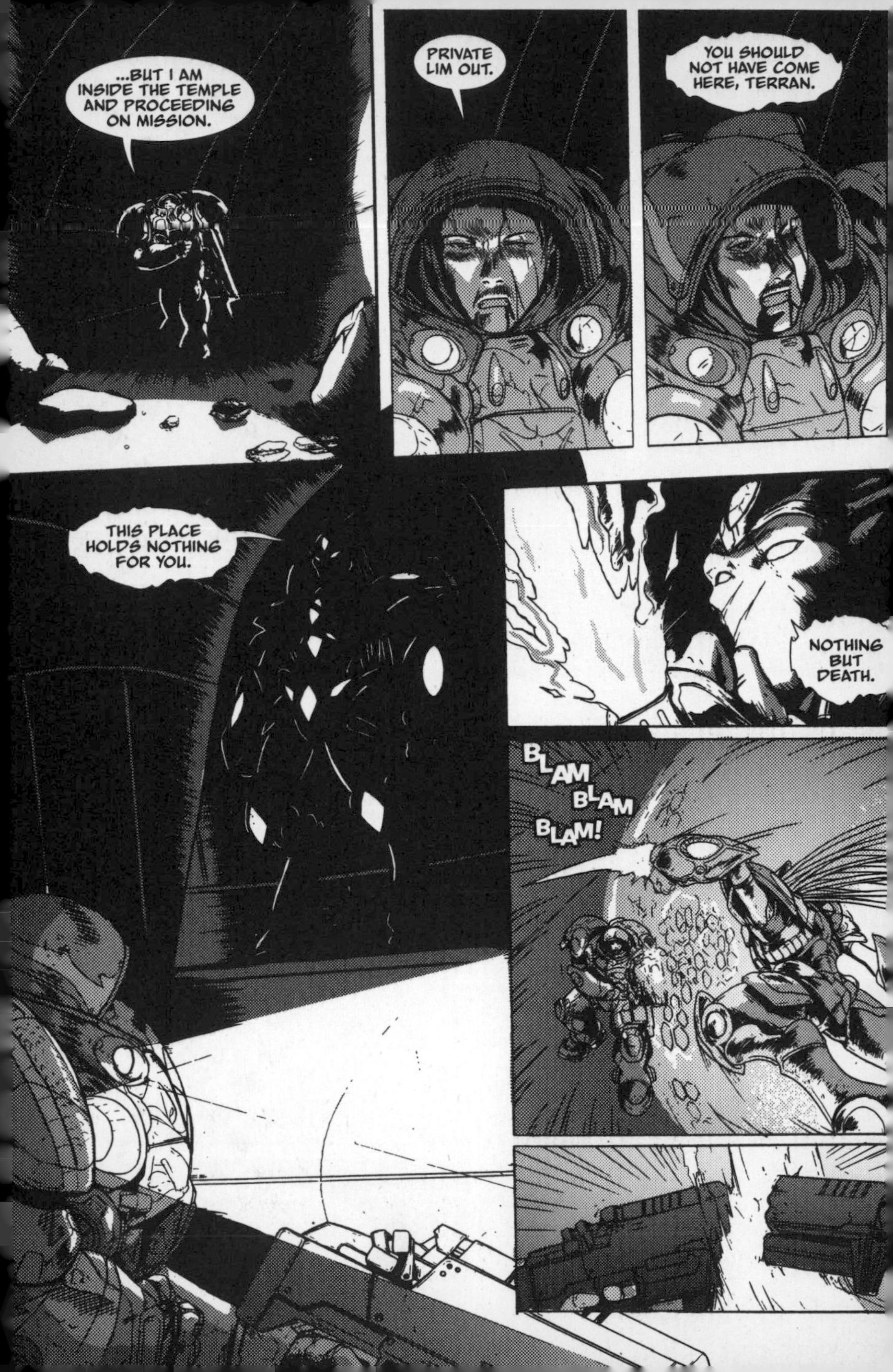
...BUT I AM INSIDE THE TEMPLE AND PROCEEDING ON MISSION.
PRIVATE LIM OUT.
YOU SHOULD NOT HAVE COME HERE, TERRAN.
THIS PLACE HOLDS NOTHING FOR YOU.
NOTHING BUT DEATH.
BLAM BLAM BLAM!

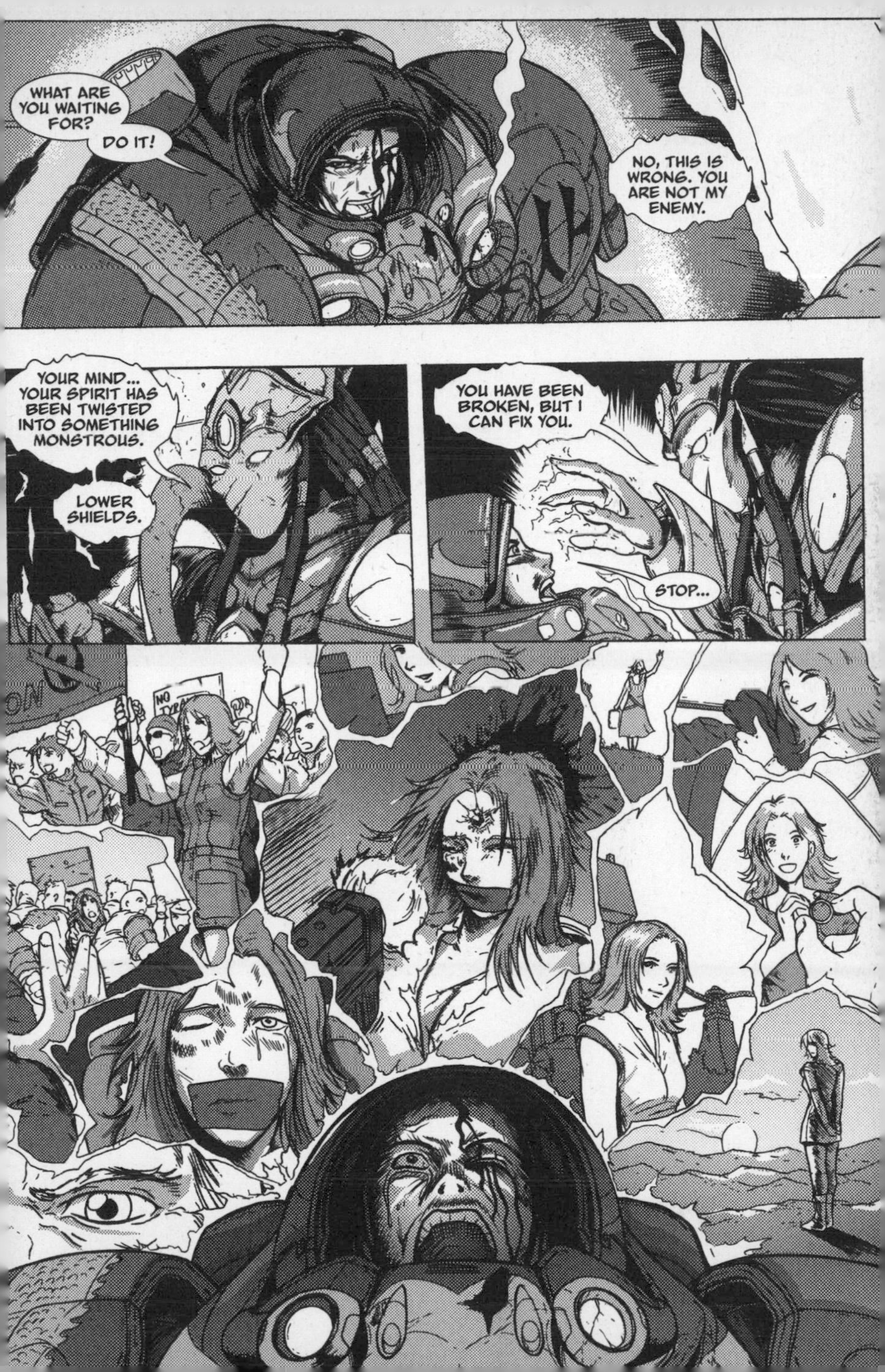
WHAT ARE YOU WAITING FOR?
DO IT!
NO, THIS IS WRONG. YOU ARE NOT MY ENEMY.
YOUR MIND... YOUR SPIRIT HAS BEEN TWISTED INTO SOMETHING MONSTROUS.
LOWER SHIELDS.
YOU HAVE BEEN BROKEN, BUT I CAN FIX YOU.
STOP...
NO

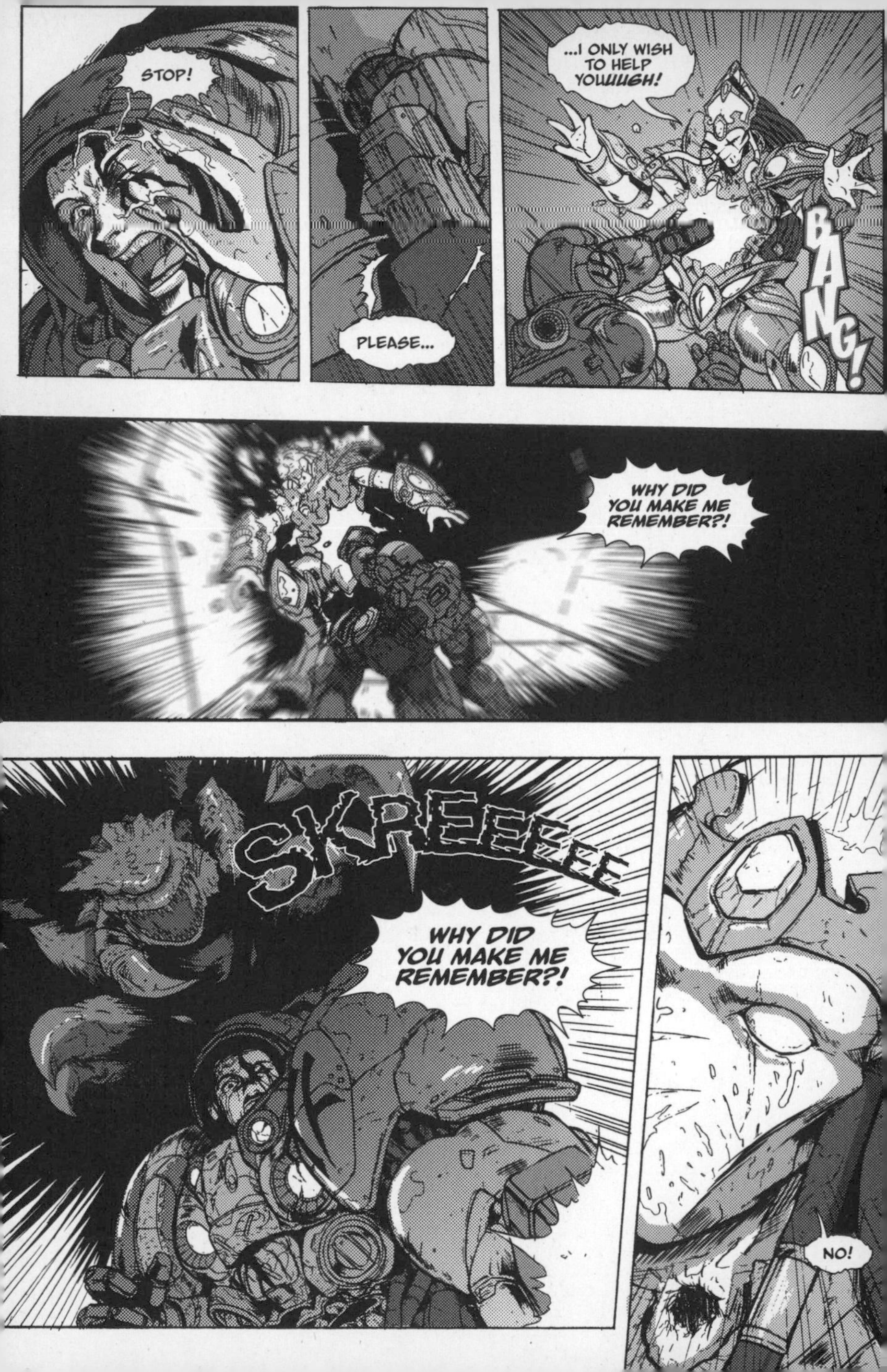
STOP!
PLEASE...
...I ONLY WISH TO HELP YOUUUGH!
BANG!
WHY DID YOU MAKE ME REMEMBER?!
SKREEEEEE
WHY DID YOU MAKE ME REMEMBER?!
NO!

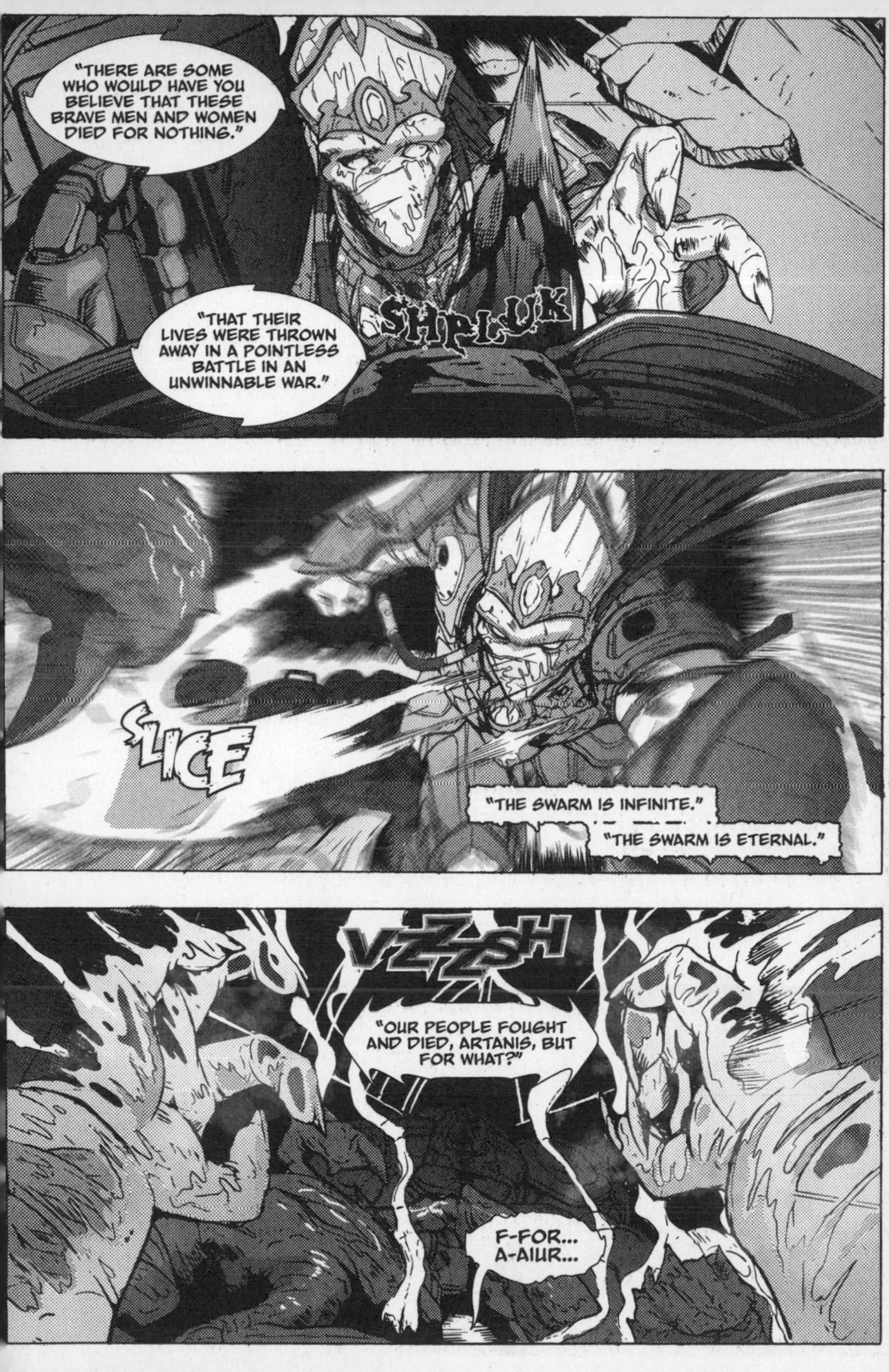
"THERE ARE SOME WHO WOULD HAVE YOU BELIEVE THAT THESE BRAVE MEN AND WOMEN DIED FOR NOTHING."
SHPLUK
"THAT THEIR LIVES WERE THROWN AWAY IN A POINTLESS BATTLE IN AN UNWINNABLE WAR."
SLICE
"THE SWARM IS INFINITE."
"THE SWARM IS ETERNAL."
VZZZSH
"OUR PEOPLE FOUGHT AND DIED, ARTANIS, BUT FOR WHAT?"
F-FOR... A-AIUR...

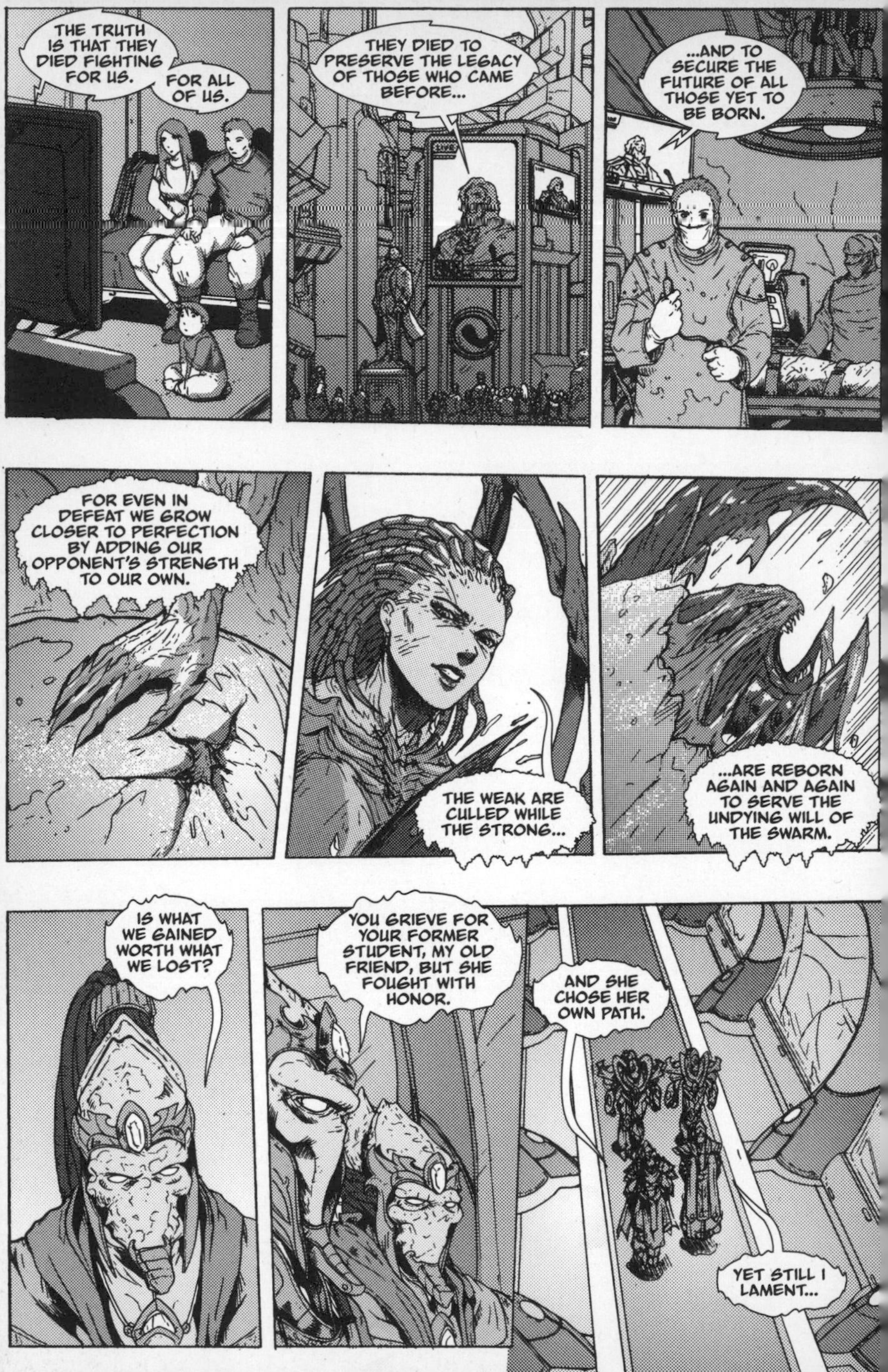
THE TRUTH IS THAT THEY DIED FIGHTING FOR US.
FOR ALL OF US.
THEY DIED TO PRESERVE THE LEGACY OF THOSE WHO CAME BEFORE...
...AND TO SECURE THE FUTURE OF ALL THOSE YET TO BE BORN.
FOR EVEN IN DEFEAT WE GROW CLOSER TO PERFECTION BY ADDING OUR OPPONENT'S STRENGTH TO OUR OWN.
THE WEAK ARE CULLED WHILE THE STRONG...
...ARE REBORN AGAIN AND AGAIN TO SERVE THE UNDYING WILL OF THE SWARM.
IS WHAT WE GAINED WORTH WHAT WE LOST?
YOU GRIEVE FOR YOUR FORMER STUDENT, MY OLD FRIEND, BUT SHE FOUGHT WITH HONOR.
AND SHE CHOSE HER OWN PATH.
YET STILL I LAMENT...

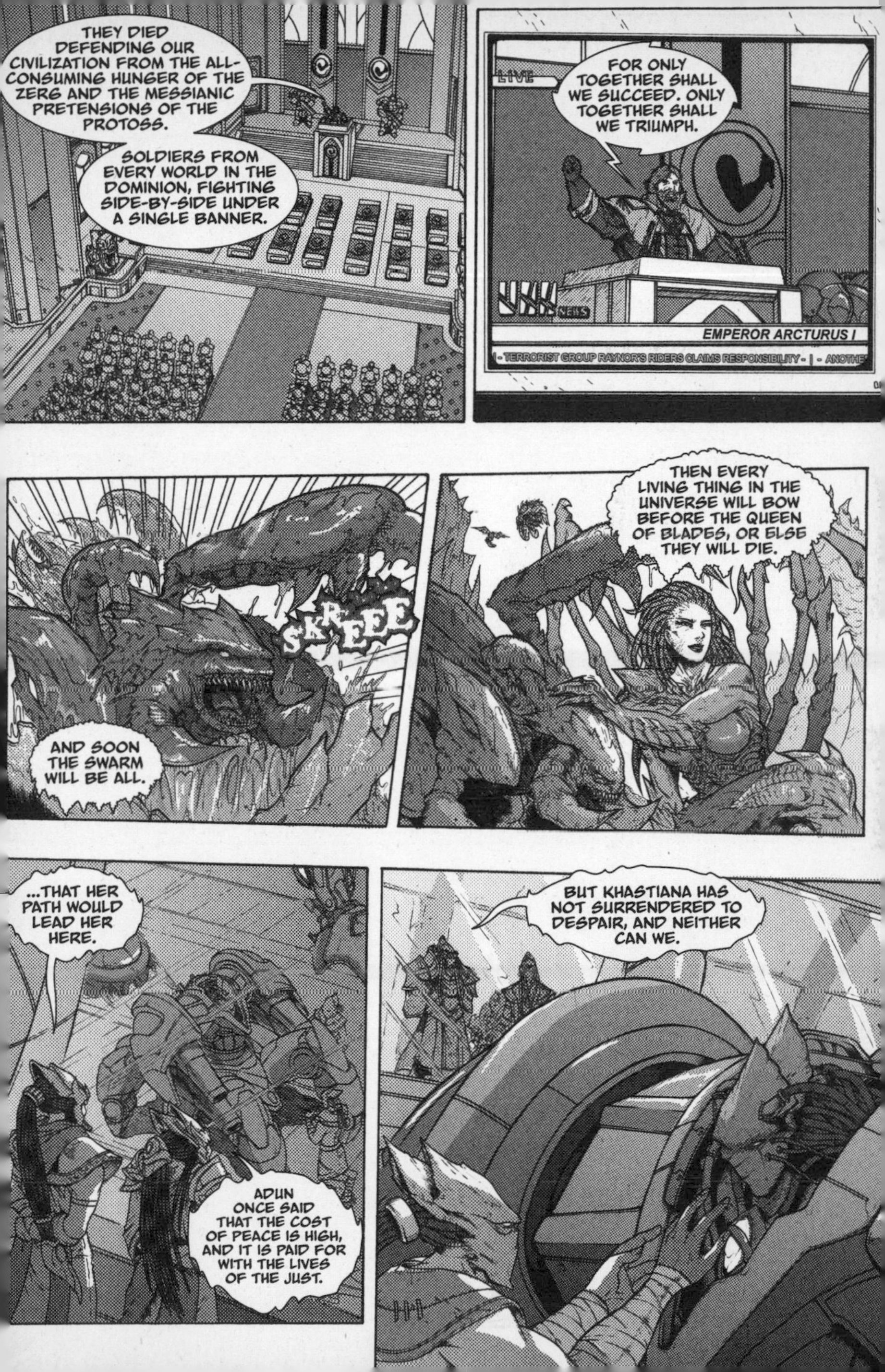
THEY DIED DEFENDING OUR CIVILIZATION FROM THE ALL-CONSUMING HUNGER OF THE ZERG AND THE MESSIANIC PRETENSIONS OF THE PROTOSS.
SOLDIERS FROM EVERY WORLD IN THE DOMINION, FIGHTING SIDE-BY-SIDE UNDER A SINGLE BANNER.
LIVE
FOR ONLY TOGETHER SHALL WE SUCCEED. ONLY TOGETHER SHALL WE TRIUMPH.
UNN NEWS
EMPEROR ARCTURUS I
- TERRORIST GROUP RAYNOR'S RIDERS CLAIMS RESPONSIBILITY - | - ANOTHE
SKREEEE
AND SOON THE SWARM WILL BE ALL.
THEN EVERY LIVING THING IN THE UNIVERSE WILL BOW BEFORE THE QUEEN OF BLADES, OR ELSE THEY WILL DIE.
...THAT HER PATH WOULD LEAD HER HERE.
ADUN ONCE SAID THAT THE COST OF PEACE IS HIGH, AND IT IS PAID FOR WITH THE LIVES OF THE JUST.
BUT KHASTIANA HAS NOT SURRENDERED TO DESPAIR, AND NEITHER CAN WE.

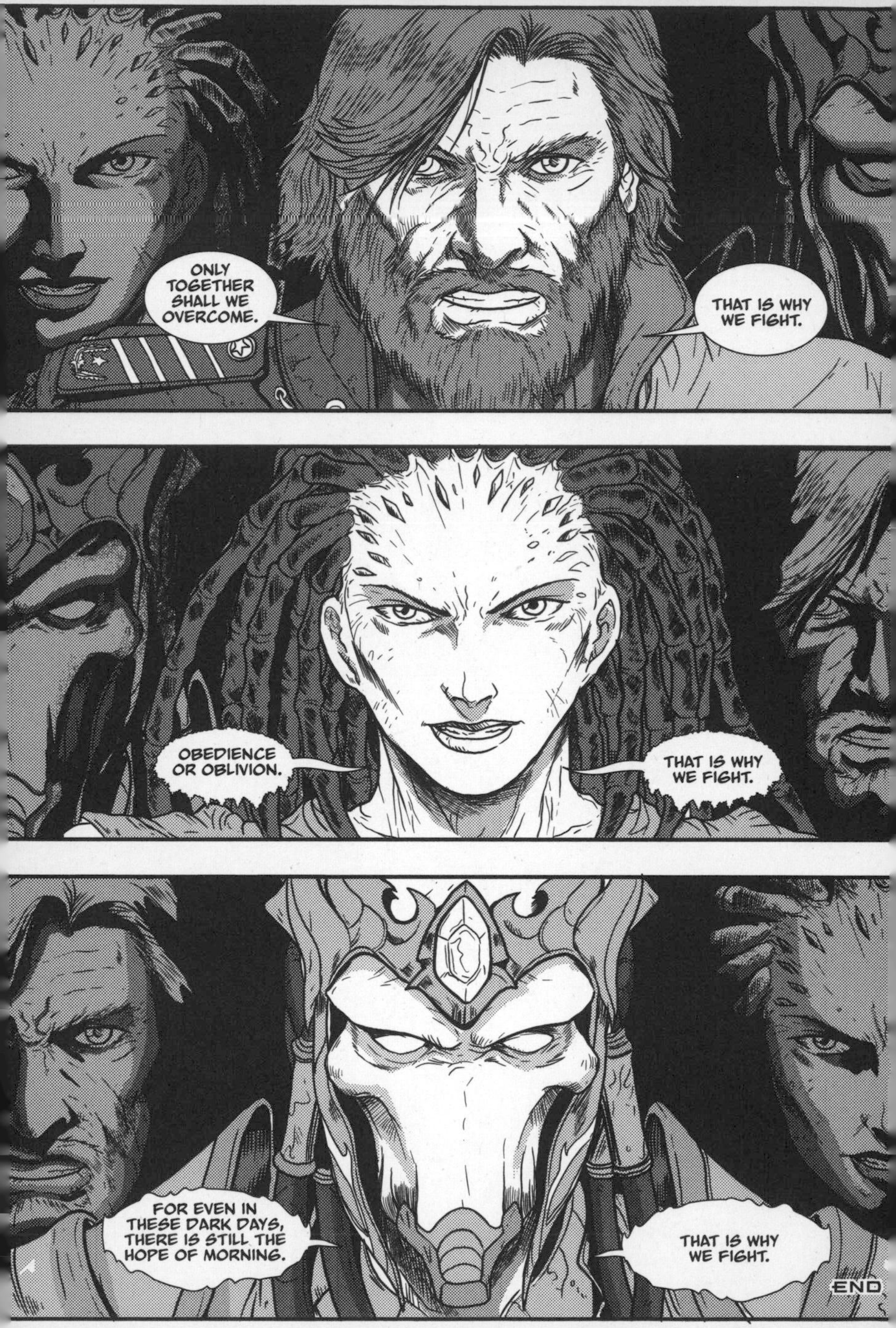
ONLY TOGETHER SHALL WE OVERCOME.
THAT IS WHY WE FIGHT.
OBEDIENCE OR OBLIVION.
THAT IS WHY WE FIGHT.
FOR EVEN IN THESE DARK DAYS, THERE IS STILL THE HOPE OF MORNING.
THAT IS WHY WE FIGHT.
END

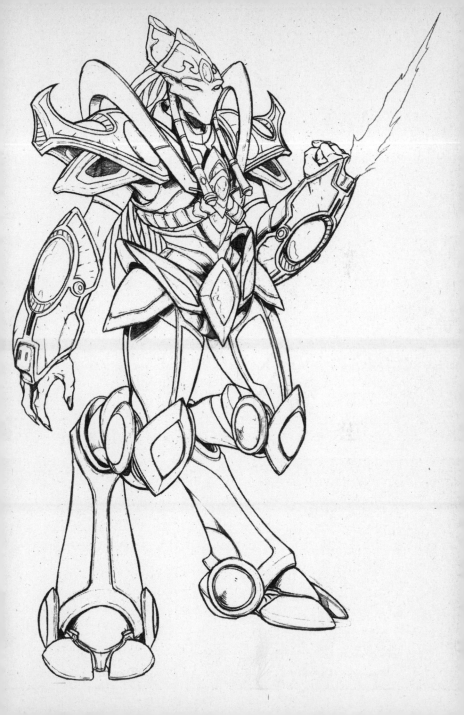

StarCraft

Frontline

Volume 1

Thunder God

Written by Richard A. Knaak

Pencils and Inks by Naohiro Washio

Art Assistants: Yoshihito Watanabe,
Kure Yon and Natsuko Kurata

Tones by Hanzow Kagehara

Contributing Editor: Rie Shiramizu
Associate Editor: Jessica Chavez
Letterers: Lucas Rivera and Michael Paolilli

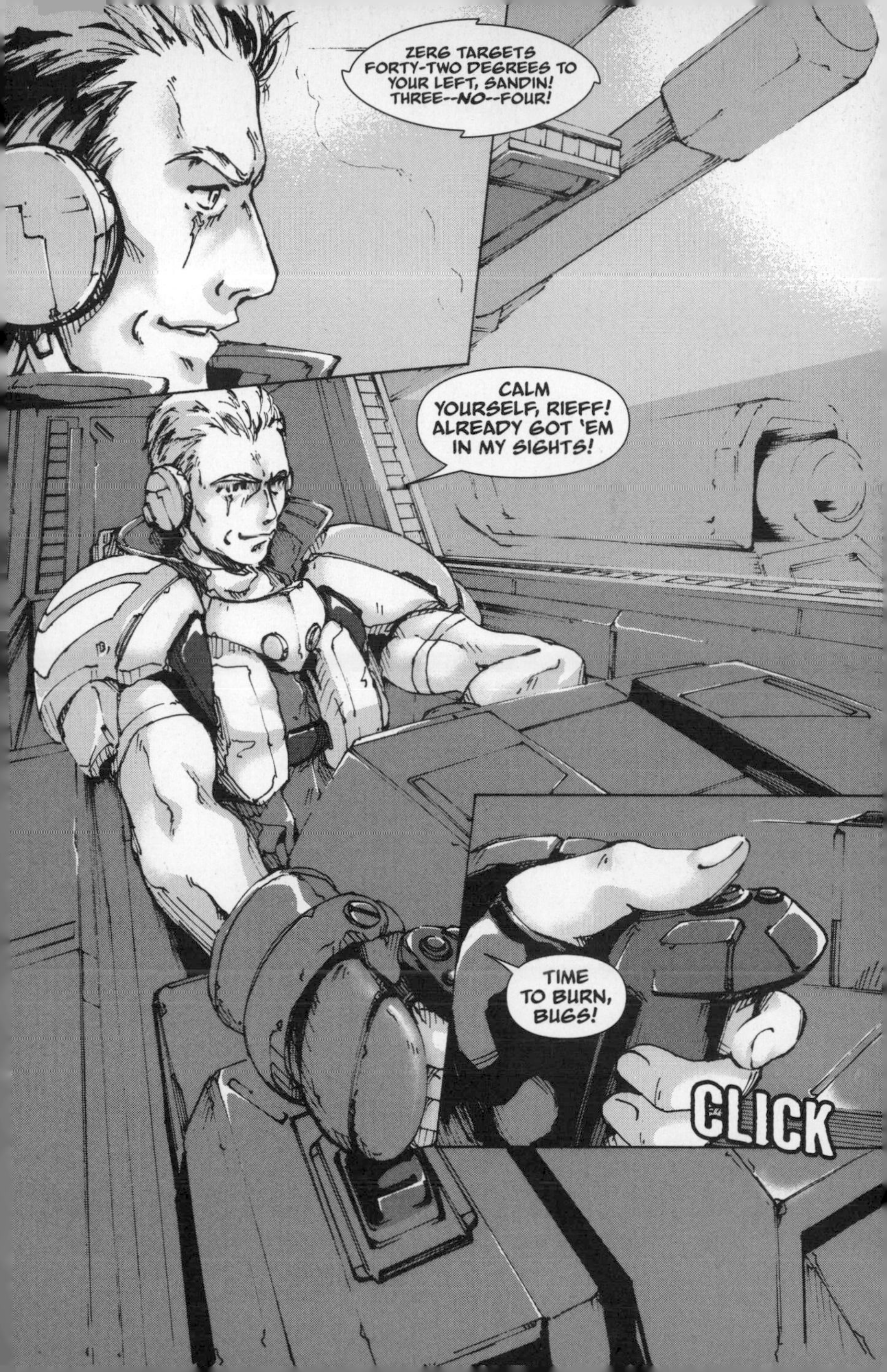
ZERG TARGETS FORTY-TWO DEGREES TO YOUR LEFT, SANDIN! THREE--*NO*--FOUR!
CALM YOURSELF, RIEFF! ALREADY GOT 'EM IN MY SIGHTS!
TIME TO BURN, BUGS!
CLICK

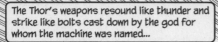
The Thor's weapons resound like thunder and strike like bolts cast down by the god for whom the machine was named...

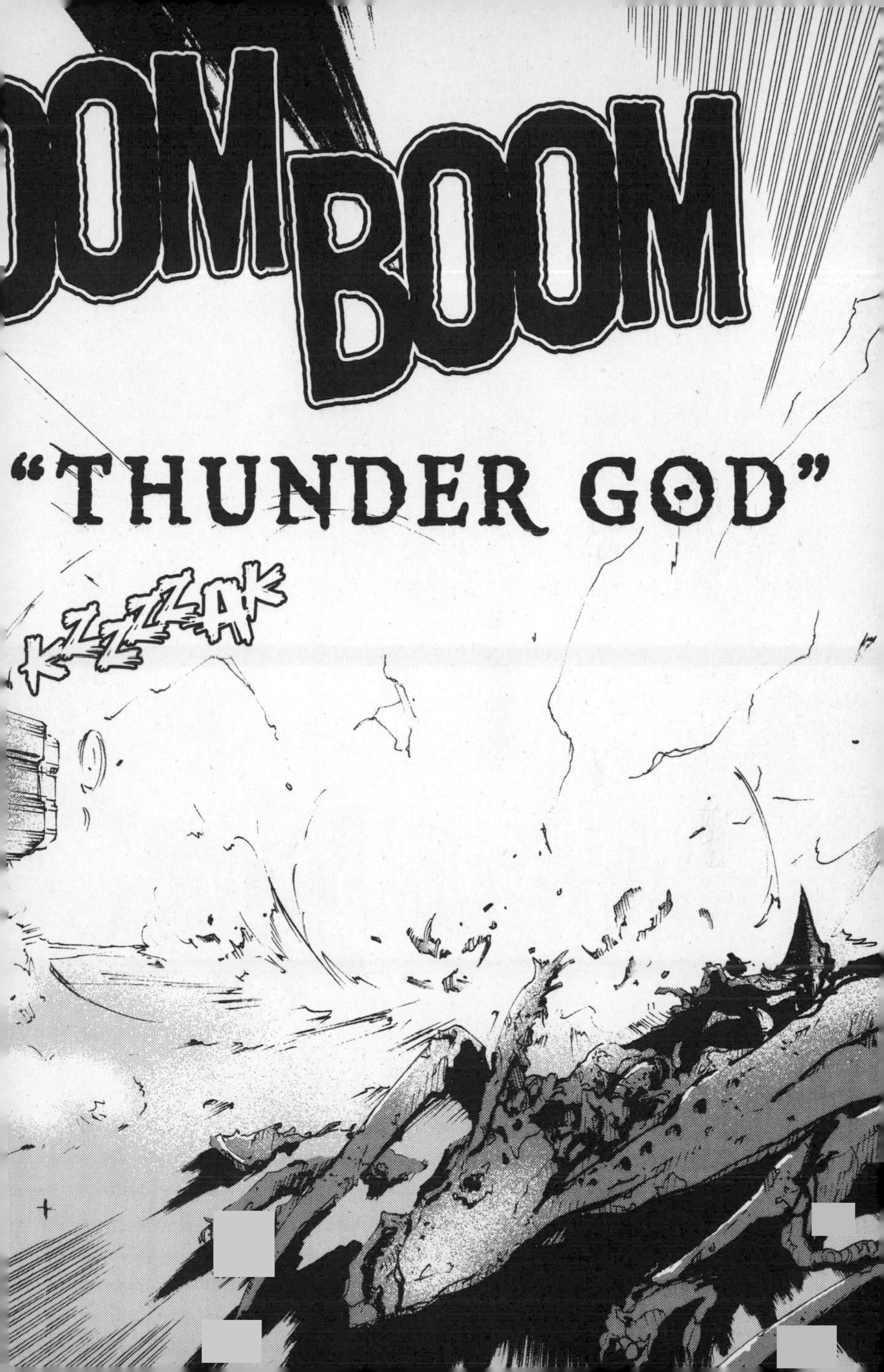
OOM
BOOM
"THUNDER GOD"
KZZZZAK

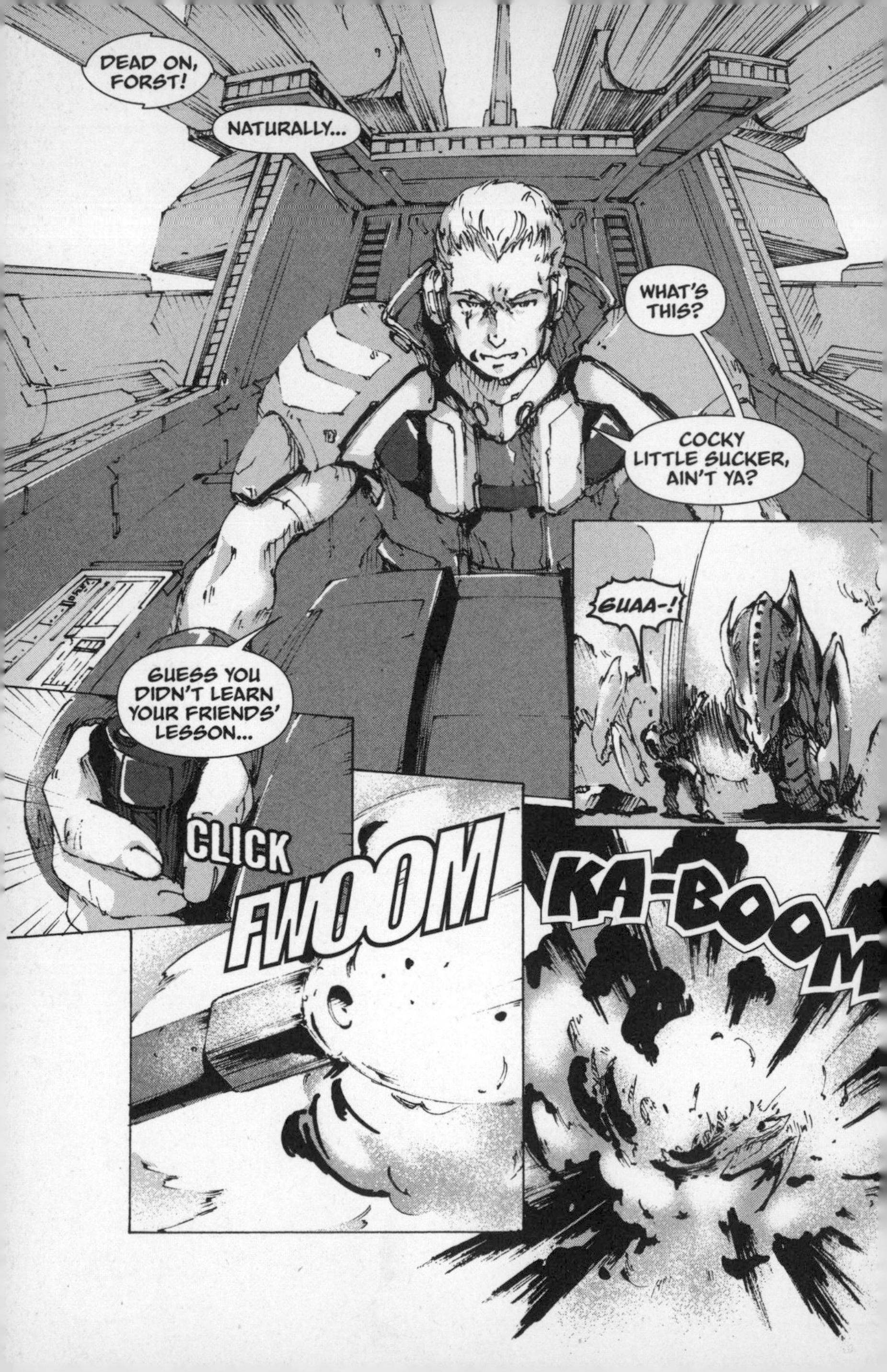
DEAD ON, FORST!
NATURALLY...
WHAT'S THIS?
COCKY LITTLE SUCKER, AIN'T YA?
GUESS YOU DIDN'T LEARN YOUR FRIENDS' LESSON...
GUAA-!
CLICK
FWOOM
KA-BOOM

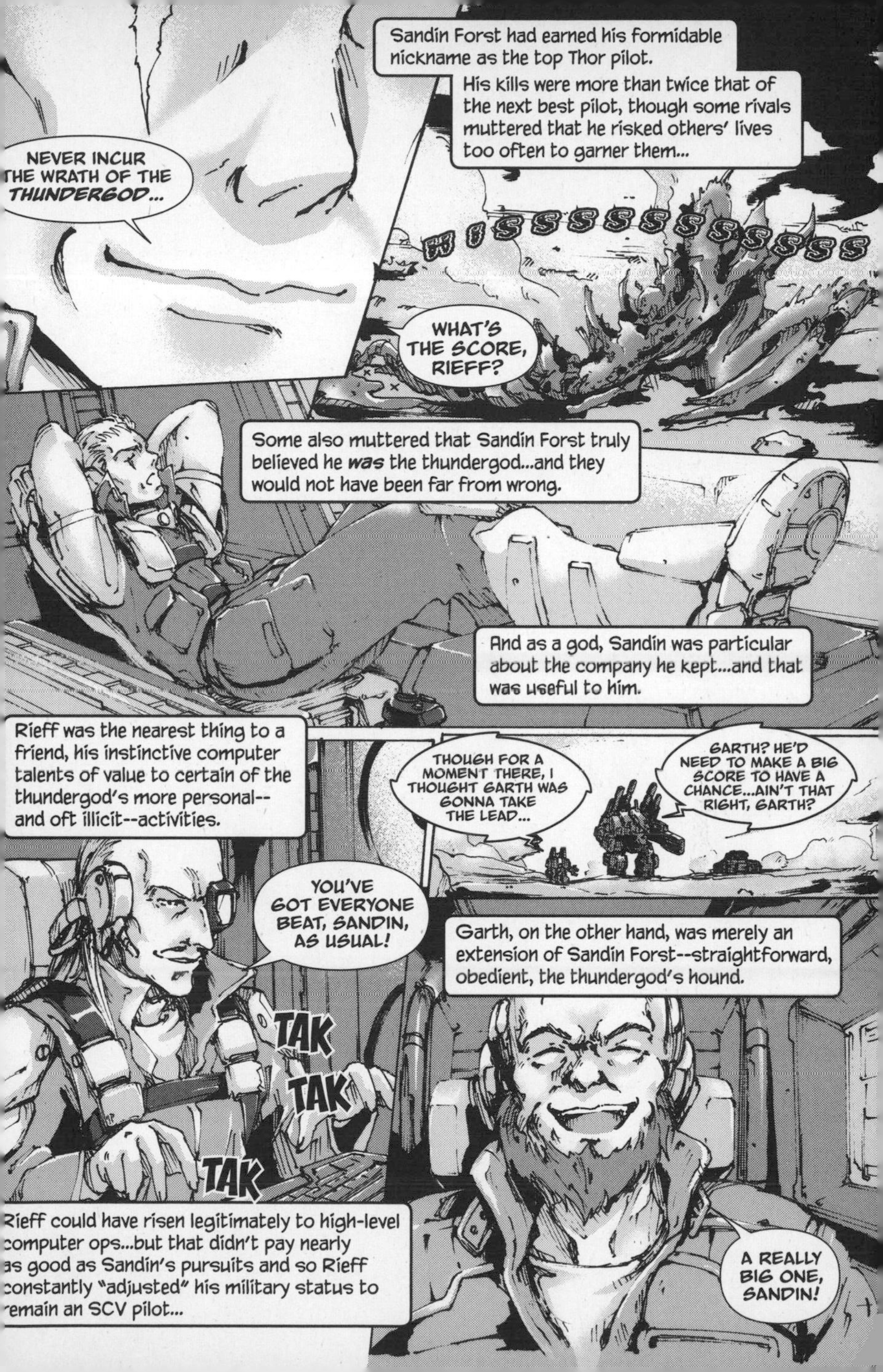
NEVER INCUR THE WRATH OF THE *THUNDERGOD*...
Sandin Forst had earned his formidable nickname as the top Thor pilot.
His kills were more than twice that of the next best pilot, though some rivals muttered that he risked others' lives too often to garner them...
HISSSSSSSSSSS
WHAT'S THE SCORE, RIEFF?
Some also muttered that Sandin Forst truly believed he ***was*** the thundergod...and they would not have been far from wrong.
And as a god, Sandin was particular about the company he kept...and that was useful to him.
Rieff was the nearest thing to a friend, his instinctive computer talents of value to certain of the thundergod's more personal--and oft illicit--activities.
THOUGH FOR A MOMENT THERE, I THOUGHT GARTH WAS GONNA TAKE THE LEAD...
GARTH? HE'D NEED TO MAKE A BIG SCORE TO HAVE A CHANCE...AIN'T THAT RIGHT, GARTH?
YOU'VE GOT EVERYONE BEAT, SANDIN, AS USUAL!
TAK
TAK
TAK
Rieff could have risen legitimately to high-level computer ops...but that didn't pay nearly as good as Sandin's pursuits and so Rieff constantly "adjusted" his military status to remain an SCV pilot...
Garth, on the other hand, was merely an extension of Sandin Forst--straightforward, obedient, the thundergod's hound.
A REALLY BIG ONE, SANDIN!

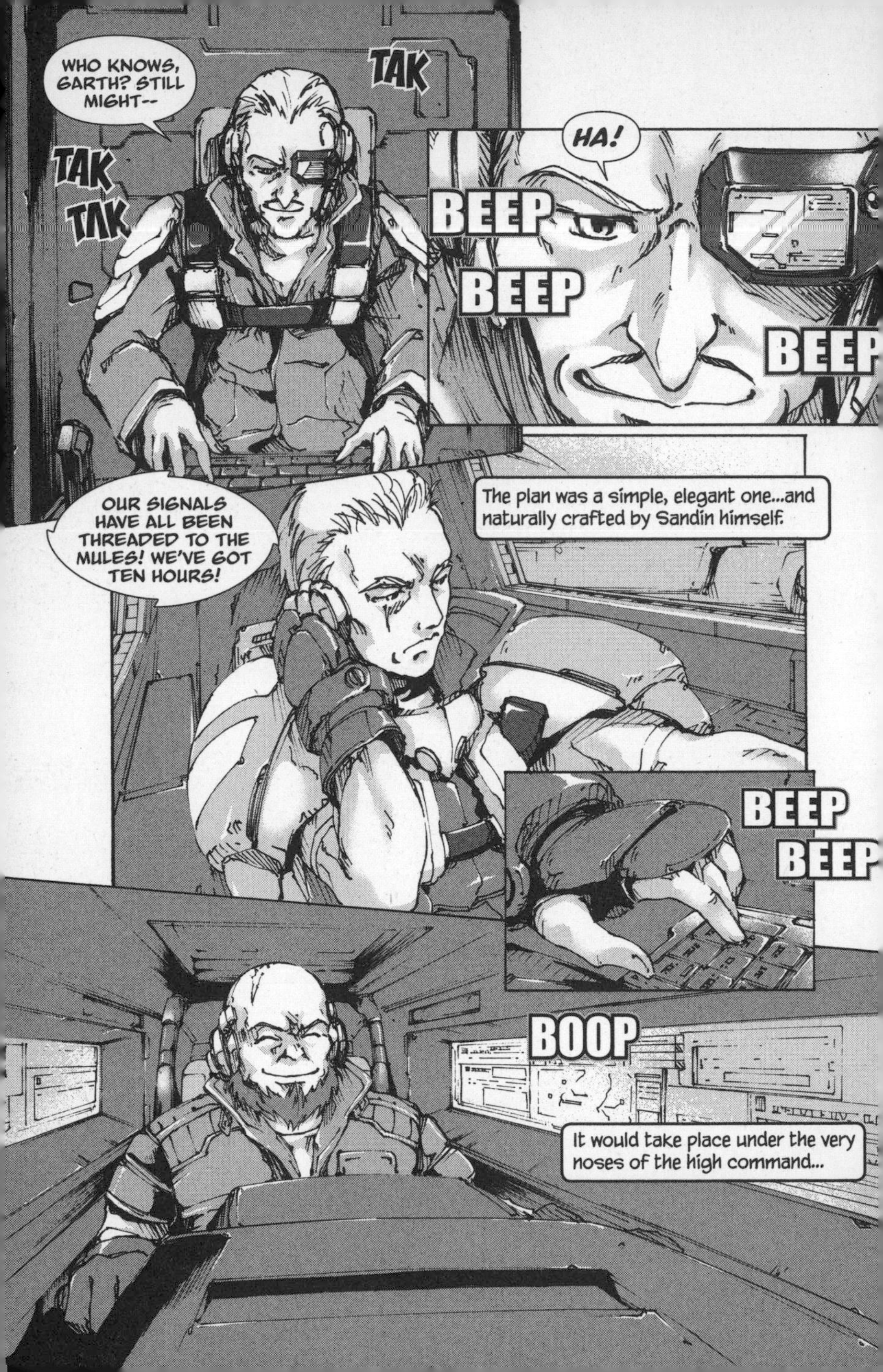
WHO KNOWS, GARTH? STILL MIGHT--
TAK
TAK
TAK
HA!
BEEP
BEEP
BEEP
OUR SIGNALS HAVE ALL BEEN THREADED TO THE MULES! WE'VE GOT TEN HOURS!
The plan was a simple, elegant one...and naturally crafted by Sandin himself.
BEEP
BEEP
BOOP
It would take place under the very noses of the high command...

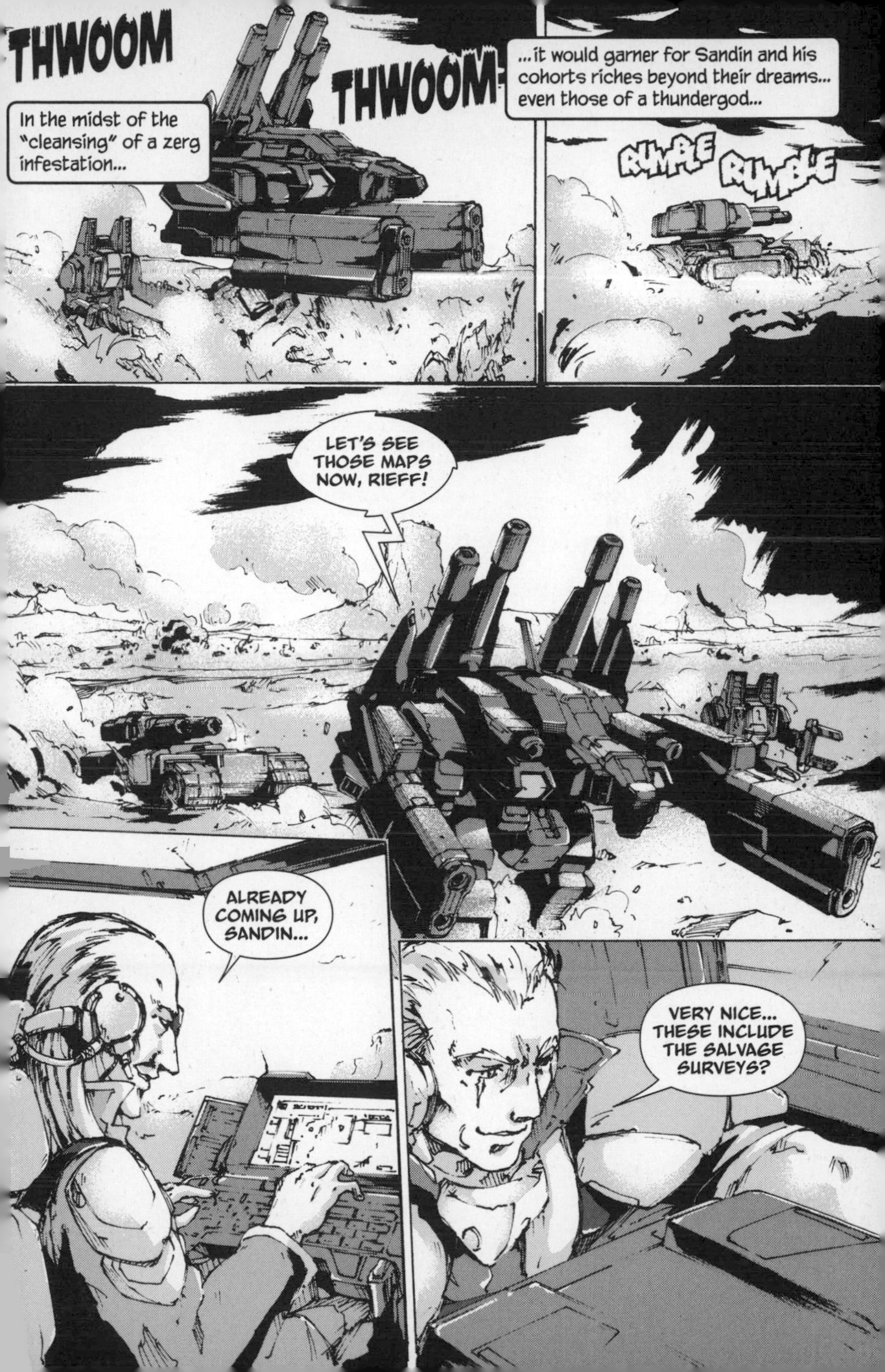
THWOOM
In the midst of the "cleansing" of a zerg infestation...
THWOOM
...it would garner for Sandin and his cohorts riches beyond their dreams... even those of a thundergod...
RUMBLE RUMBLE
LET'S SEE THOSE MAPS NOW, RIEFF!
ALREADY COMING UP, SANDIN...
VERY NICE... THESE INCLUDE THE SALVAGE SURVEYS?

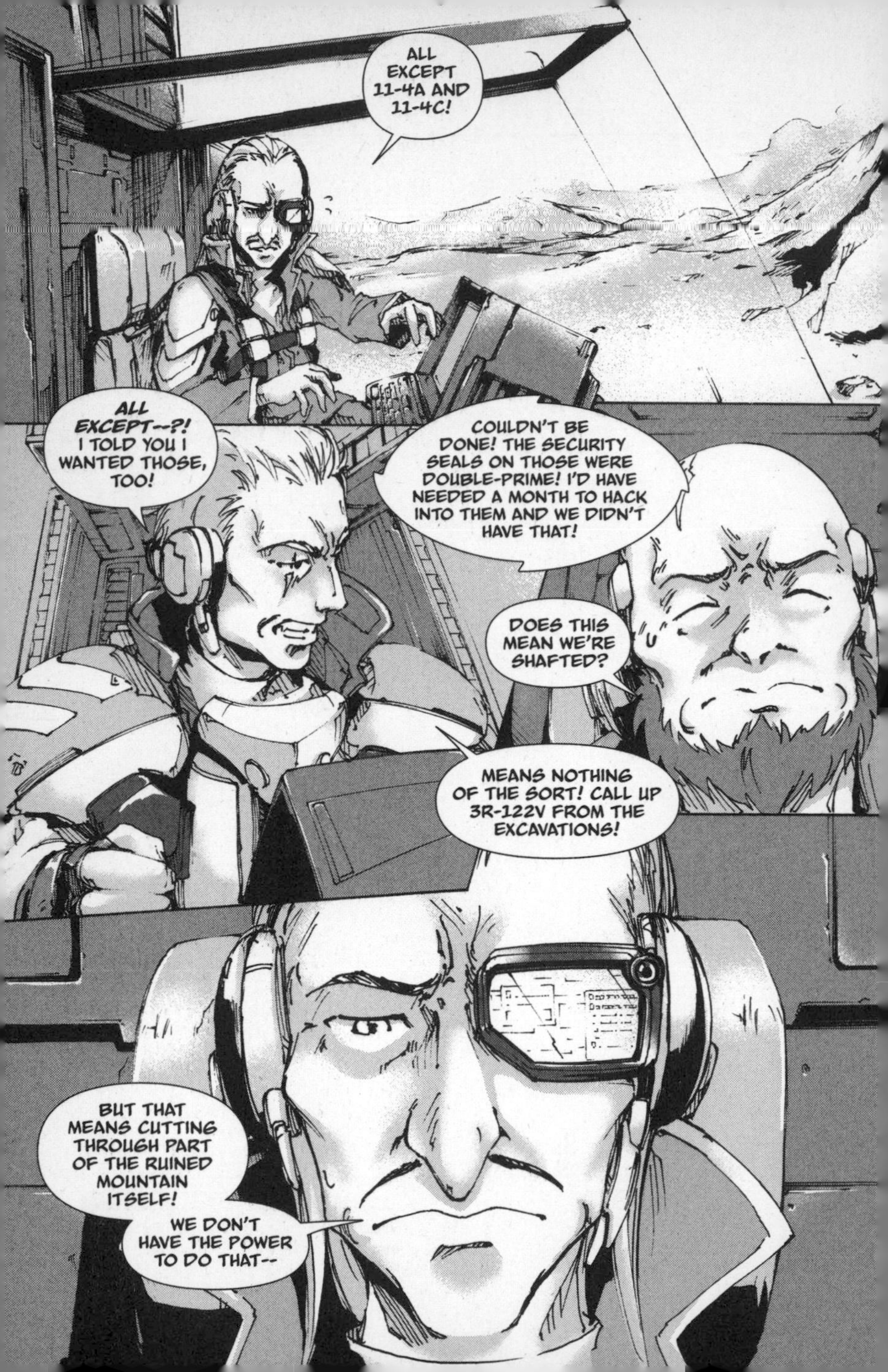
ALL EXCEPT 11-4A AND 11-4C!
ALL EXCEPT--?! I TOLD YOU I WANTED THOSE, TOO!
COULDN'T BE DONE! THE SECURITY SEALS ON THOSE WERE DOUBLE-PRIME! I'D HAVE NEEDED A MONTH TO HACK INTO THEM AND WE DIDN'T HAVE THAT!
DOES THIS MEAN WE'RE SHAFTED?
MEANS NOTHING OF THE SORT! CALL UP 3R-122V FROM THE EXCAVATIONS!
BUT THAT MEANS CUTTING THROUGH PART OF THE RUINED MOUNTAIN ITSELF!
WE DON'T HAVE THE POWER TO DO THAT--

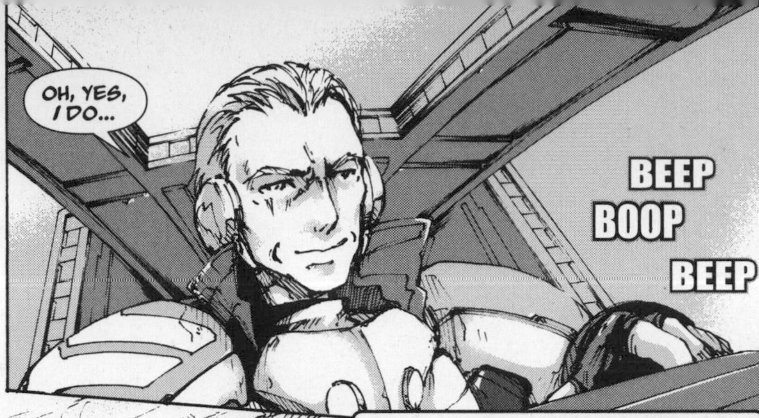
OH, YES, I DO...
BEEP
BOOP
BEEP

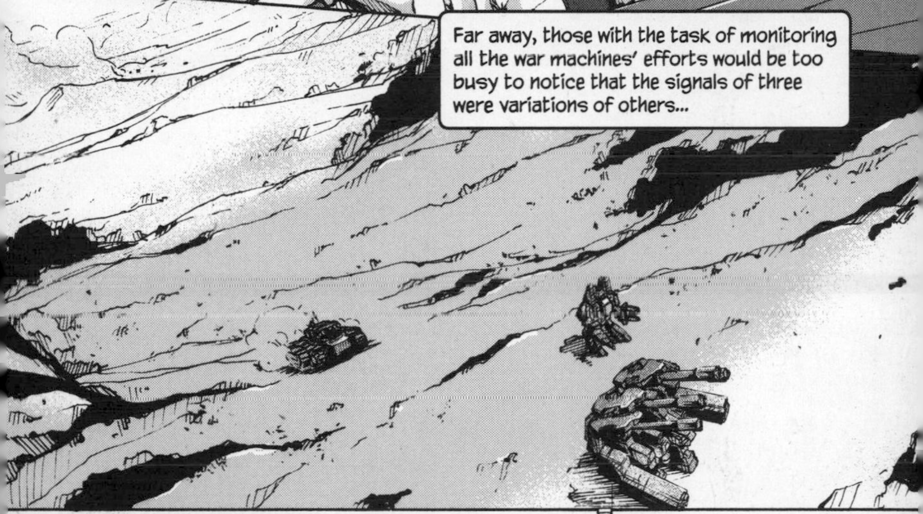
Far away, those with the task of monitoring all the war machines' efforts would be too busy to notice that the signals of three were variations of others...

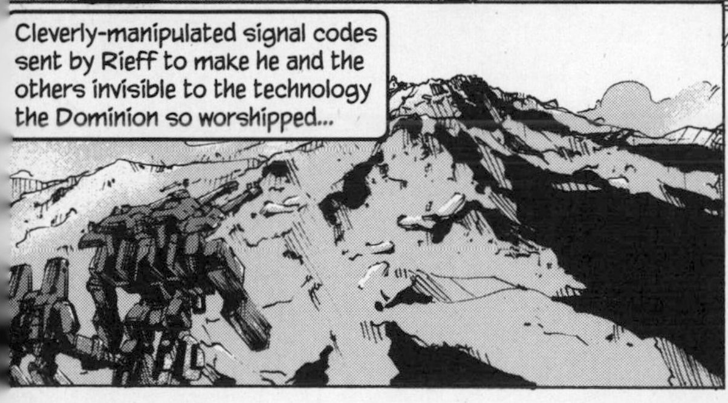
Cleverly-manipulated signal codes sent by Rieff to make he and the others invisible to the technology the Dominion so worshipped...

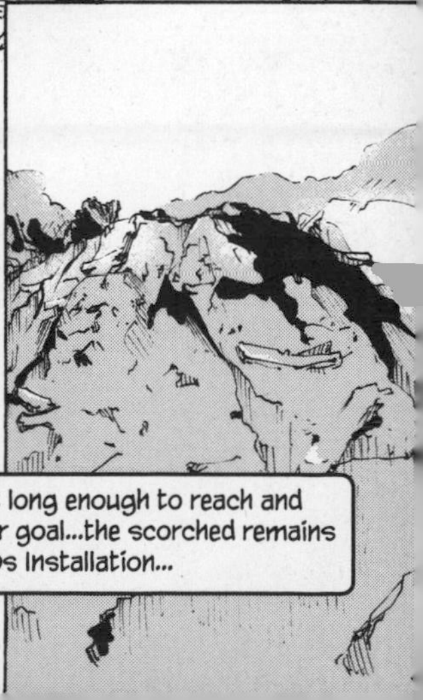
Invisible just long enough to reach and ransack their goal...the scorched remains of the Jacobs Installation...

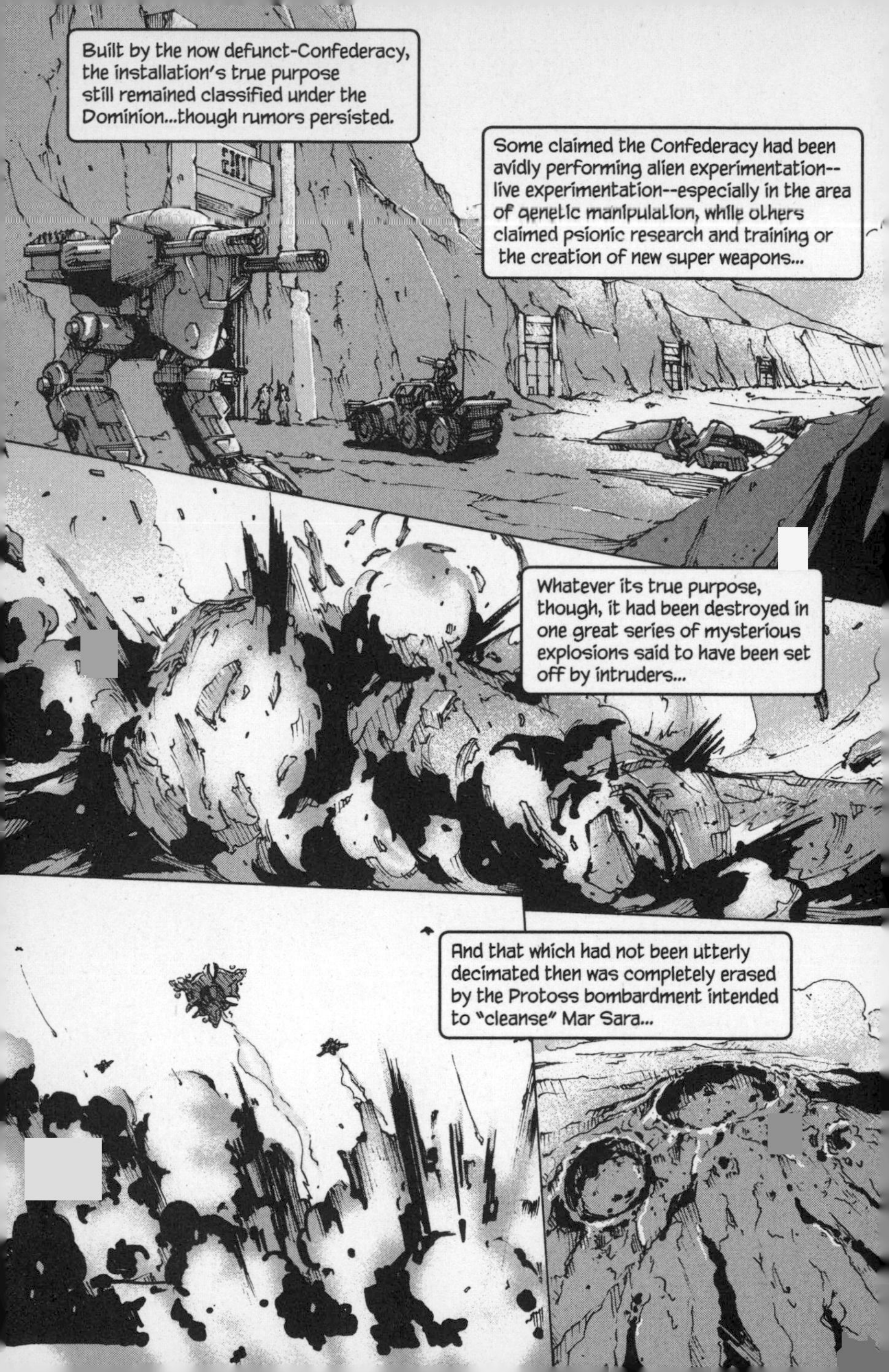
Built by the now defunct-Confederacy, the installation's true purpose still remained classified under the Dominion...though rumors persisted.
Some claimed the Confederacy had been avidly performing alien experimentation--live experimentation--especially in the area of genetic manipulation, while others claimed psionic research and training or the creation of new super weapons...
Whatever its true purpose, though, it had been destroyed in one great series of mysterious explosions said to have been set off by intruders...
And that which had not been utterly decimated then was completely erased by the Protoss bombardment intended to "cleanse" Mar Sara...

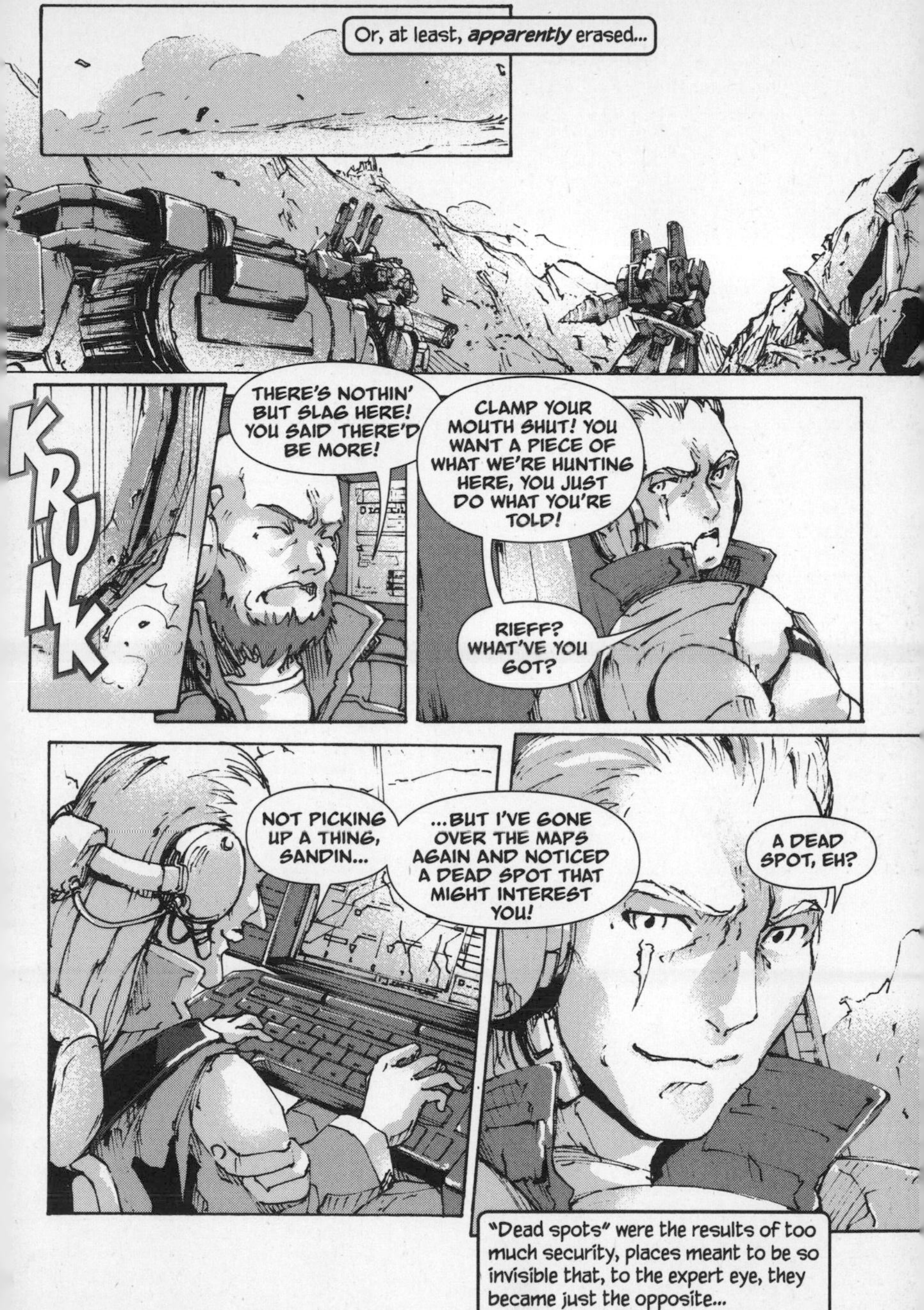
Or, at least, *apparently* erased...
KRUNK
THERE'S NOTHIN' BUT SLAG HERE! YOU SAID THERE'D BE MORE!
CLAMP YOUR MOUTH SHUT! YOU WANT A PIECE OF WHAT WE'RE HUNTING HERE, YOU JUST DO WHAT YOU'RE TOLD!
RIEFF? WHAT'VE YOU GOT?
NOT PICKING UP A THING, SANDIN...
...BUT I'VE GONE OVER THE MAPS AGAIN AND NOTICED A DEAD SPOT THAT MIGHT INTEREST YOU!
A DEAD SPOT, EH?
"Dead spots" were the results of too much security, places meant to be so invisible that, to the expert eye, they became just the opposite...

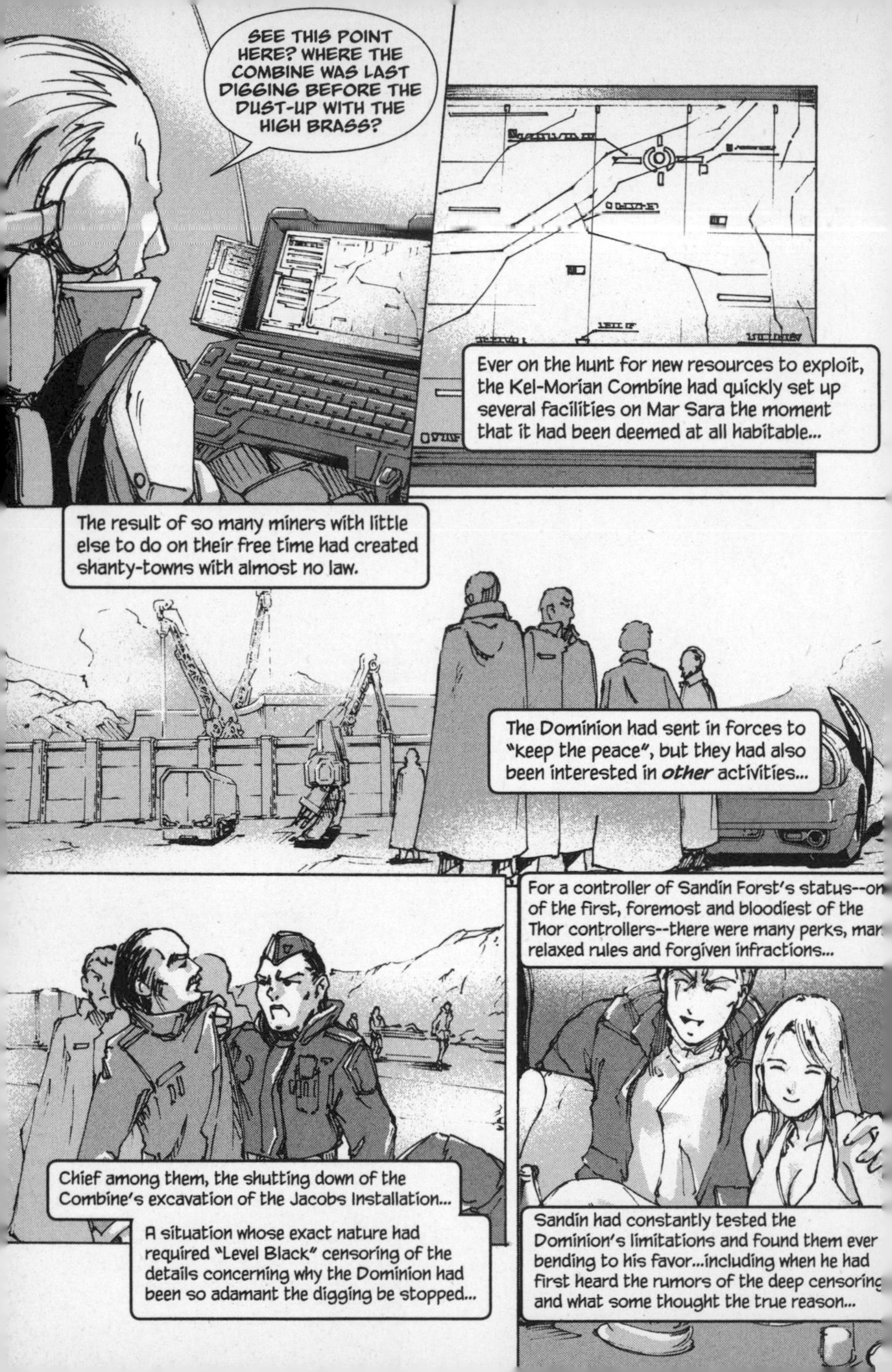
SEE THIS POINT HERE? WHERE THE COMBINE WAS LAST DIGGING BEFORE THE DUST-UP WITH THE HIGH BRASS?
Ever on the hunt for new resources to exploit, the Kel-Morian Combine had quickly set up several facilities on Mar Sara the moment that it had been deemed at all habitable...
The result of so many miners with little else to do on their free time had created shanty-towns with almost no law.
The Dominion had sent in forces to "keep the peace", but they had also been interested in *other* activities...
Chief among them, the shutting down of the Combine's excavation of the Jacobs Installation...
A situation whose exact nature had required "Level Black" censoring of the details concerning why the Dominion had been so adamant the digging be stopped...
For a controller of Sandin Forst's status--on of the first, foremost and bloodiest of the Thor controllers--there were many perks, man relaxed rules and forgiven infractions...
Sandin had constantly tested the Dominion's limitations and found them ever bending to his favor...including when he had first heard the rumors of the deep censoring and what some thought the true reason...

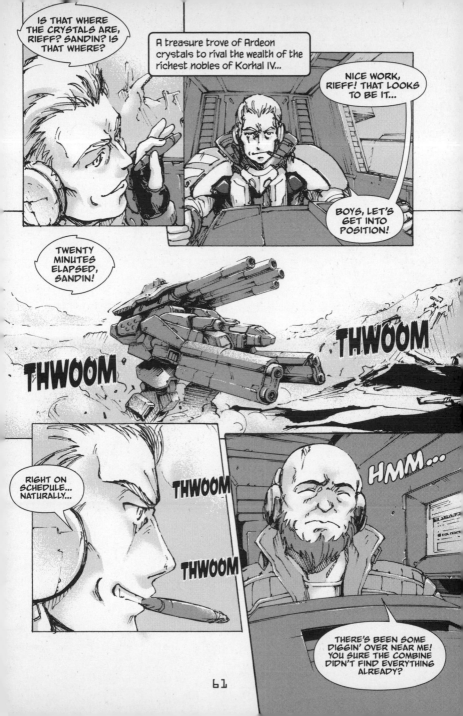

IS THAT WHERE THE CRYSTALS ARE, RIEFF? SANDIN? IS THAT WHERE?

A treasure trove of Ardeon crystals to rival the wealth of the richest nobles of Korhal IV...

NICE WORK, RIEFF! THAT LOOKS TO BE IT...

BOYS, LET'S GET INTO POSITION!

TWENTY MINUTES ELAPSED, SANDIN!

THWOOM

THWOOM

THWOOM

RIGHT ON SCHEDULE... NATURALLY...

THWOOM

THWOOM

HMM...

THERE'S BEEN SOME DIGGIN' OVER NEAR ME! YOU SURE THE COMBINE DIDN'T FIND EVERYTHING ALREADY?

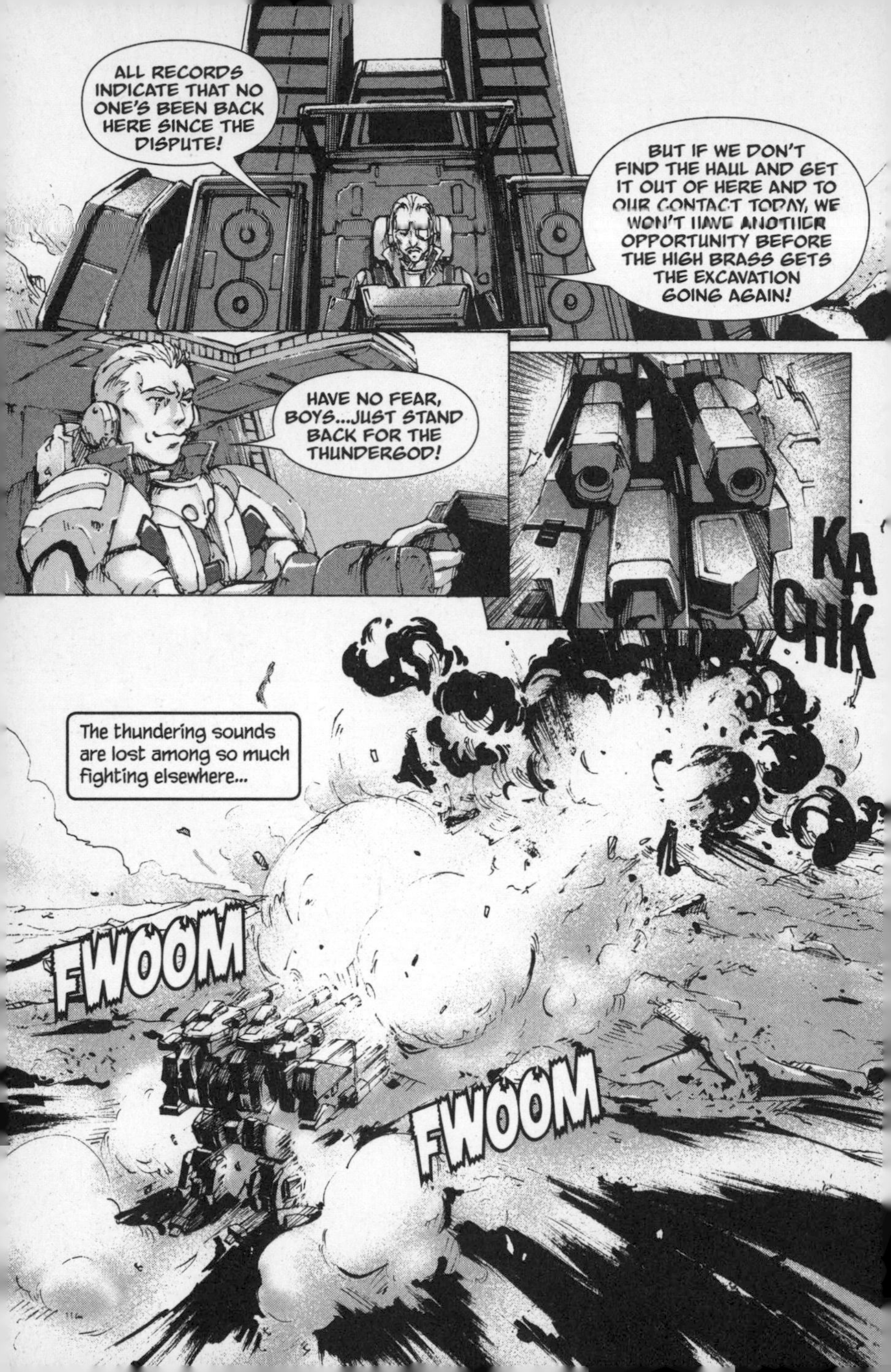

ALL RECORDS INDICATE THAT NO ONE'S BEEN BACK HERE SINCE THE DISPUTE!
BUT IF WE DON'T FIND THE HAUL AND GET IT OUT OF HERE AND TO OUR CONTACT TODAY, WE WON'T HAVE ANOTHER OPPORTUNITY BEFORE THE HIGH BRASS GETS THE EXCAVATION GOING AGAIN!
HAVE NO FEAR, BOYS...JUST STAND BACK FOR THE THUNDERGOD!
KA CHK
The thundering sounds are lost among so much fighting elsewhere...
FWOOM
FWOOM

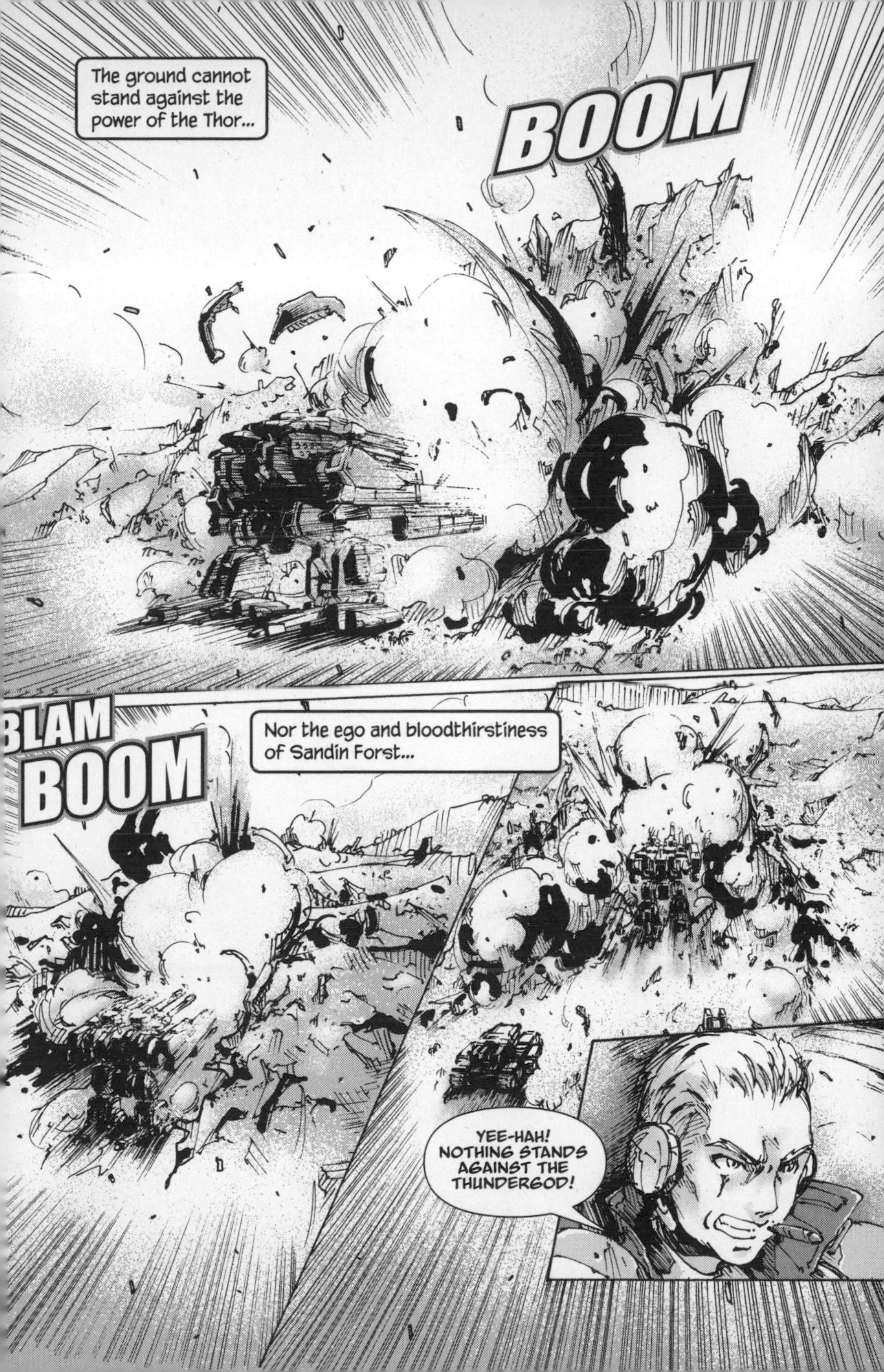
The ground cannot stand against the power of the Thor...
BOOM
BLAM
BOOM
Nor the ego and bloodthirstiness of Sandin Forst...
YEE-HAH! NOTHING STANDS AGAINST THE THUNDERGOD!

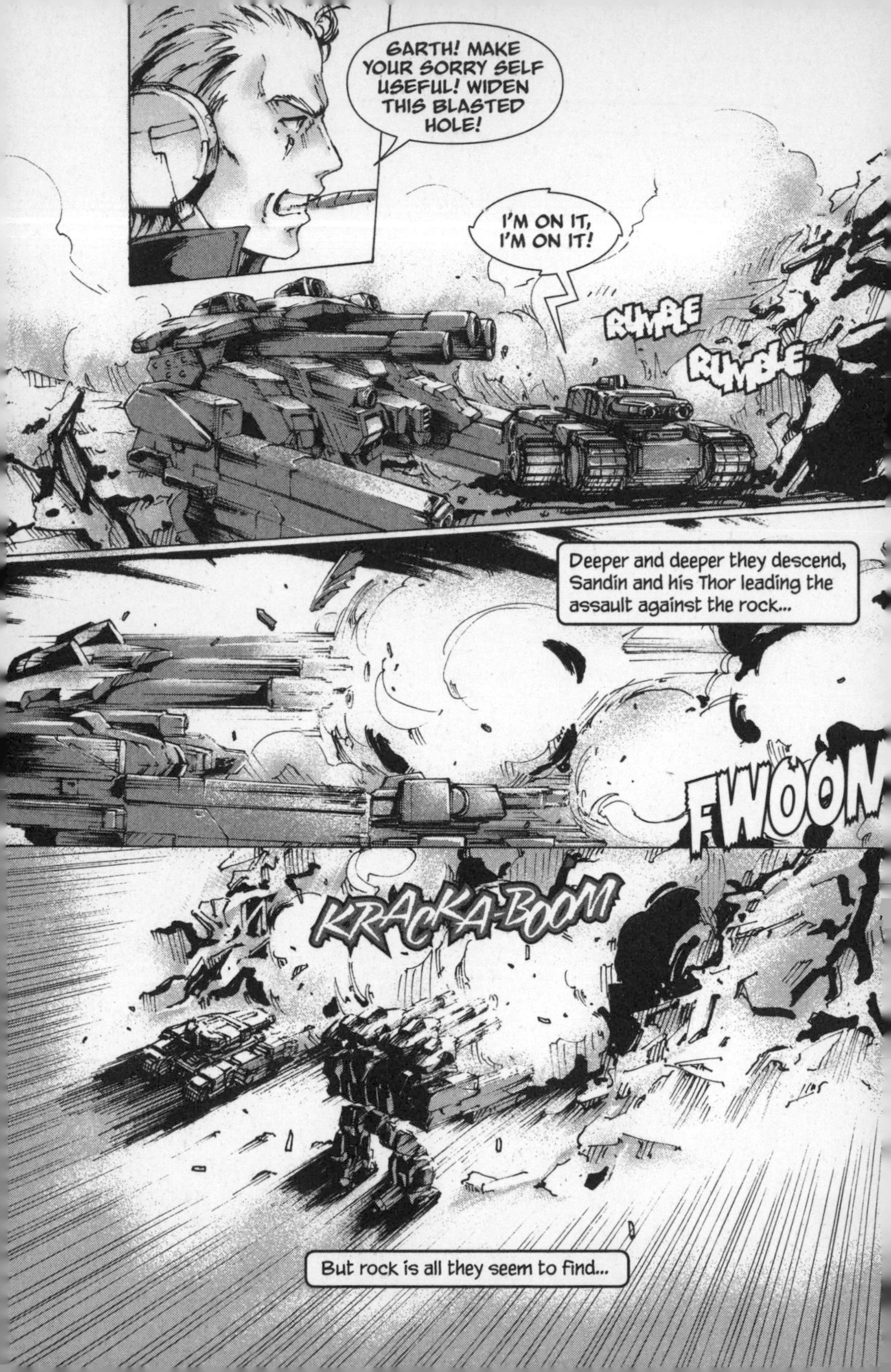

GARTH! MAKE YOUR SORRY SELF USEFUL! WIDEN THIS BLASTED HOLE!
I'M ON IT, I'M ON IT!
RUMBLE
RUMBLE
Deeper and deeper they descend, Sandin and his Thor leading the assault against the rock...
FWOOM
KRACKA-BOOM
But rock is all they seem to find...

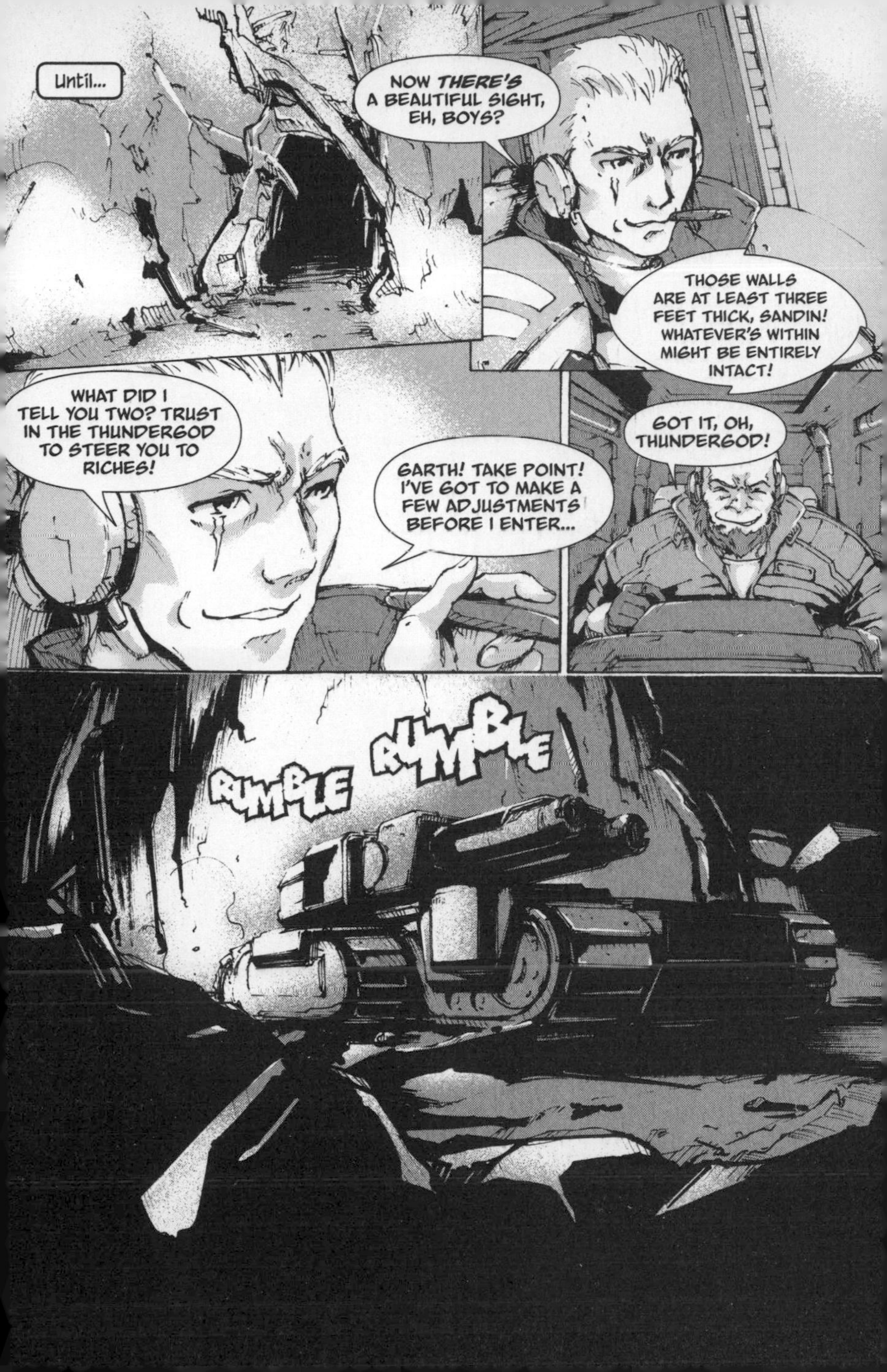
Until...
NOW THERE'S A BEAUTIFUL SIGHT, EH, BOYS?
THOSE WALLS ARE AT LEAST THREE FEET THICK, SANDIN! WHATEVER'S WITHIN MIGHT BE ENTIRELY INTACT!
WHAT DID I TELL YOU TWO? TRUST IN THE THUNDERGOD TO STEER YOU TO RICHES!
GARTH! TAKE POINT! I'VE GOT TO MAKE A FEW ADJUSTMENTS BEFORE I ENTER...
GOT IT, OH, THUNDERGOD!
RUMBLE
RUMBLE

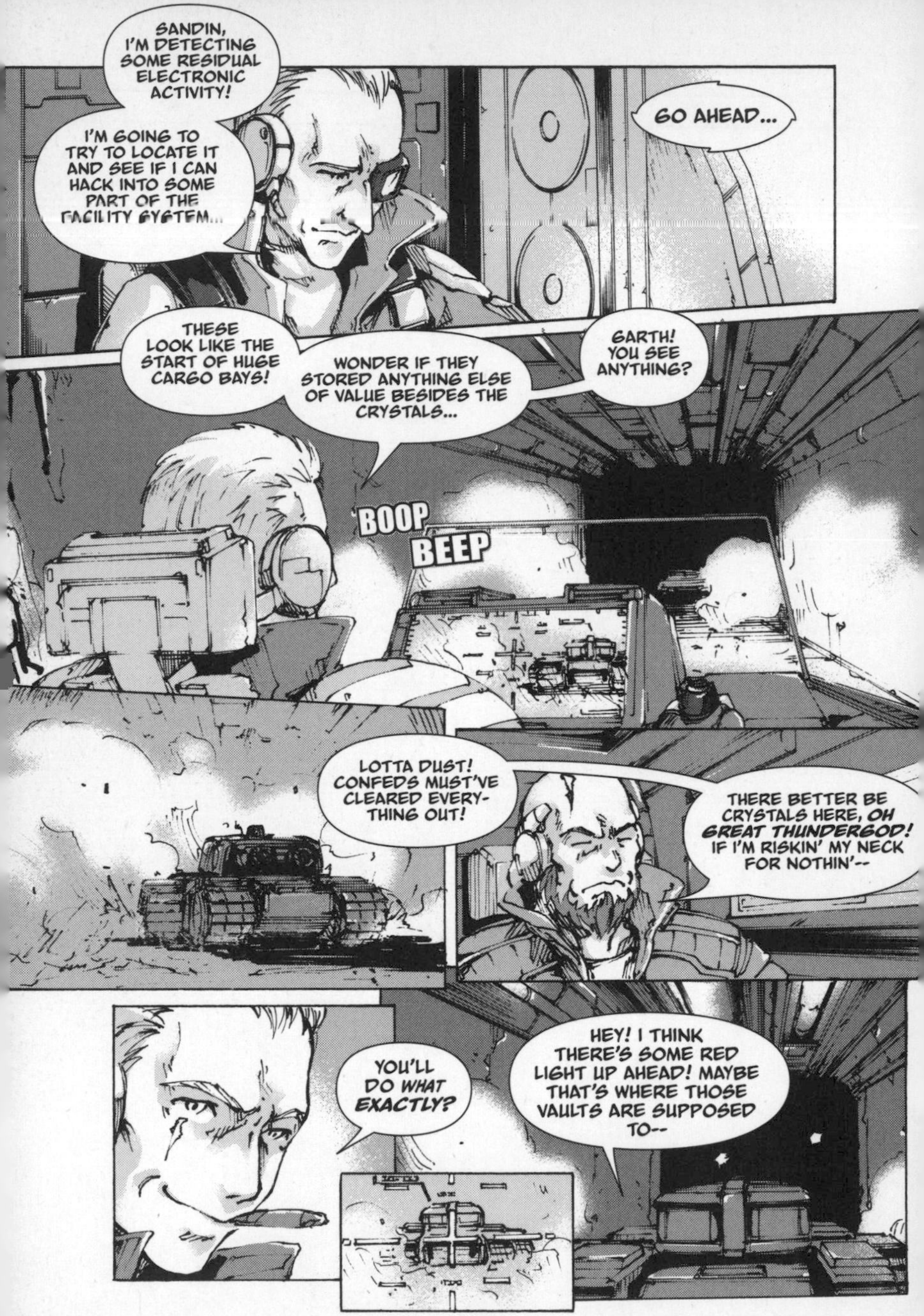
SANDIN, I'M DETECTING SOME RESIDUAL ELECTRONIC ACTIVITY!
I'M GOING TO TRY TO LOCATE IT AND SEE IF I CAN HACK INTO SOME PART OF THE FACILITY SYSTEM...
GO AHEAD...
THESE LOOK LIKE THE START OF HUGE CARGO BAYS!
WONDER IF THEY STORED ANYTHING ELSE OF VALUE BESIDES THE CRYSTALS...
GARTH! YOU SEE ANYTHING?
BOOP
BEEP
LOTTA DUST! CONFEDS MUST'VE CLEARED EVERY-THING OUT!
THERE BETTER BE CRYSTALS HERE, *OH GREAT THUNDERGOD!* IF I'M RISKIN' MY NECK FOR NOTHIN'--
YOU'LL DO *WHAT* ***EXACTLY?***
HEY! I THINK THERE'S SOME RED LIGHT UP AHEAD! MAYBE THAT'S WHERE THOSE VAULTS ARE SUPPOSED TO--

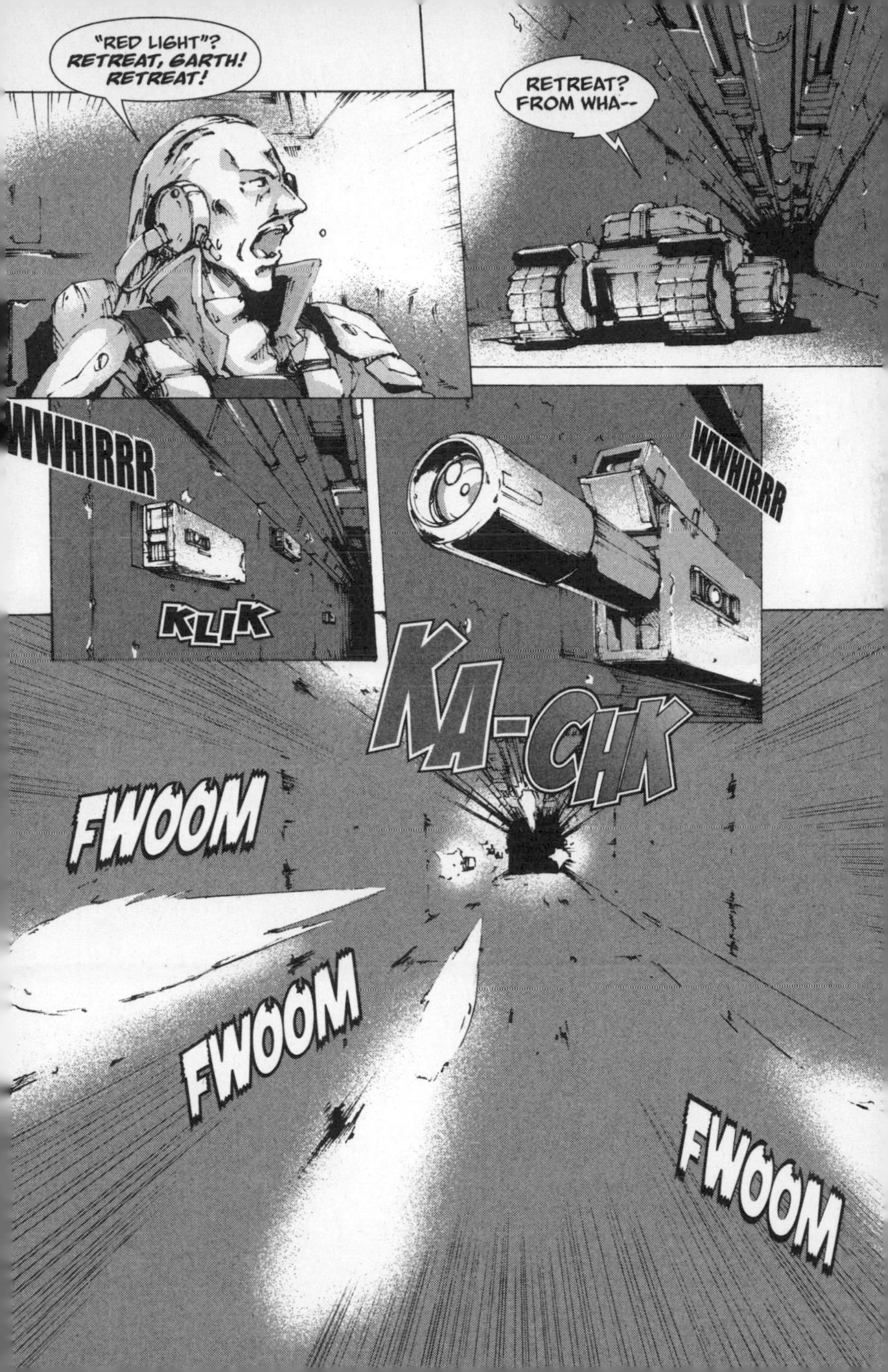
"RED LIGHT"? RETREAT, GARTH! RETREAT!
RETREAT? FROM WHA--
WWHIRRR
KLIK
WWHIRRR
KA-CHK
FWOOM
FWOOM
FWOOM

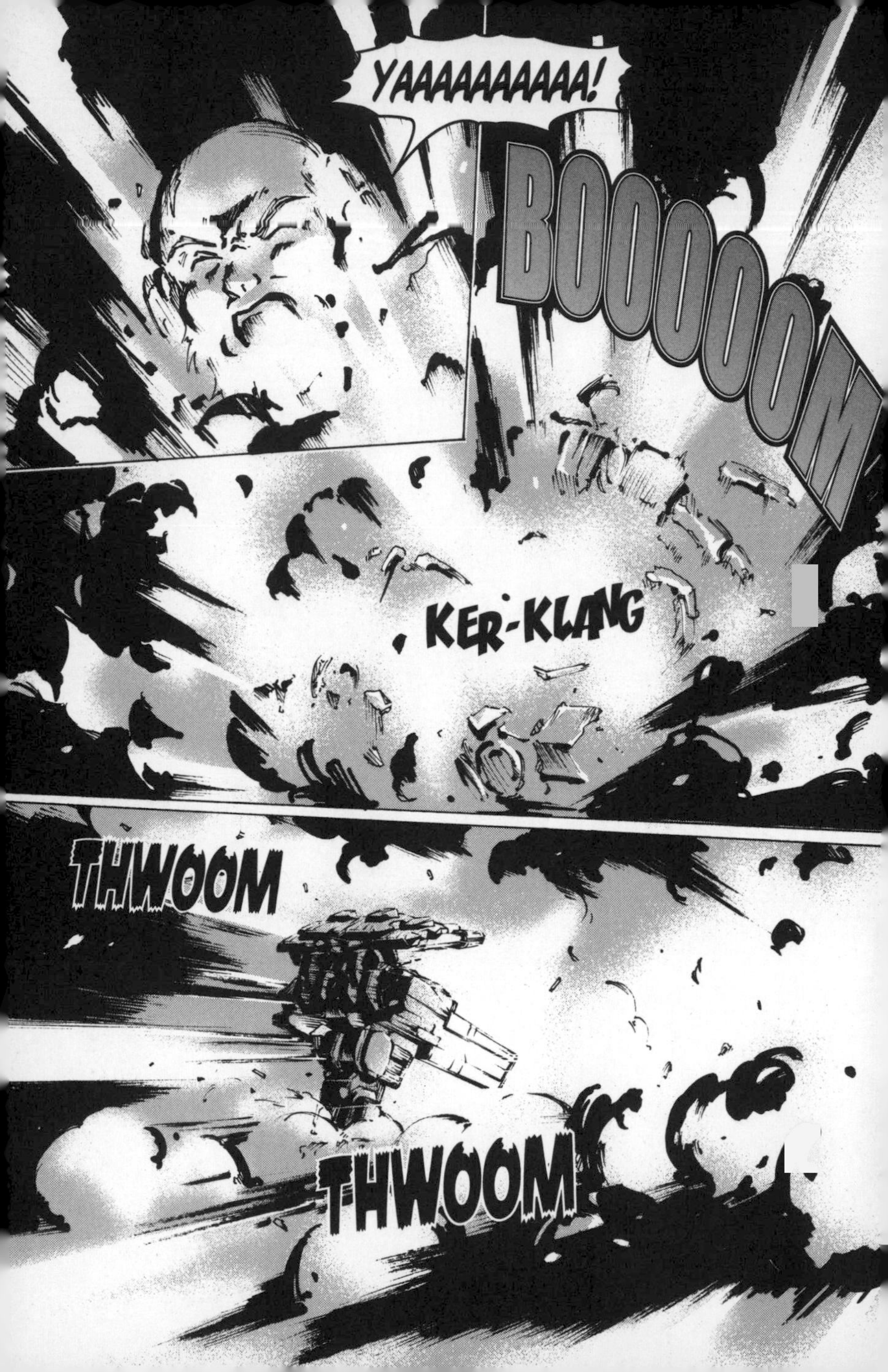
YAAAAAAAAAA!
BOOOOOM
KER-KLANG
THWOOM
THWOOM

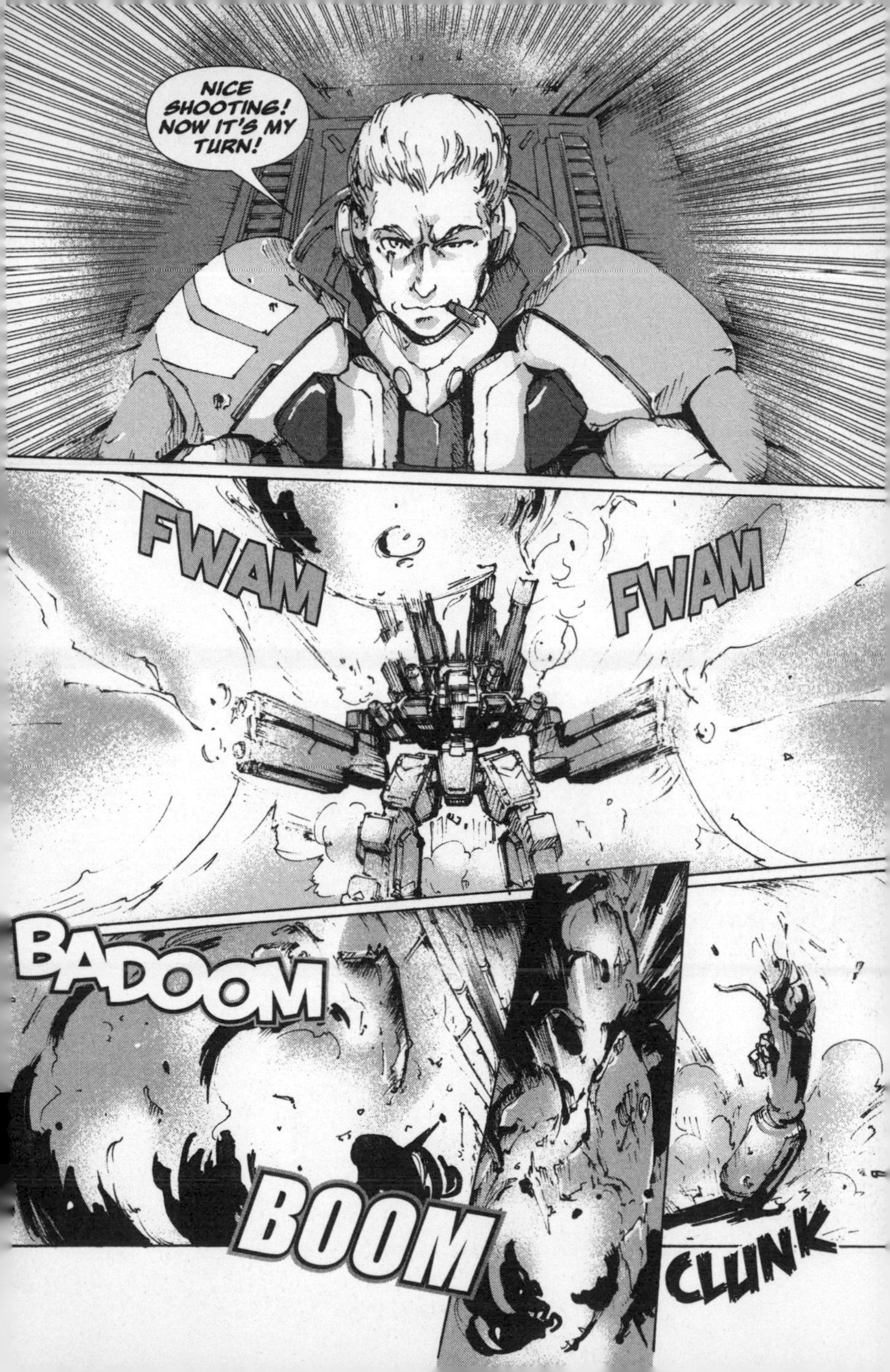
NICE SHOOTING! NOW IT'S MY TURN!
FWAM
FWAM
BADOOM
BOOM
CLUNK

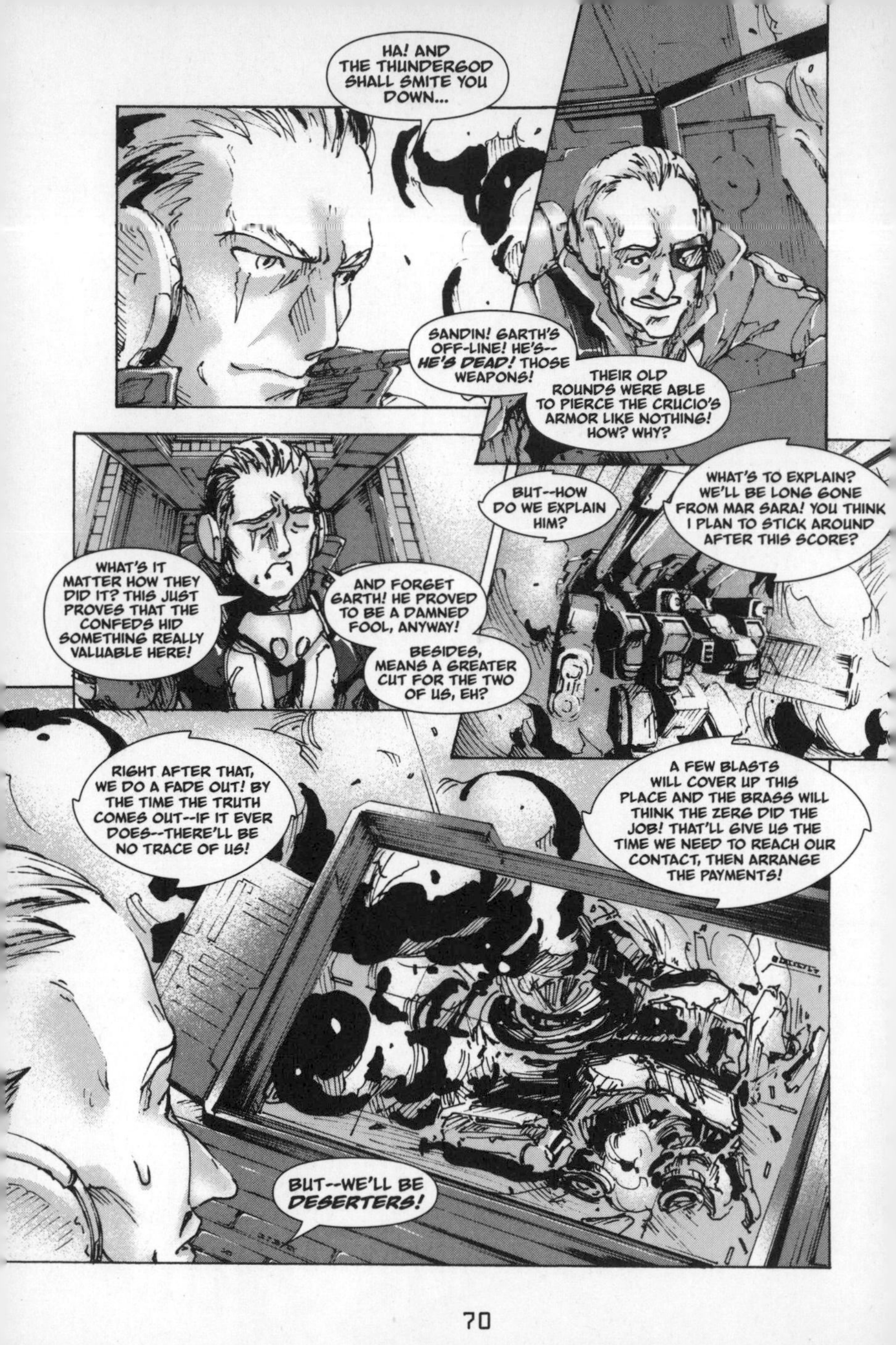
HA! AND THE THUNDERGOD SHALL SMITE YOU DOWN...
SANDIN! GARTH'S OFF-LINE! HE'S-- *HE'S DEAD!* THOSE WEAPONS!
THEIR OLD ROUNDS WERE ABLE TO PIERCE THE CRUCIO'S ARMOR LIKE NOTHING! HOW? WHY?
WHAT'S IT MATTER HOW THEY DID IT? THIS JUST PROVES THAT THE CONFEDS HID SOMETHING REALLY VALUABLE HERE!
AND FORGET GARTH! HE PROVED TO BE A DAMNED FOOL, ANYWAY!
BESIDES, MEANS A GREATER CUT FOR THE TWO OF US, EH?
BUT--HOW DO WE EXPLAIN HIM?
WHAT'S TO EXPLAIN? WE'LL BE LONG GONE FROM MAR SARA! YOU THINK I PLAN TO STICK AROUND AFTER THIS SCORE?
RIGHT AFTER THAT, WE DO A FADE OUT! BY THE TIME THE TRUTH COMES OUT--IF IT EVER DOES--THERE'LL BE NO TRACE OF US!
A FEW BLASTS WILL COVER UP THIS PLACE AND THE BRASS WILL THINK THE ZERG DID THE JOB! THAT'LL GIVE US THE TIME WE NEED TO REACH OUR CONTACT, THEN ARRANGE THE PAYMENTS!
BUT--WE'LL BE *DESERTERS!*

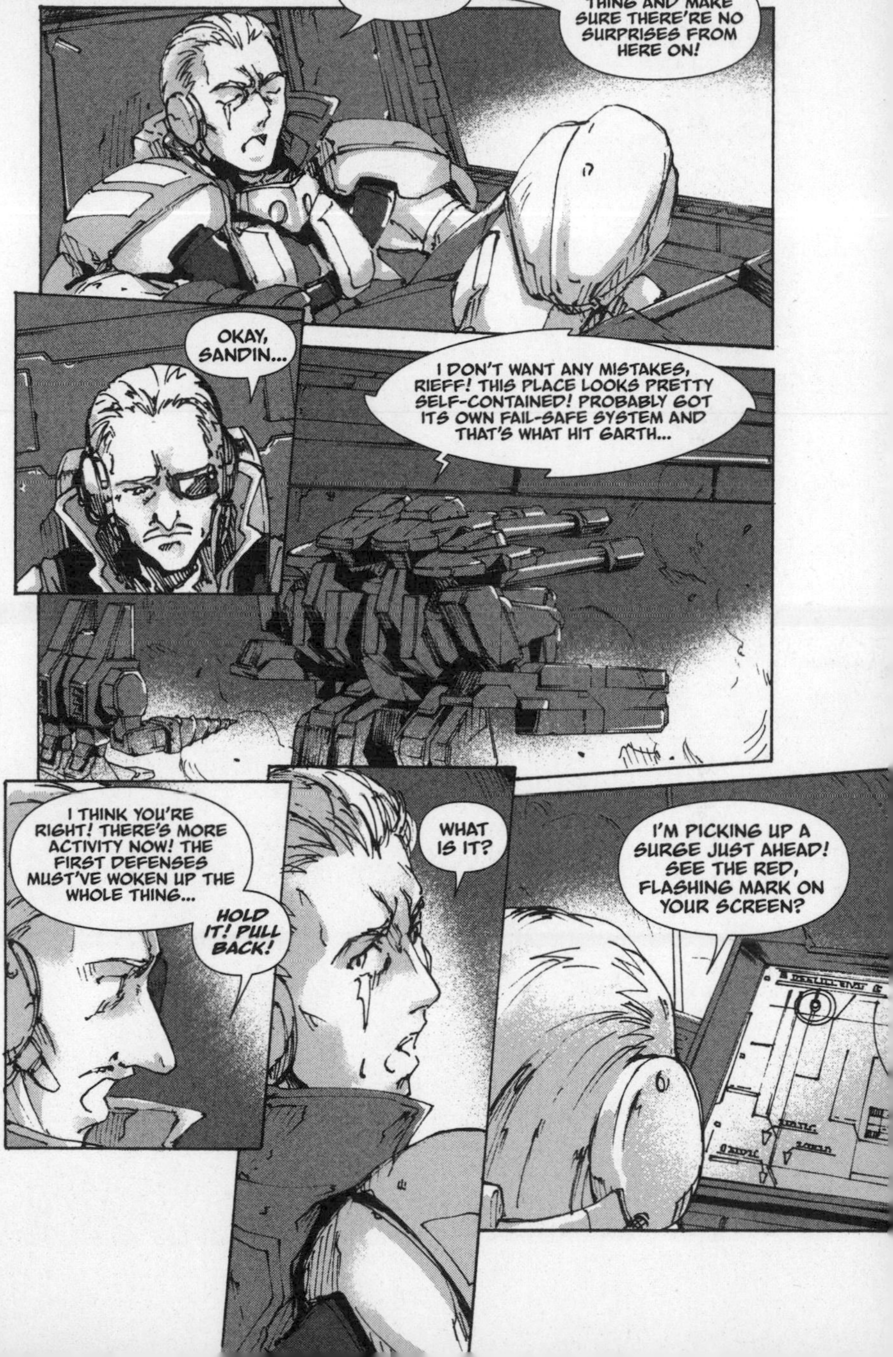
YEAH... RICH ONES!
NOW DO YOUR THING AND MAKE SURE THERE'RE NO SURPRISES FROM HERE ON!
OKAY, SANDIN...
I DON'T WANT ANY MISTAKES, RIEFF! THIS PLACE LOOKS PRETTY SELF-CONTAINED! PROBABLY GOT ITS OWN FAIL-SAFE SYSTEM AND THAT'S WHAT HIT GARTH...
I THINK YOU'RE RIGHT! THERE'S MORE ACTIVITY NOW! THE FIRST DEFENSES MUST'VE WOKEN UP THE WHOLE THING...
HOLD IT! PULL BACK!
WHAT IS IT?
I'M PICKING UP A SURGE JUST AHEAD! SEE THE RED, FLASHING MARK ON YOUR SCREEN?

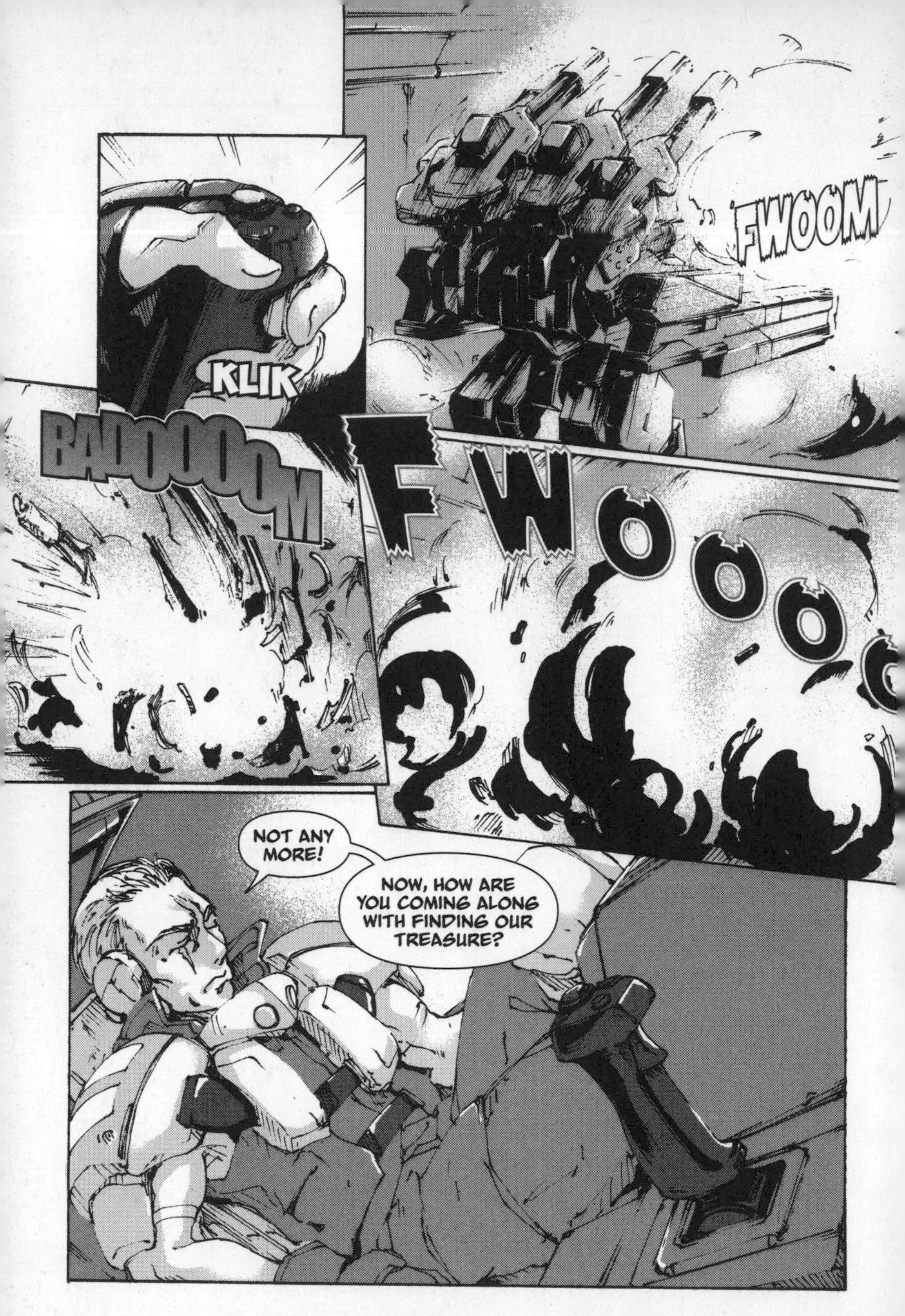
KLIK
FWOOM
BADOOOOM
FWOOOO
NOT ANY MORE!
NOW, HOW ARE YOU COMING ALONG WITH FINDING OUR TREASURE?

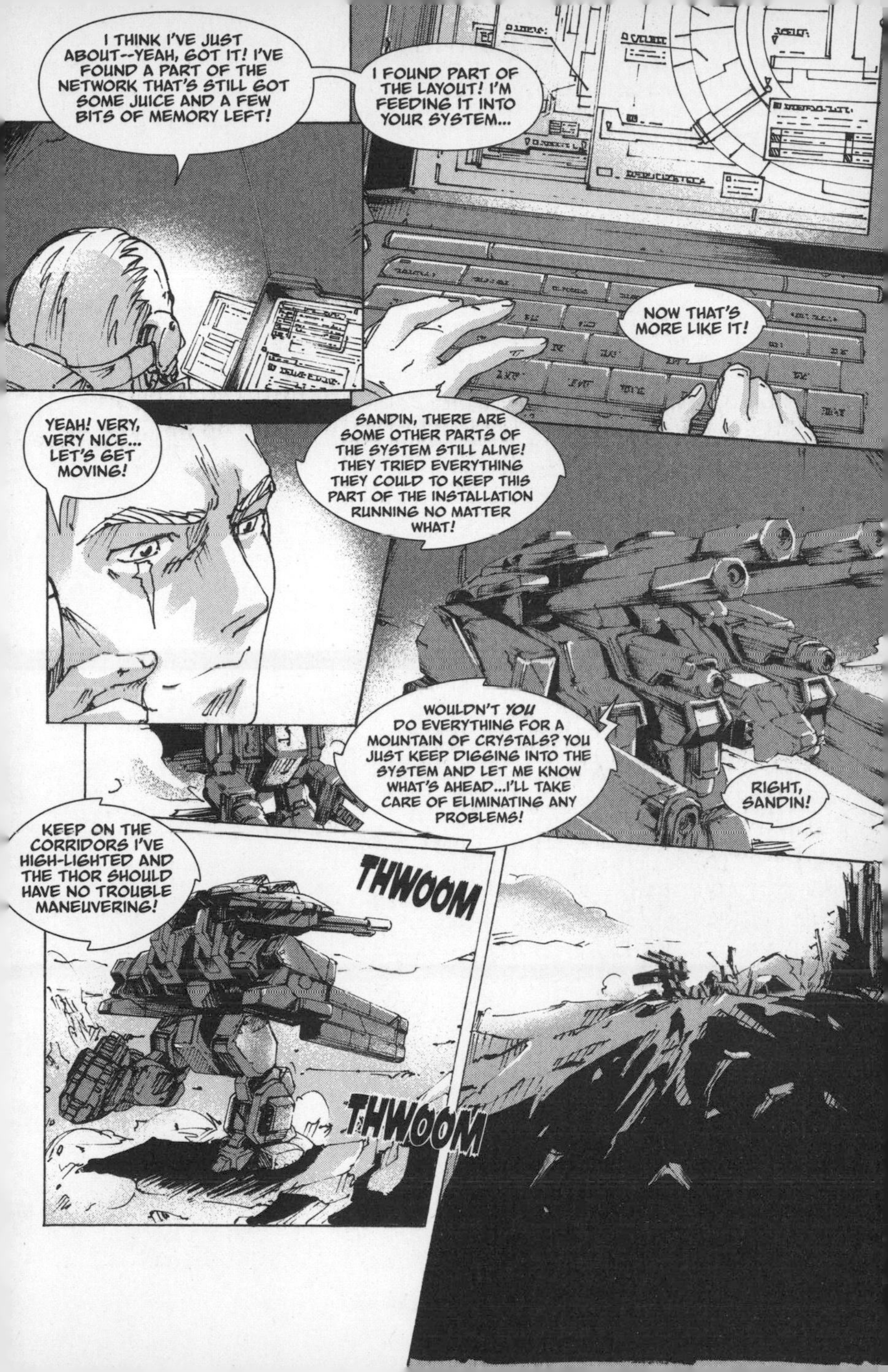
I THINK I'VE JUST ABOUT--YEAH, GOT IT! I'VE FOUND A PART OF THE NETWORK THAT'S STILL GOT SOME JUICE AND A FEW BITS OF MEMORY LEFT!
I FOUND PART OF THE LAYOUT! I'M FEEDING IT INTO YOUR SYSTEM...
NOW THAT'S MORE LIKE IT!
YEAH! VERY, VERY NICE... LET'S GET MOVING!
SANDIN, THERE ARE SOME OTHER PARTS OF THE SYSTEM STILL ALIVE! THEY TRIED EVERYTHING THEY COULD TO KEEP THIS PART OF THE INSTALLATION RUNNING NO MATTER WHAT!
WOULDN'T *YOU* DO EVERYTHING FOR A MOUNTAIN OF CRYSTALS? YOU JUST KEEP DIGGING INTO THE SYSTEM AND LET ME KNOW WHAT'S AHEAD...I'LL TAKE CARE OF ELIMINATING ANY PROBLEMS!
RIGHT, SANDIN!
KEEP ON THE CORRIDORS I'VE HIGH-LIGHTED AND THE THOR SHOULD HAVE NO TROUBLE MANEUVERING!
THWOOM
THWOOM

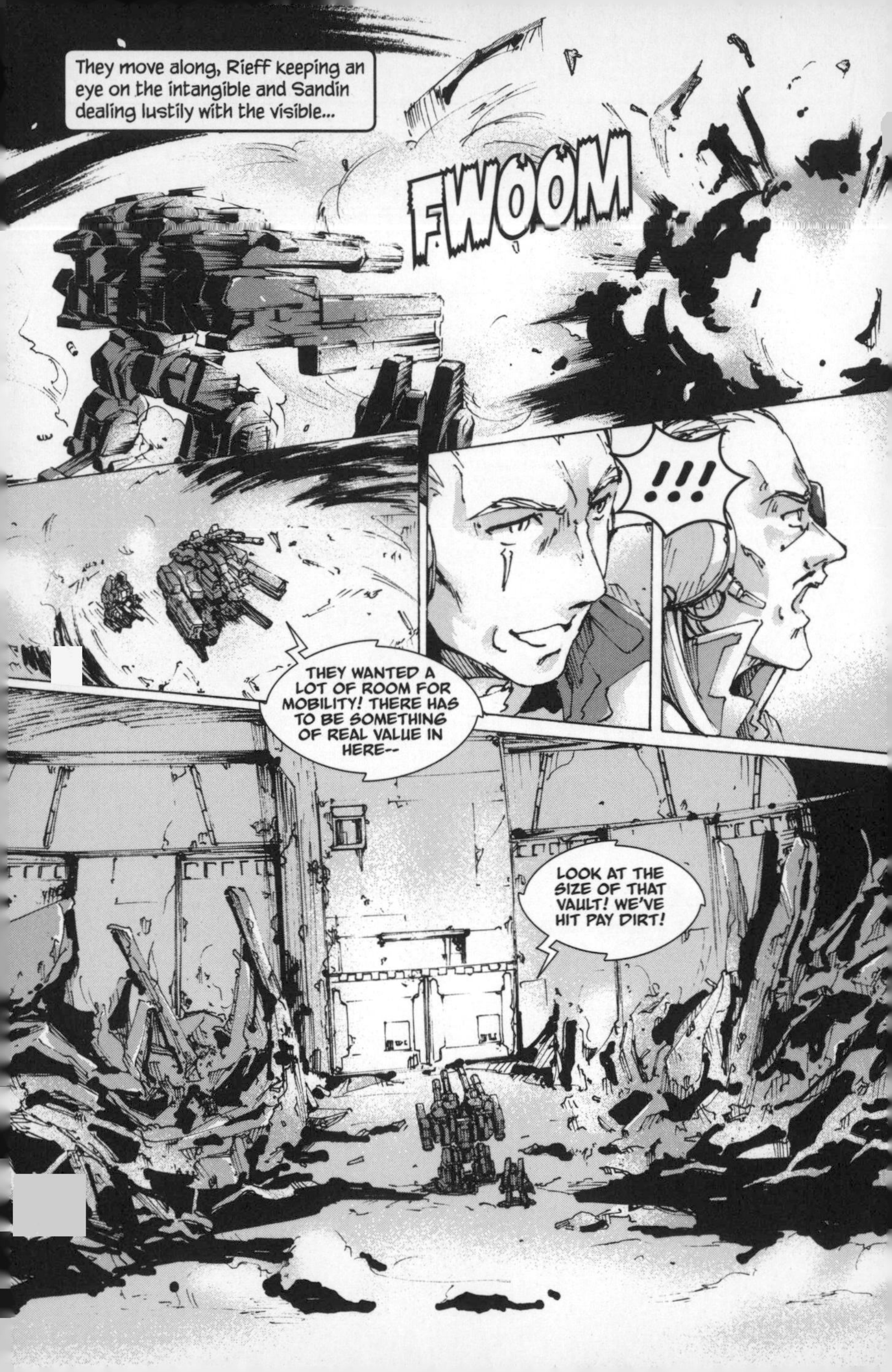
They move along, Rieff keeping an eye on the intangible and Sandin dealing lustily with the visible...
FWOOM
!!!
THEY WANTED A LOT OF ROOM FOR MOBILITY! THERE HAS TO BE SOMETHING OF REAL VALUE IN HERE--
LOOK AT THE SIZE OF THAT VAULT! WE'VE HIT PAY DIRT!

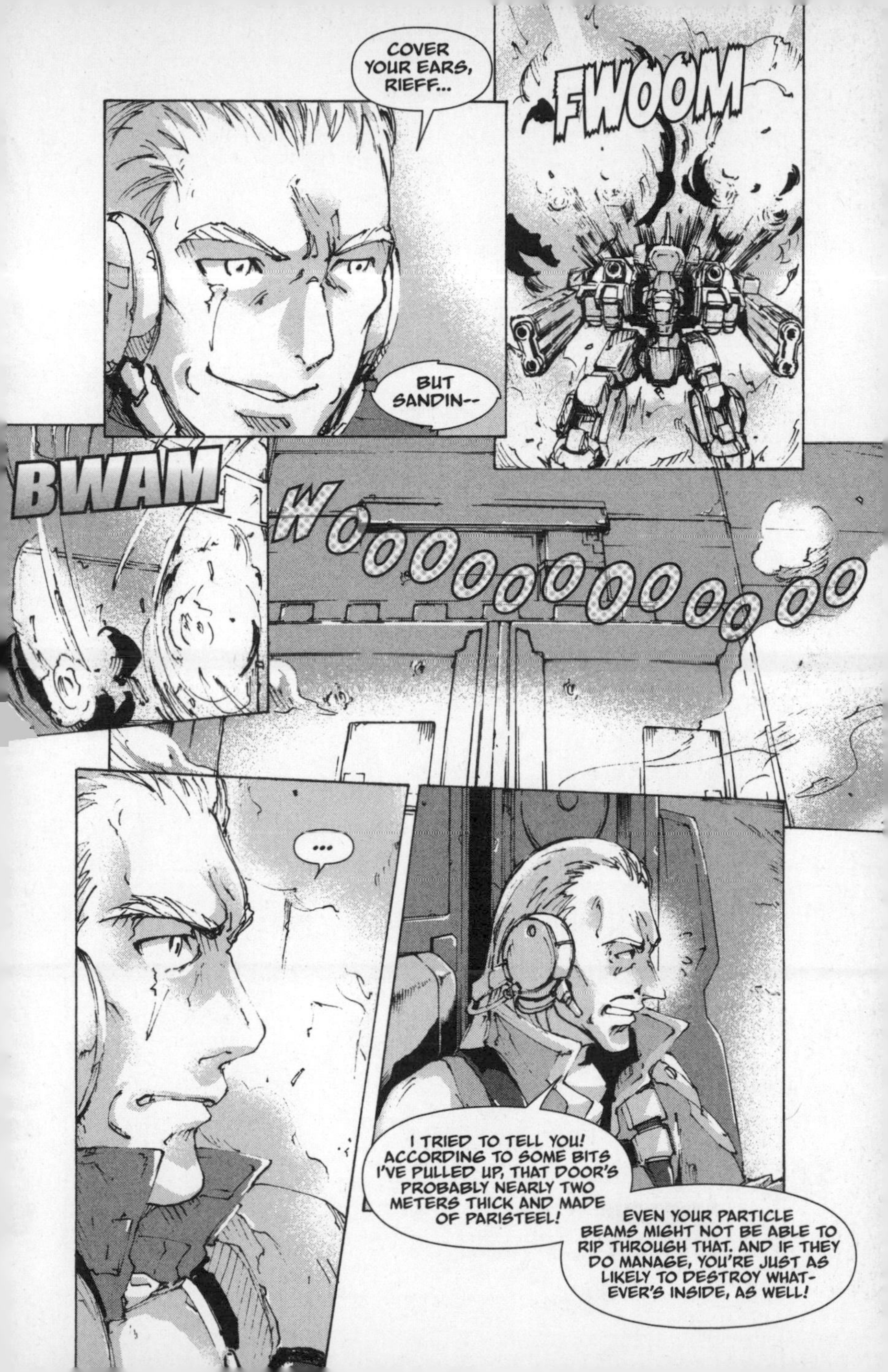
COVER YOUR EARS, RIEFF...
BUT SANDIN--
FWOOM
BWAM
WOOOOOOOOOOOO
...
I TRIED TO TELL YOU! ACCORDING TO SOME BITS I'VE PULLED UP, THAT DOOR'S PROBABLY NEARLY TWO METERS THICK AND MADE OF PARISTEEL!
EVEN YOUR PARTICLE BEAMS MIGHT NOT BE ABLE TO RIP THROUGH THAT. AND IF THEY DO MANAGE, YOU'RE JUST AS LIKELY TO DESTROY WHAT-EVER'S INSIDE, AS WELL!

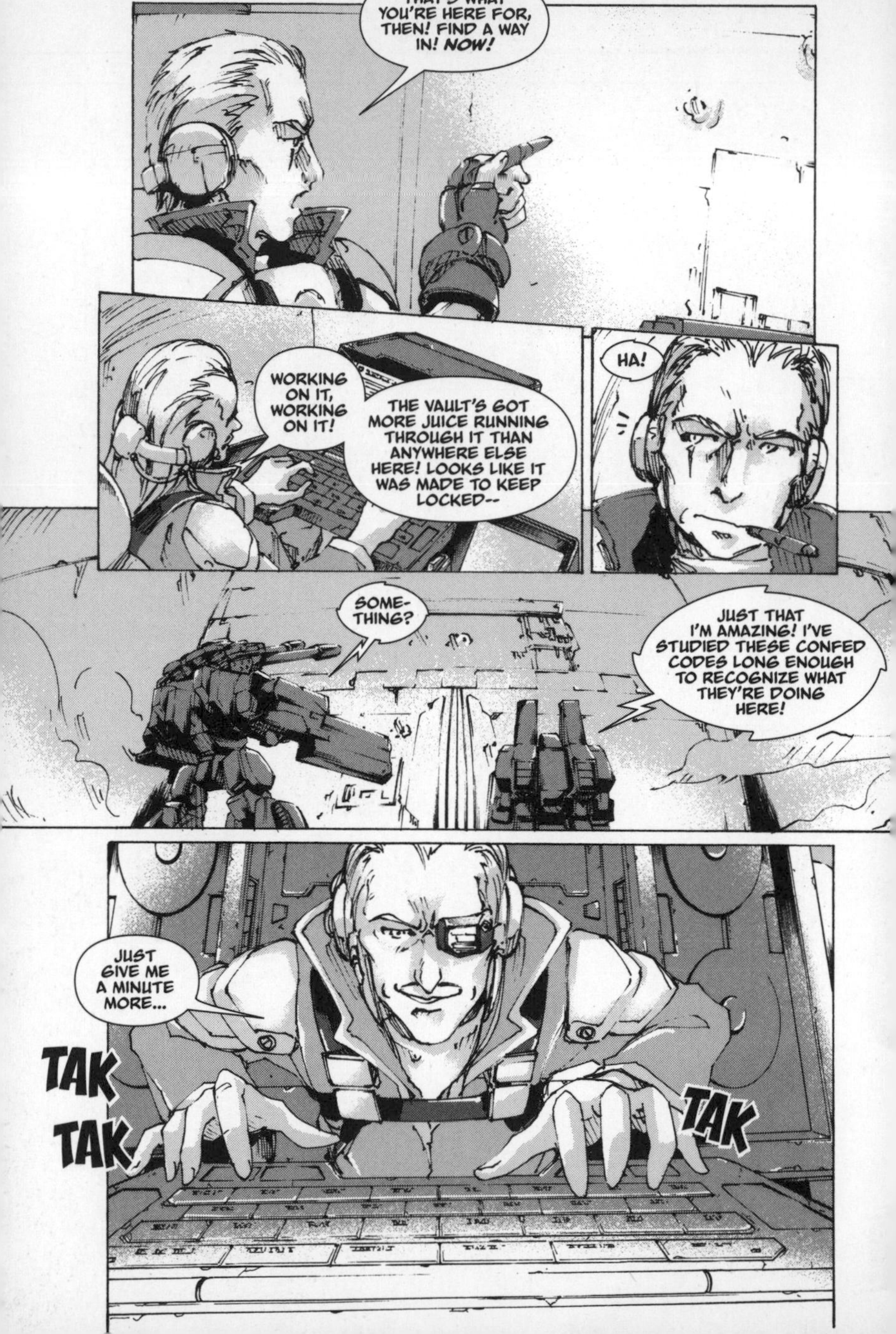
THAT'S WHAT YOU'RE HERE FOR, THEN! FIND A WAY IN! NOW!
WORKING ON IT, WORKING ON IT!
THE VAULT'S GOT MORE JUICE RUNNING THROUGH IT THAN ANYWHERE ELSE HERE! LOOKS LIKE IT WAS MADE TO KEEP LOCKED--
HA!
SOME-THING?
JUST THAT I'M AMAZING! I'VE STUDIED THESE CONFED CODES LONG ENOUGH TO RECOGNIZE WHAT THEY'RE DOING HERE!
JUST GIVE ME A MINUTE MORE...
TAK
TAK
TAK

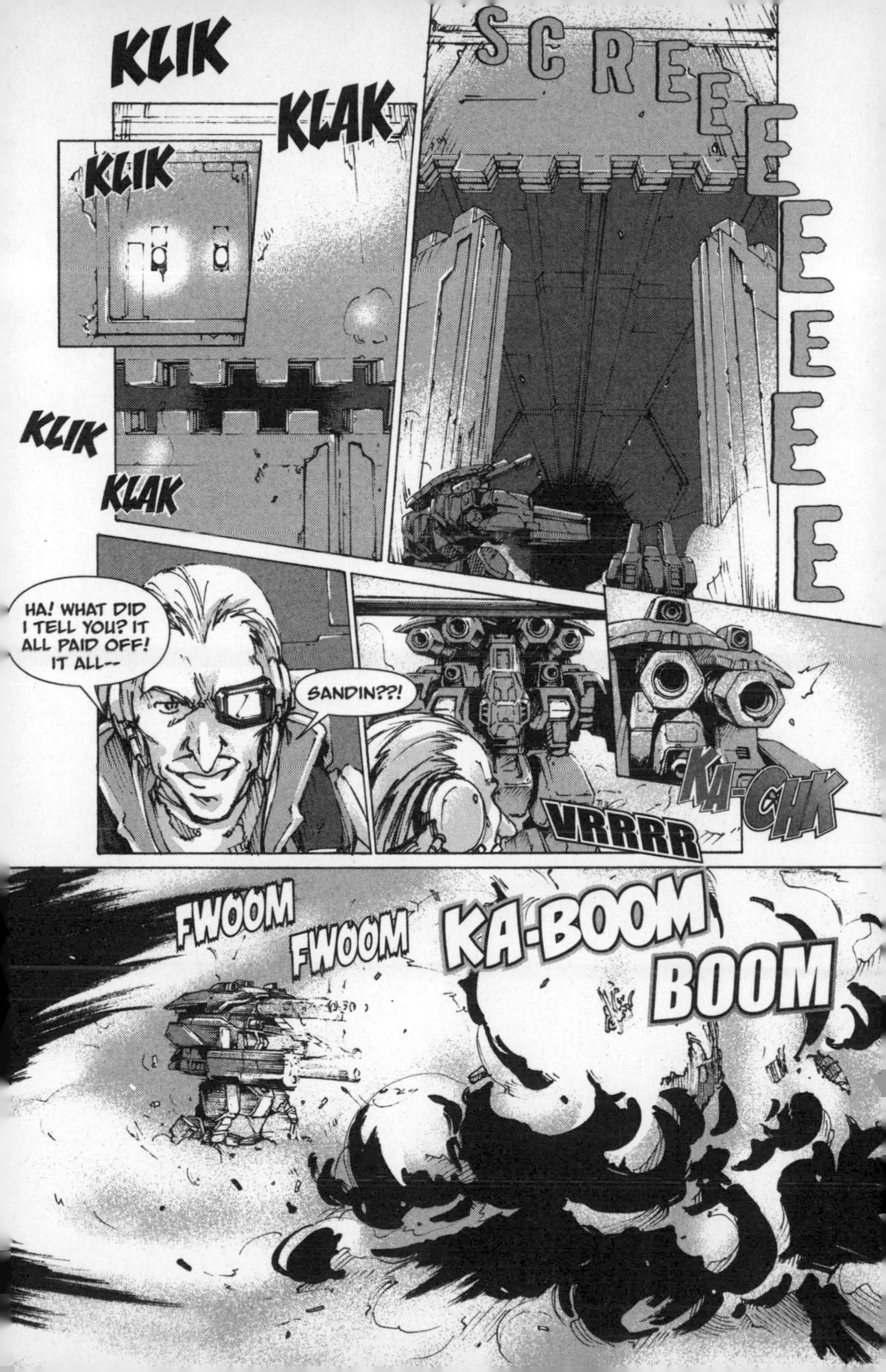
KLIK
KLAK
KLIK
KLIK
KLAK
SCREEEEEEEEE
HA! WHAT DID I TELL YOU? IT ALL PAID OFF! IT ALL--
SANDIN??!
VRRRR
KA-CHK
FWOOM
FWOOM
KA-BOOM
BOOM

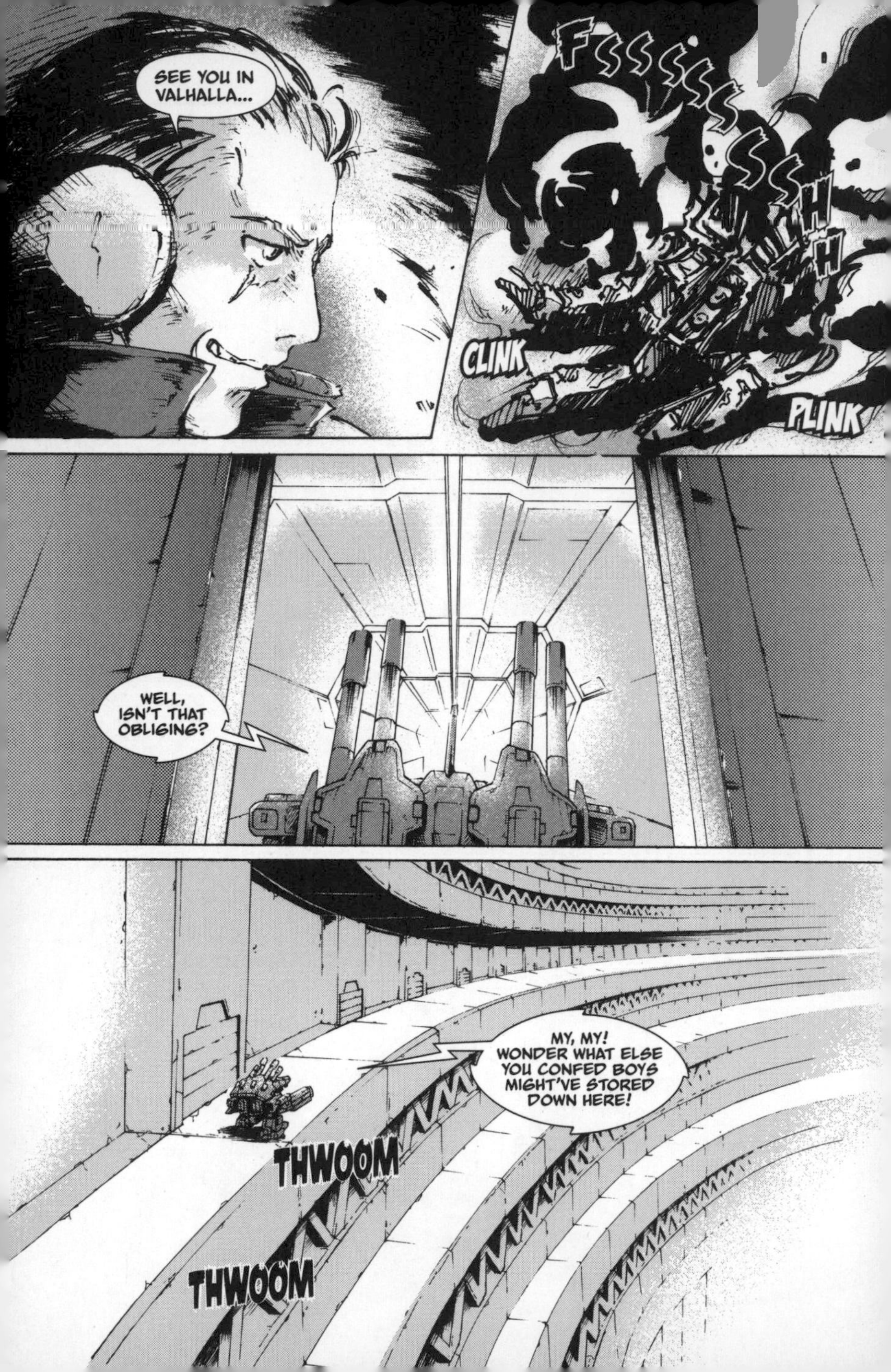
SEE YOU IN VALHALLA...
FSSSSSSSHH
CLINK
PLINK
WELL, ISN'T THAT OBLIGING?
MY, MY! WONDER WHAT ELSE YOU CONFED BOYS MIGHT'VE STORED DOWN HERE!
THWOOM
THWOOM

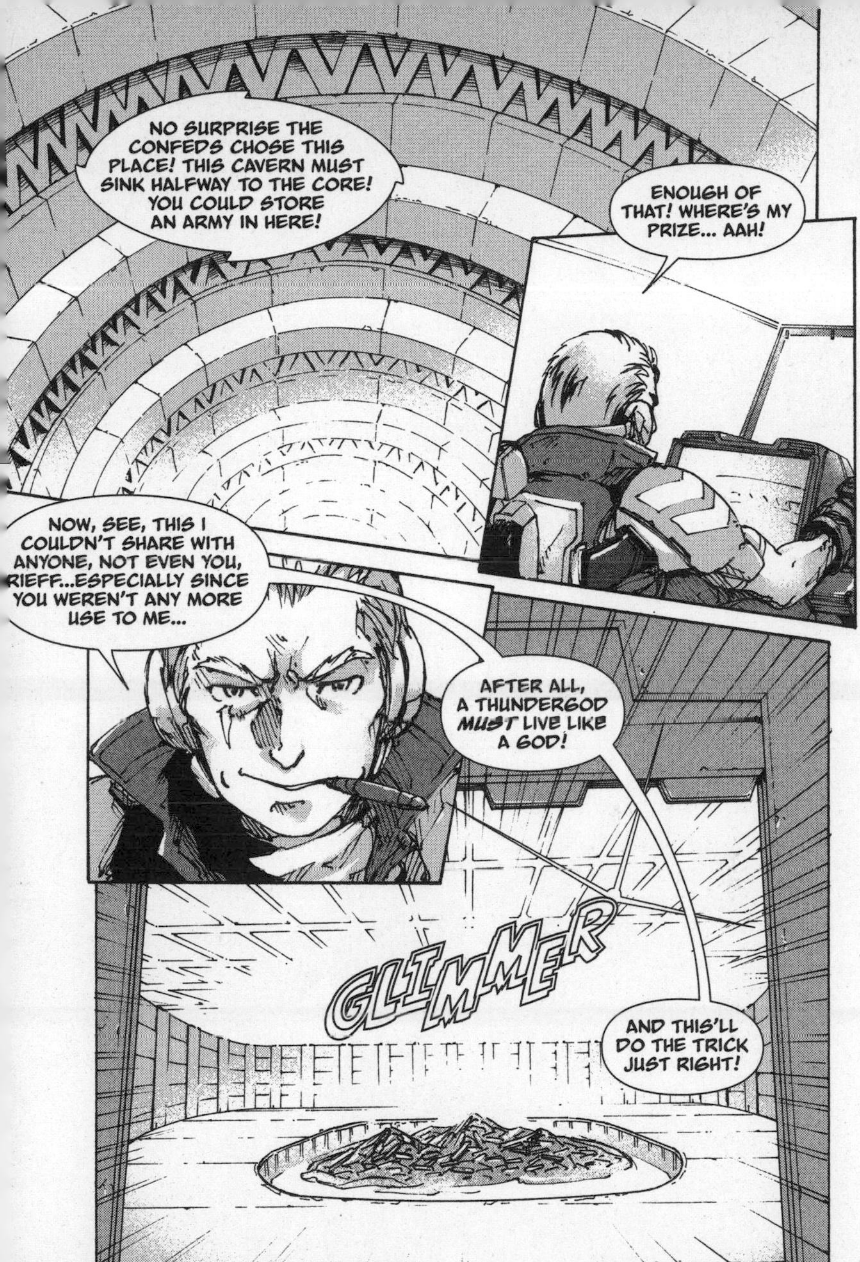
NO SURPRISE THE CONFEDS CHOSE THIS PLACE! THIS CAVERN MUST SINK HALFWAY TO THE CORE! YOU COULD STORE AN ARMY IN HERE!
ENOUGH OF THAT! WHERE'S MY PRIZE... AAH!
NOW, SEE, THIS I COULDN'T SHARE WITH ANYONE, NOT EVEN YOU, RIEFF...ESPECIALLY SINCE YOU WEREN'T ANY MORE USE TO ME...
AFTER ALL, A THUNDERGOD *MUST* LIVE LIKE A GOD!
GLIMMER
AND THIS'LL DO THE TRICK JUST RIGHT!

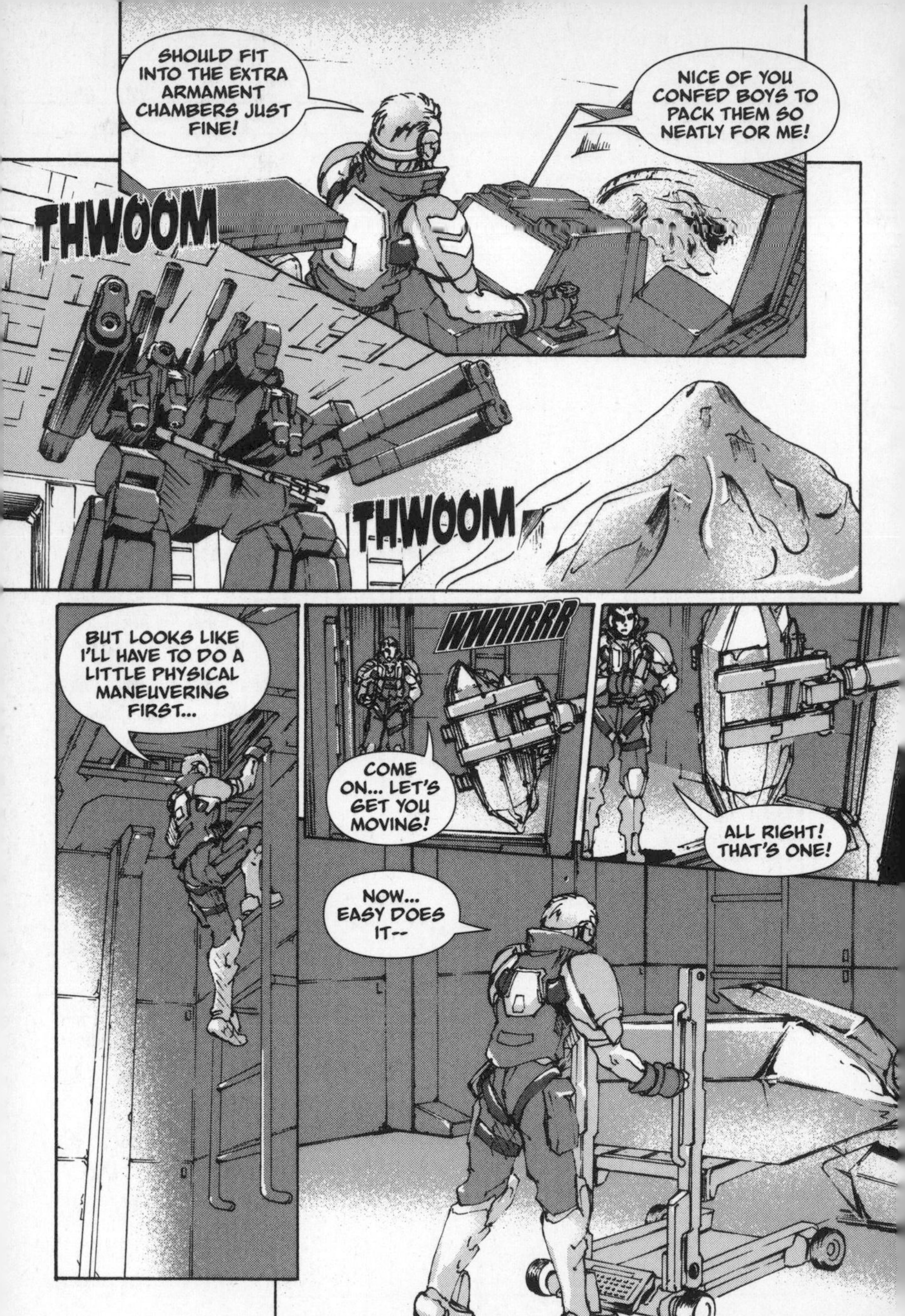
SHOULD FIT INTO THE EXTRA ARMAMENT CHAMBERS JUST FINE!
NICE OF YOU CONFED BOYS TO PACK THEM SO NEATLY FOR ME!
THWOOM
THWOOM
BUT LOOKS LIKE I'LL HAVE TO DO A LITTLE PHYSICAL MANEUVERING FIRST...
WWHIRRR
COME ON... LET'S GET YOU MOVING!
ALL RIGHT! THAT'S ONE!
NOW... EASY DOES IT--

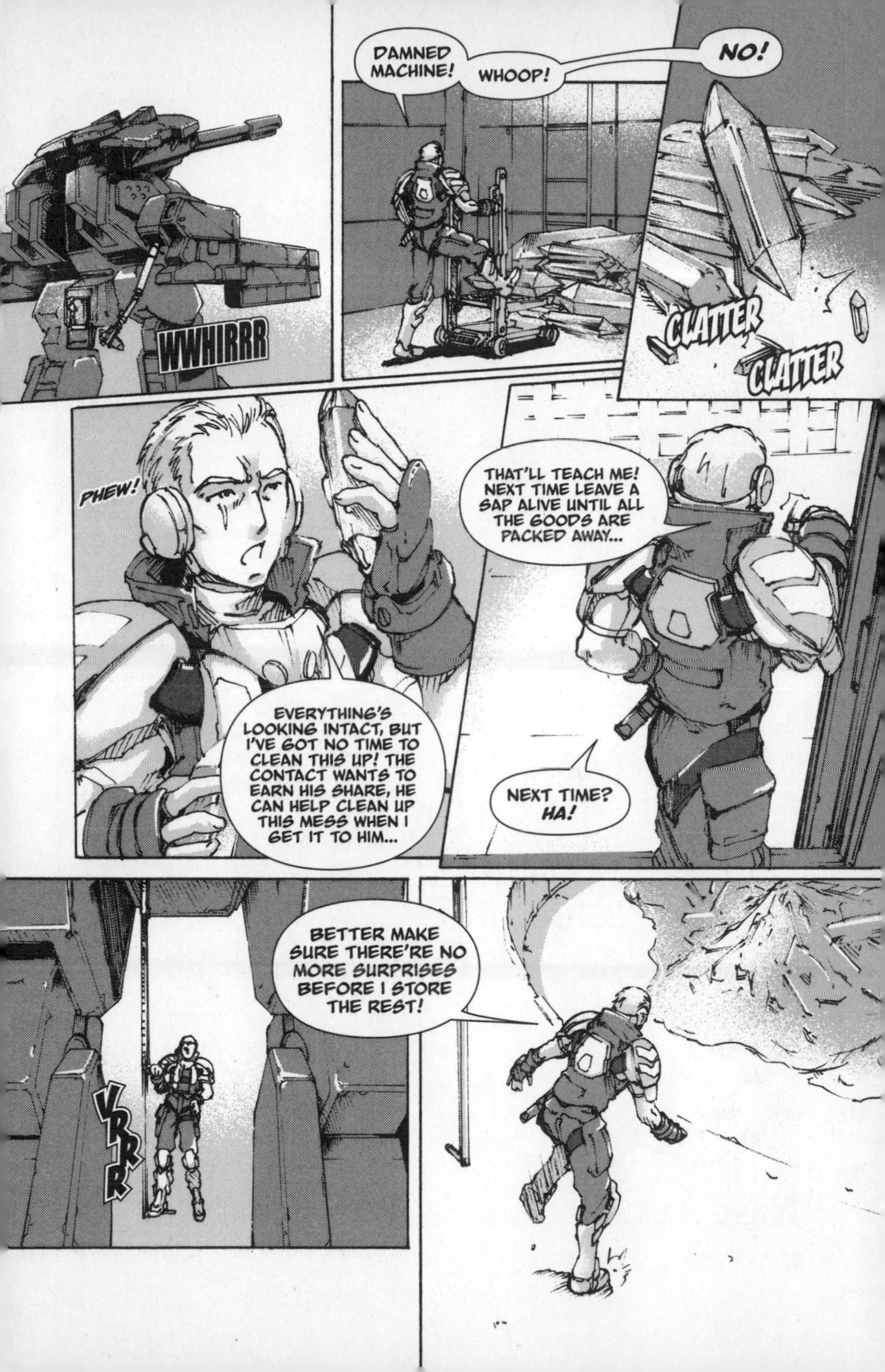
WWHIRRR
DAMNED MACHINE!
WHOOP!
NO!
CLATTER
CLATTER
PHEW!
EVERYTHING'S LOOKING INTACT, BUT I'VE GOT NO TIME TO CLEAN THIS UP! THE CONTACT WANTS TO EARN HIS SHARE, HE CAN HELP CLEAN UP THIS MESS WHEN I GET IT TO HIM...
THAT'LL TEACH ME! NEXT TIME LEAVE A SAP ALIVE UNTIL ALL THE GOODS ARE PACKED AWAY...
NEXT TIME? HA!
VRRRR
BETTER MAKE SURE THERE'RE NO MORE SURPRISES BEFORE I STORE THE REST!

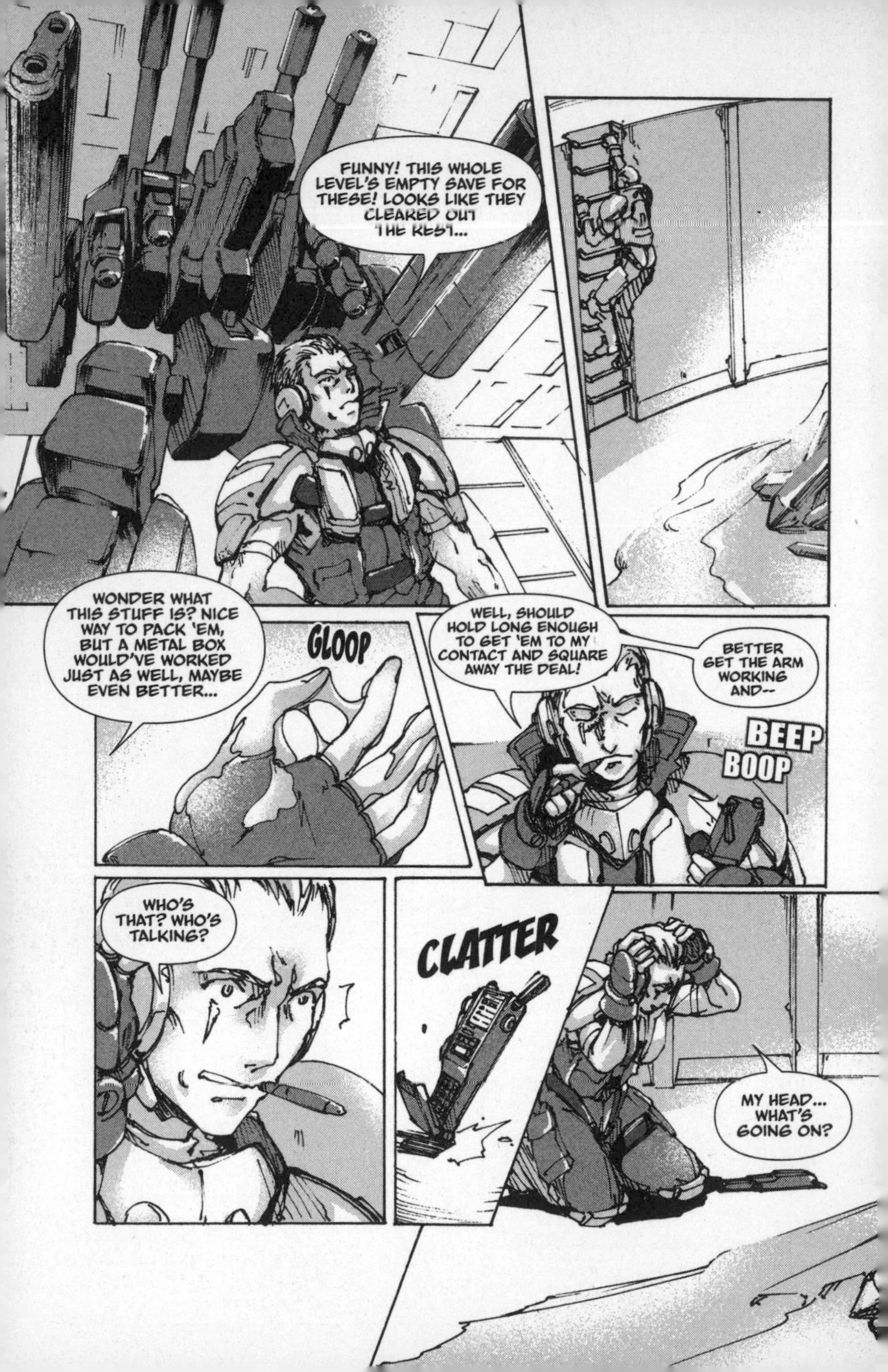
FUNNY! THIS WHOLE LEVEL'S EMPTY SAVE FOR THESE! LOOKS LIKE THEY CLEARED OUT THE REST...
WONDER WHAT THIS STUFF IS? NICE WAY TO PACK 'EM, BUT A METAL BOX WOULD'VE WORKED JUST AS WELL, MAYBE EVEN BETTER...
GLOOP
WELL, SHOULD HOLD LONG ENOUGH TO GET 'EM TO MY CONTACT AND SQUARE AWAY THE DEAL!
BETTER GET THE ARM WORKING AND--
BEEP
BOOP
WHO'S THAT? WHO'S TALKING?
CLATTER
MY HEAD... WHAT'S GOING ON?

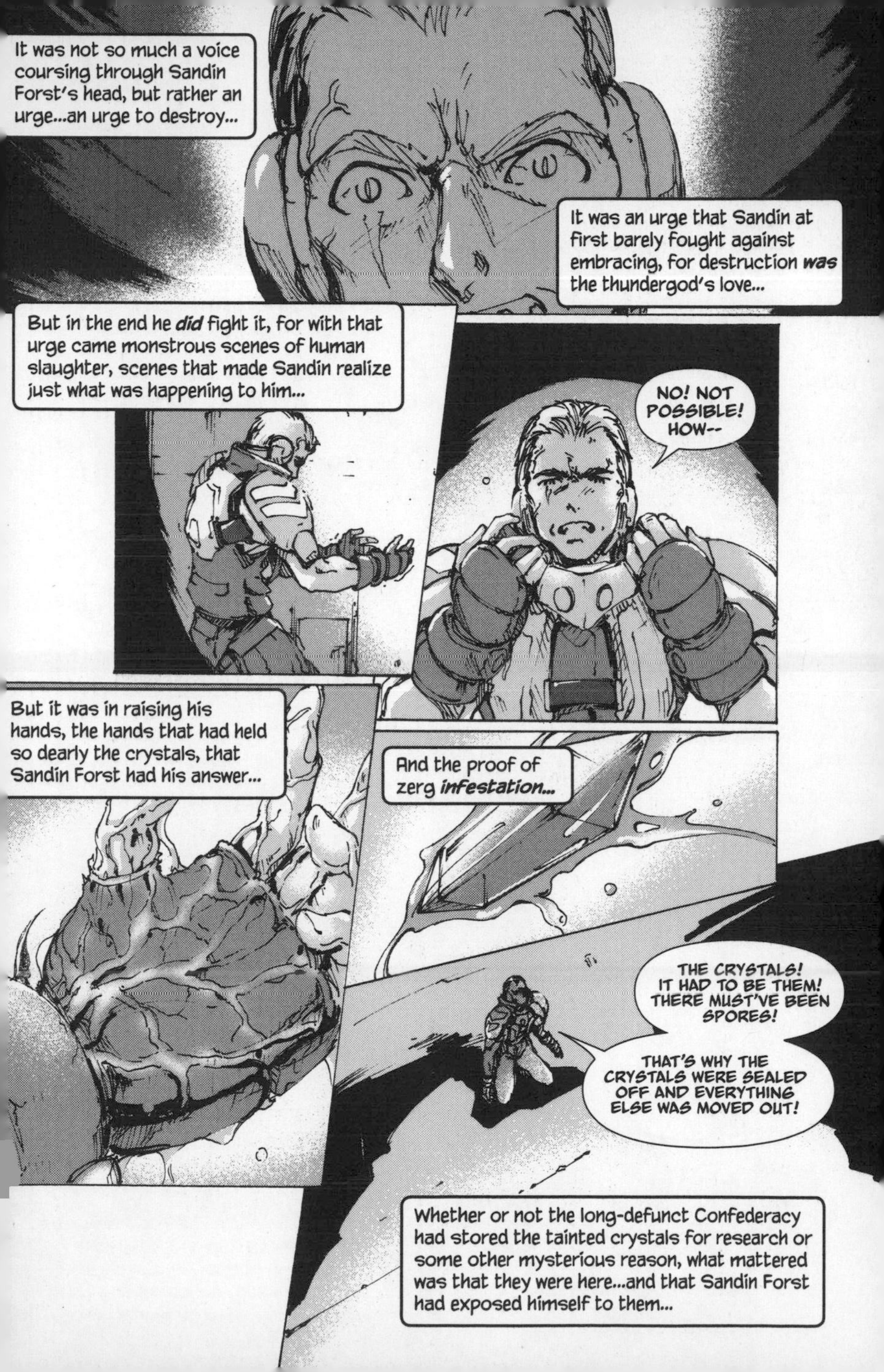
It was not so much a voice coursing through Sandin Forst's head, but rather an urge...an urge to destroy...
It was an urge that Sandin at first barely fought against embracing, for destruction *was* the thundergod's love...
But in the end he *did* fight it, for with that urge came monstrous scenes of human slaughter, scenes that made Sandin realize just what was happening to him...
NO! NOT POSSIBLE! HOW--
But it was in raising his hands, the hands that had held so dearly the crystals, that Sandin Forst had his answer...
And the proof of zerg *infestation...*
THE CRYSTALS! IT HAD TO BE THEM! THERE MUST'VE BEEN SPORES!
THAT'S WHY THE CRYSTALS WERE SEALED OFF AND EVERYTHING ELSE WAS MOVED OUT!
Whether or not the long-defunct Confederacy had stored the tainted crystals for research or some other mysterious reason, what mattered was that they were here...and that Sandin Forst had exposed himself to them...

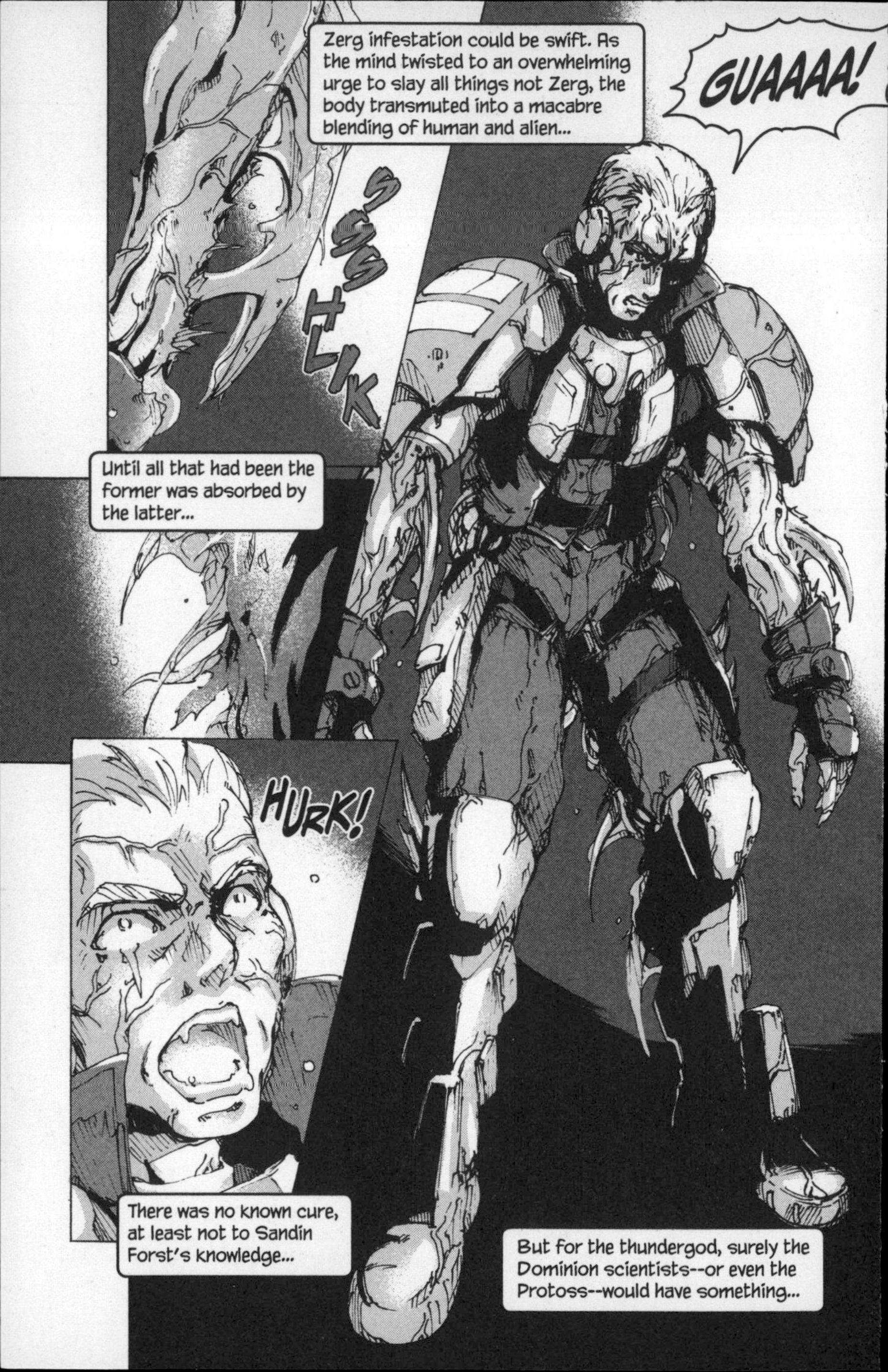
Zerg infestation could be swift. As the mind twisted to an overwhelming urge to slay all things not Zerg, the body transmuted into a macabre blending of human and alien...
SSSHLIK
GUAAAA!
Until all that had been the former was absorbed by the latter...
HURK!
There was no known cure, at least not to Sandin Forst's knowledge...
But for the thundergod, surely the Dominion scientists--or even the Protoss--would have something...

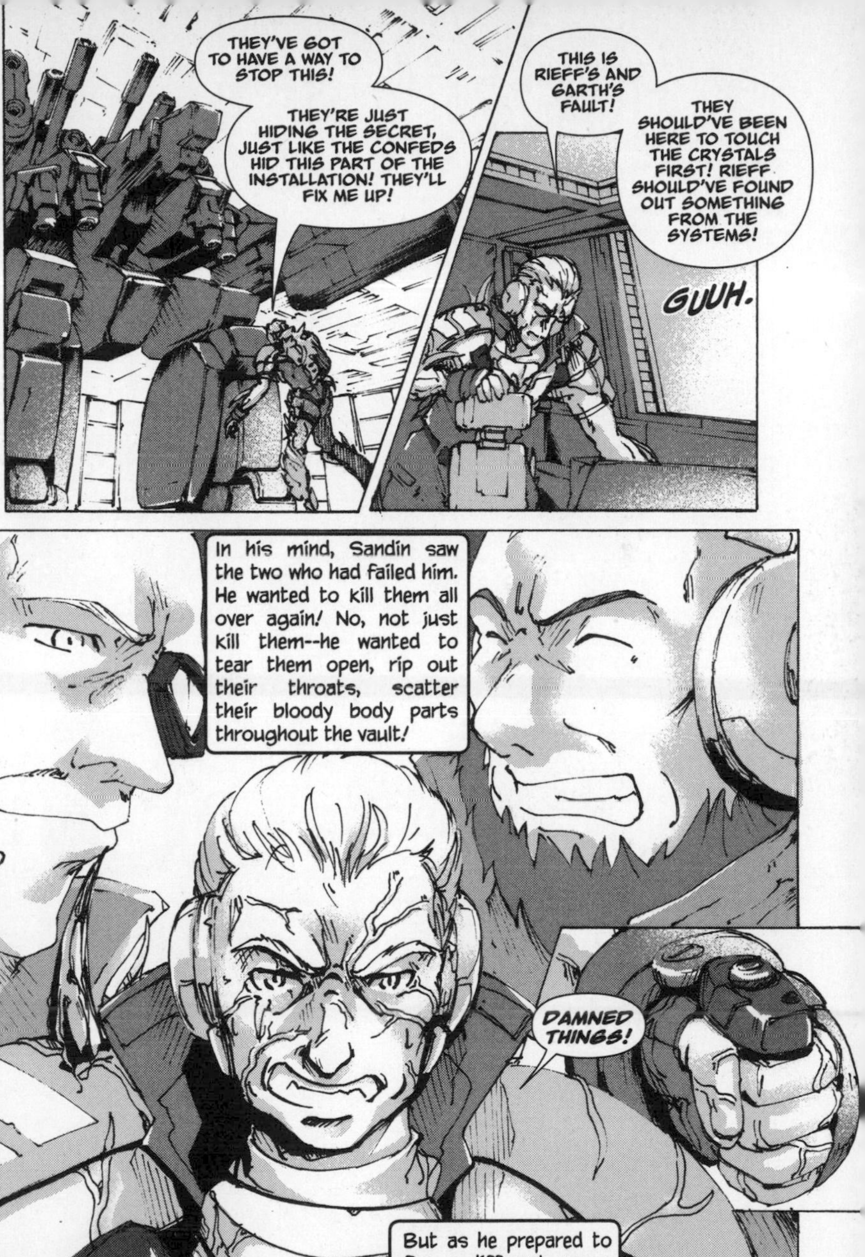
THEY'VE GOT TO HAVE A WAY TO STOP THIS!
THEY'RE JUST HIDING THE SECRET, JUST LIKE THE CONFEDS HID THIS PART OF THE INSTALLATION! THEY'LL FIX ME UP!
THIS IS RIEFF'S AND GARTH'S FAULT!
THEY SHOULD'VE BEEN HERE TO TOUCH THE CRYSTALS FIRST! RIEFF SHOULD'VE FOUND OUT SOMETHING FROM THE SYSTEMS!
GUUH.
In his mind, Sandin saw the two who had failed him. He wanted to kill them all over again! No, not just kill them--he wanted to tear them open, rip out their throats, scatter their bloody body parts throughout the vault!
DAMNED THINGS!
But as he prepared to fire, a different enemy became his focus...

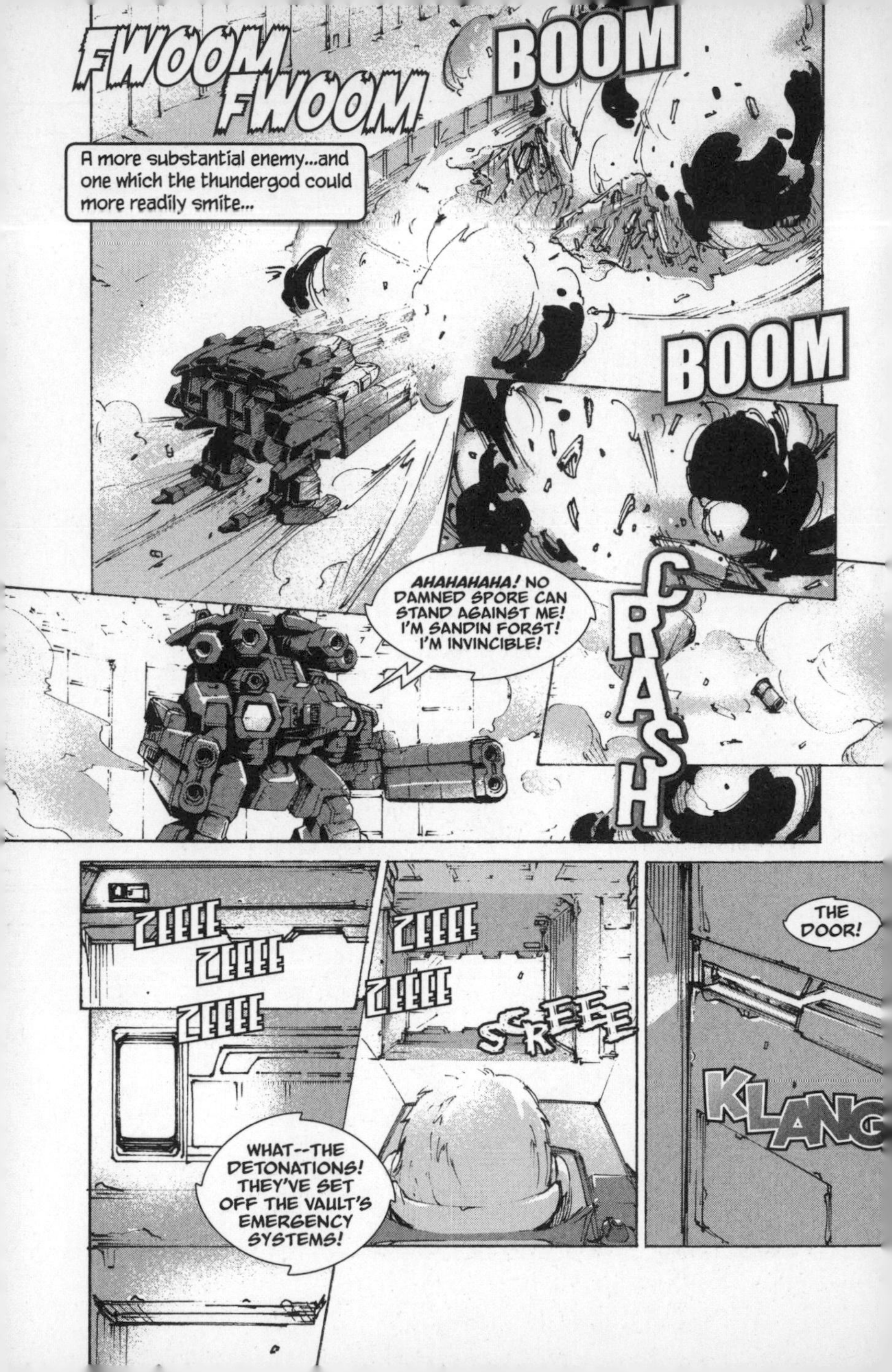
FWOOM
FWOOM
BOOM
A more substantial enemy...and one which the thundergod could more readily smite...
BOOM
AHAHAHAHA! NO DAMNED SPORE CAN STAND AGAINST ME! I'M SANDIN FORST! I'M INVINCIBLE!
CRASH
ZEEEE
ZEEEE
ZEEEE
ZEEEE
ZEEEE
SCREEEE
WHAT--THE DETONATIONS! THEY'VE SET OFF THE VAULT'S EMERGENCY SYSTEMS!
THE DOOR!
KLANG

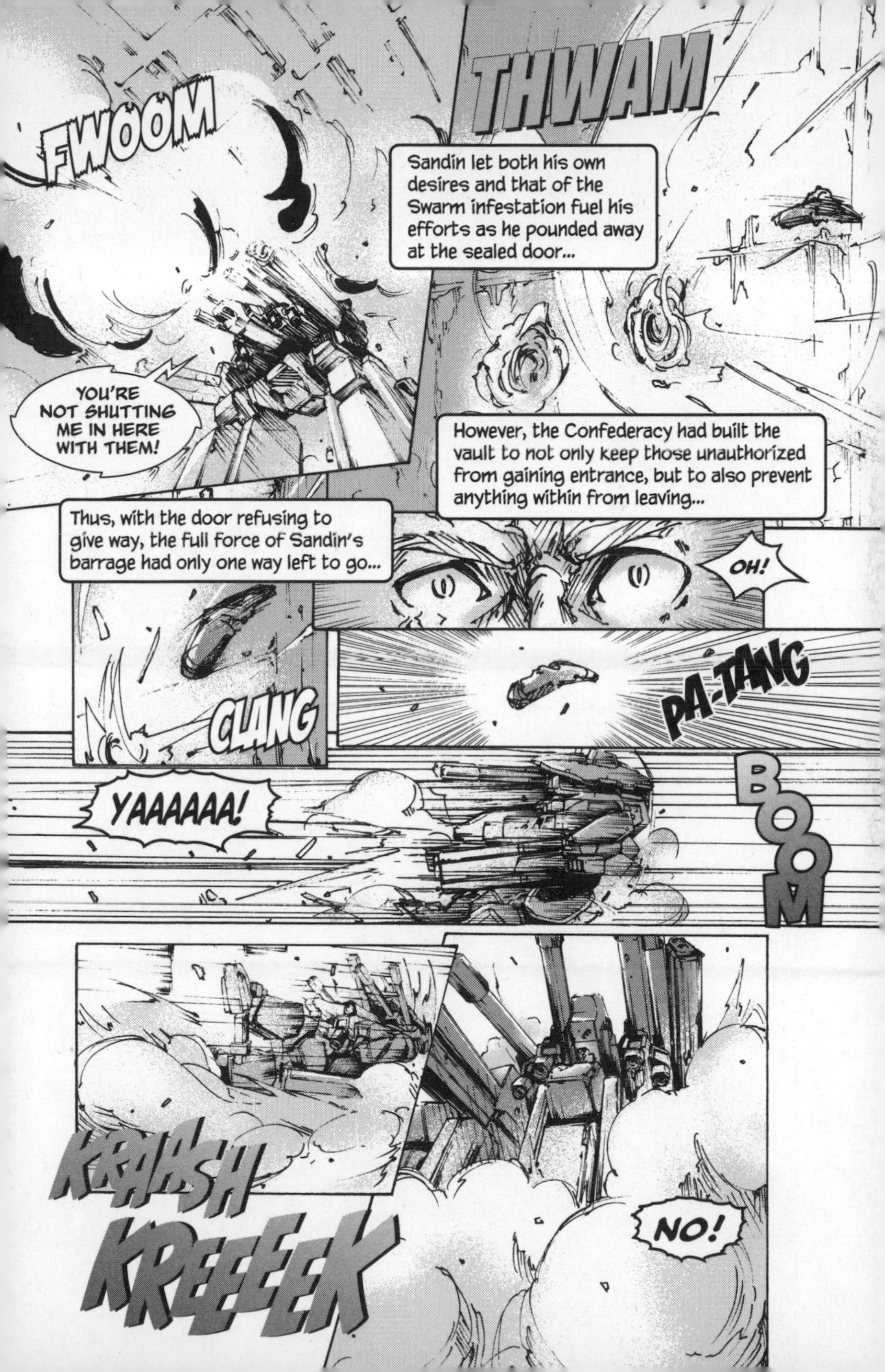
FWOOM
YOU'RE NOT SHUTTING ME IN HERE WITH THEM!
THWAM
Sandin let both his own desires and that of the Swarm infestation fuel his efforts as he pounded away at the sealed door...
However, the Confederacy had built the vault to not only keep those unauthorized from gaining entrance, but to also prevent anything within from leaving...
Thus, with the door refusing to give way, the full force of Sandin's barrage had only one way left to go...
OH!
CLANG
PA-TANG
YAAAAAA!
BOOOM
KRAASH
KREEEEK
NO!

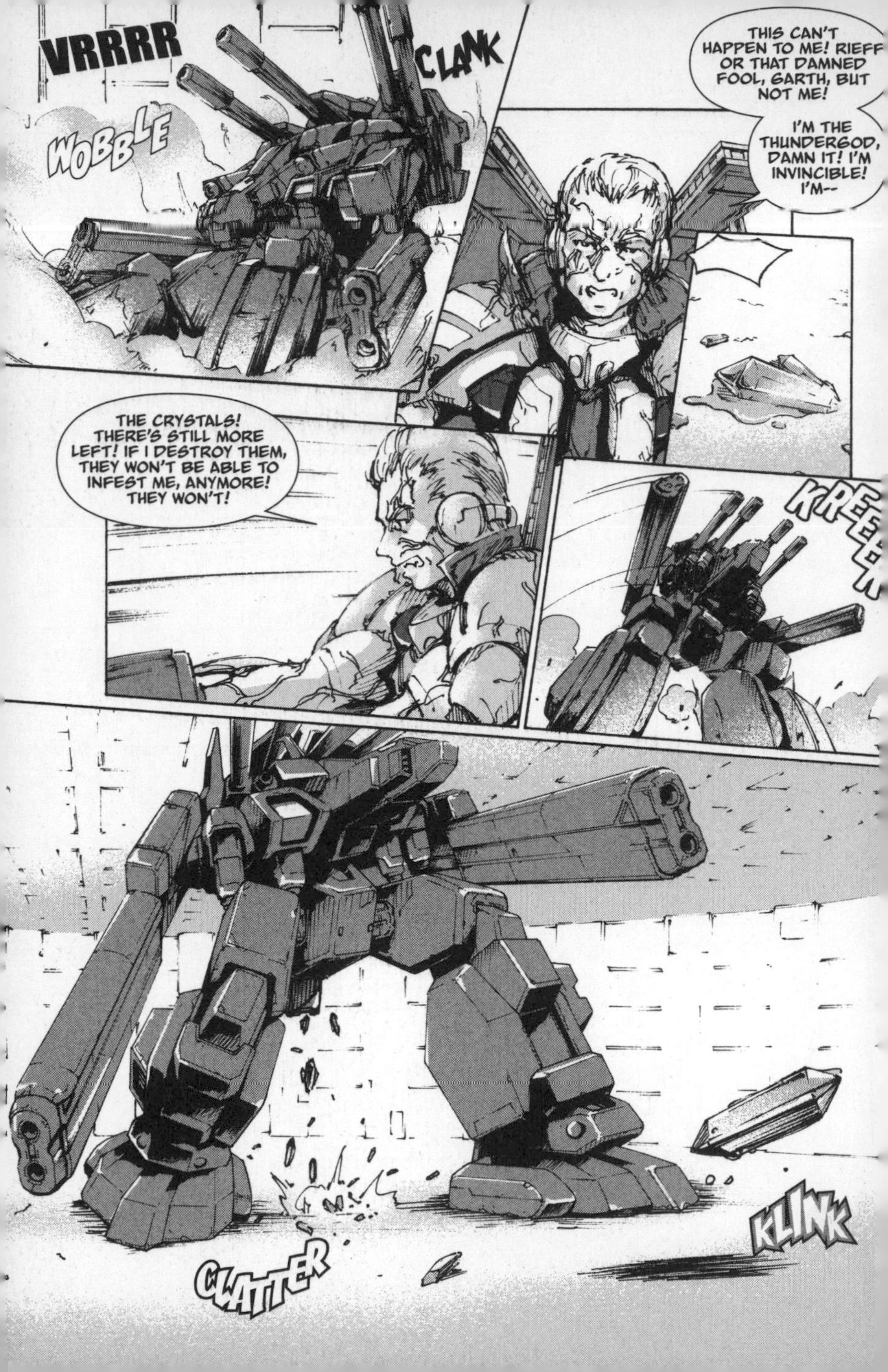
VRRRR
CLANK
WOBBLE
THIS CAN'T HAPPEN TO ME! RIEFF OR THAT DAMNED FOOL, GARTH, BUT NOT ME!
I'M THE THUNDERGOD, DAMN IT! I'M INVINCIBLE! I'M--
THE CRYSTALS! THERE'S STILL MORE LEFT! IF I DESTROY THEM, THEY WON'T BE ABLE TO INFEST ME, ANYMORE! THEY WON'T!
KREEE
CLATTER
KLINK

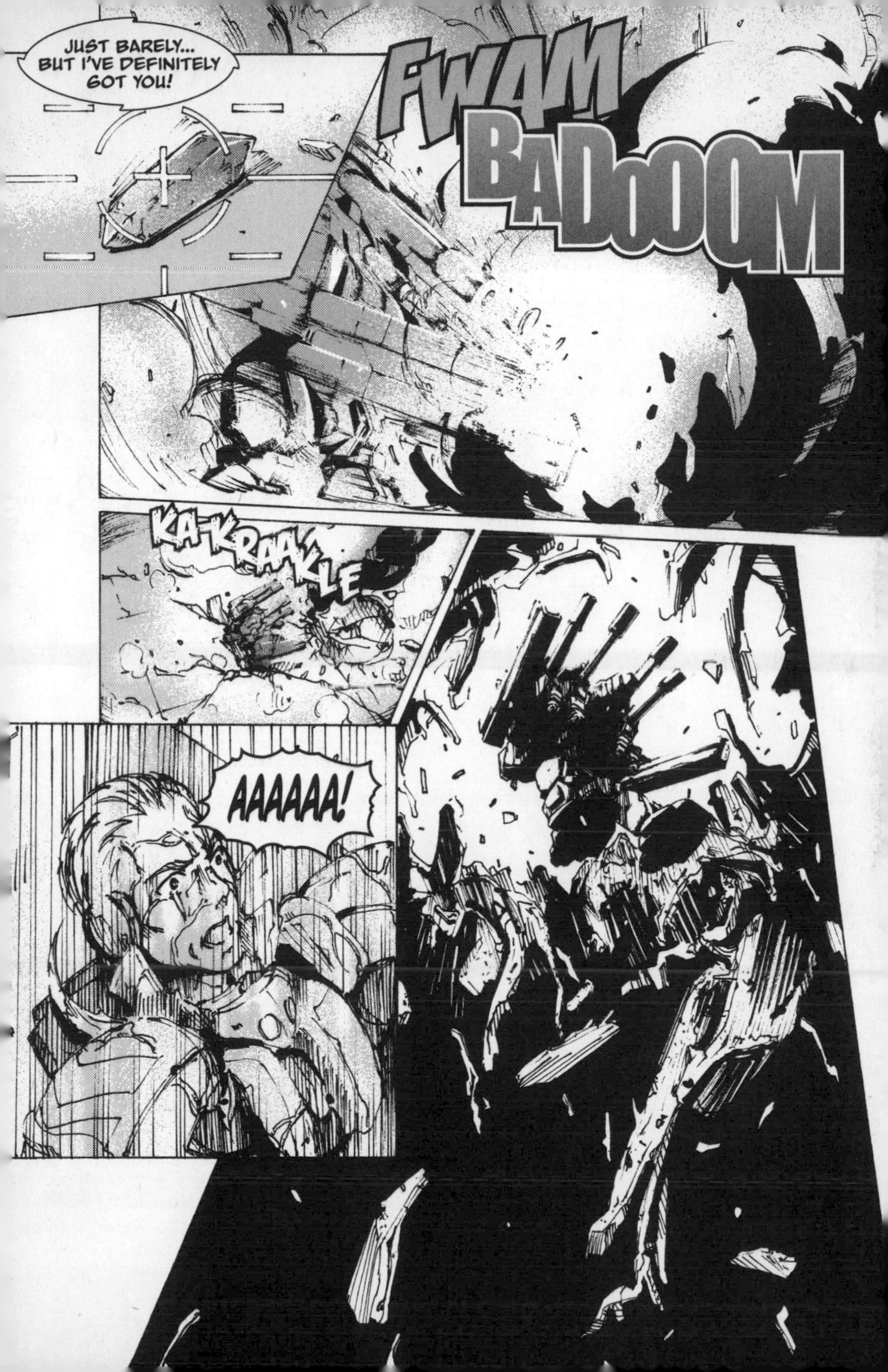
JUST BARELY... BUT I'VE DEFINITELY GOT YOU!
FWAM
BADOOOM
KA-KRAAKLE
AAAAAA!

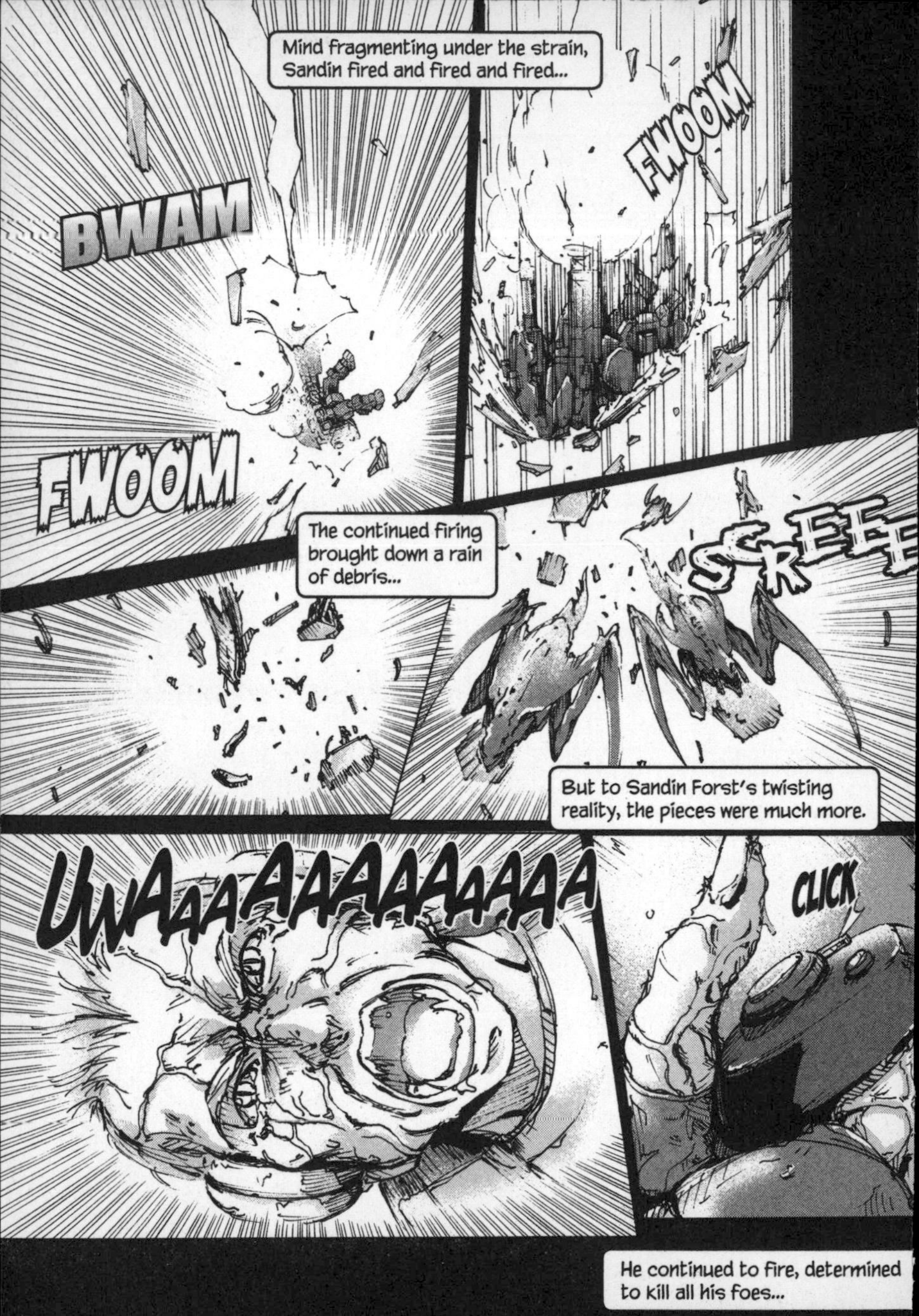
Mind fragmenting under the strain, Sandin fired and fired and fired...
BWAM
FWOOM
FWOOM
The continued firing brought down a rain of debris...
SCREEE
But to Sandin Forst's twisting reality, the pieces were much more.
UWAAAAAAAAAAAAA
CLICK
He continued to fire, determined to kill all his foes...

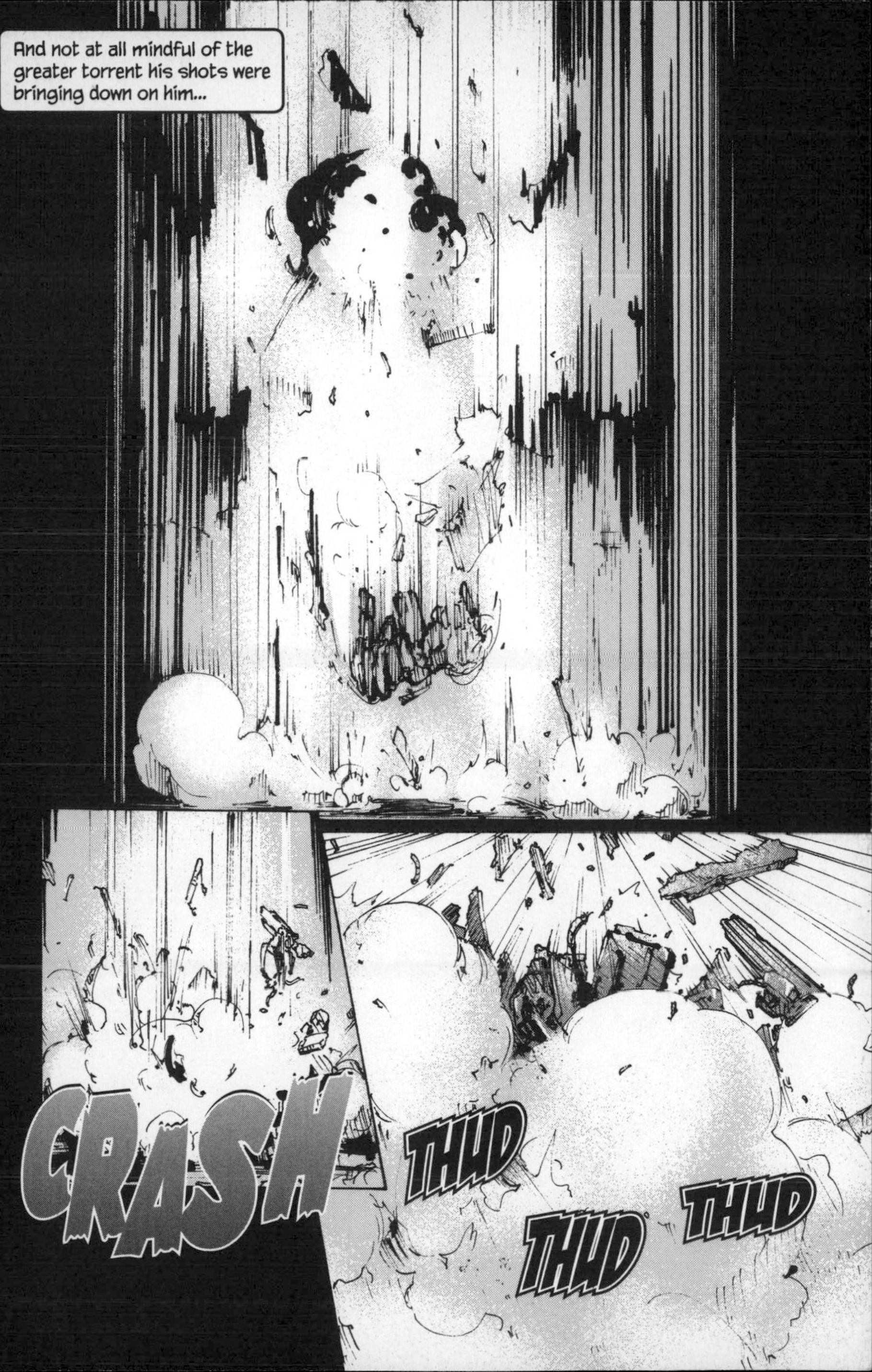
And not at all mindful of the greater torrent his shots were bringing down on him...
CRASH
THUD
THUD
THUD

WOOOOO OOOOO OO

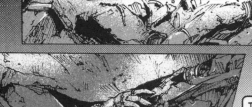

Perhaps here, then, is a lesson the Dominion should heed if they ever discover--and survive said discovery of--Sandin Forst and his Thor...

That greed and the most minute of weapons can combine to bring down the most gargantuan of war machines...

And that the greatest of empires, and even *thundergods,* are destined to suffer their downfall...

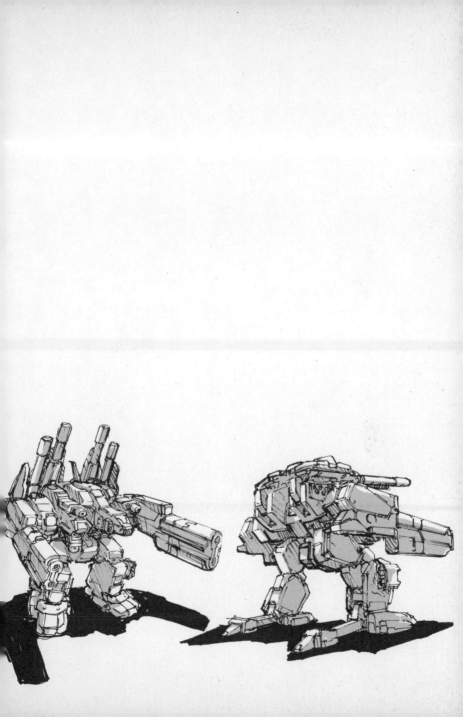

StarCraft

Frontline

Volume 1

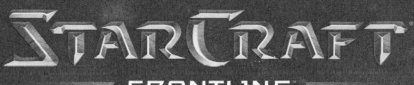

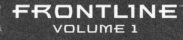

Weapon of War

Written by Paul Benjamin & Dave Shramek

Art by Hector Sevilla

Letterer: Lucas Rivera

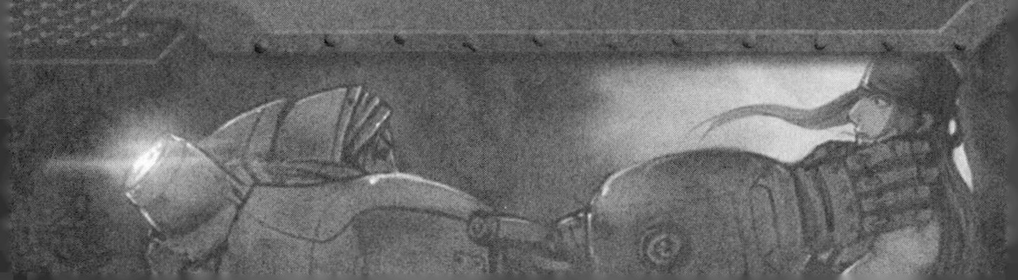

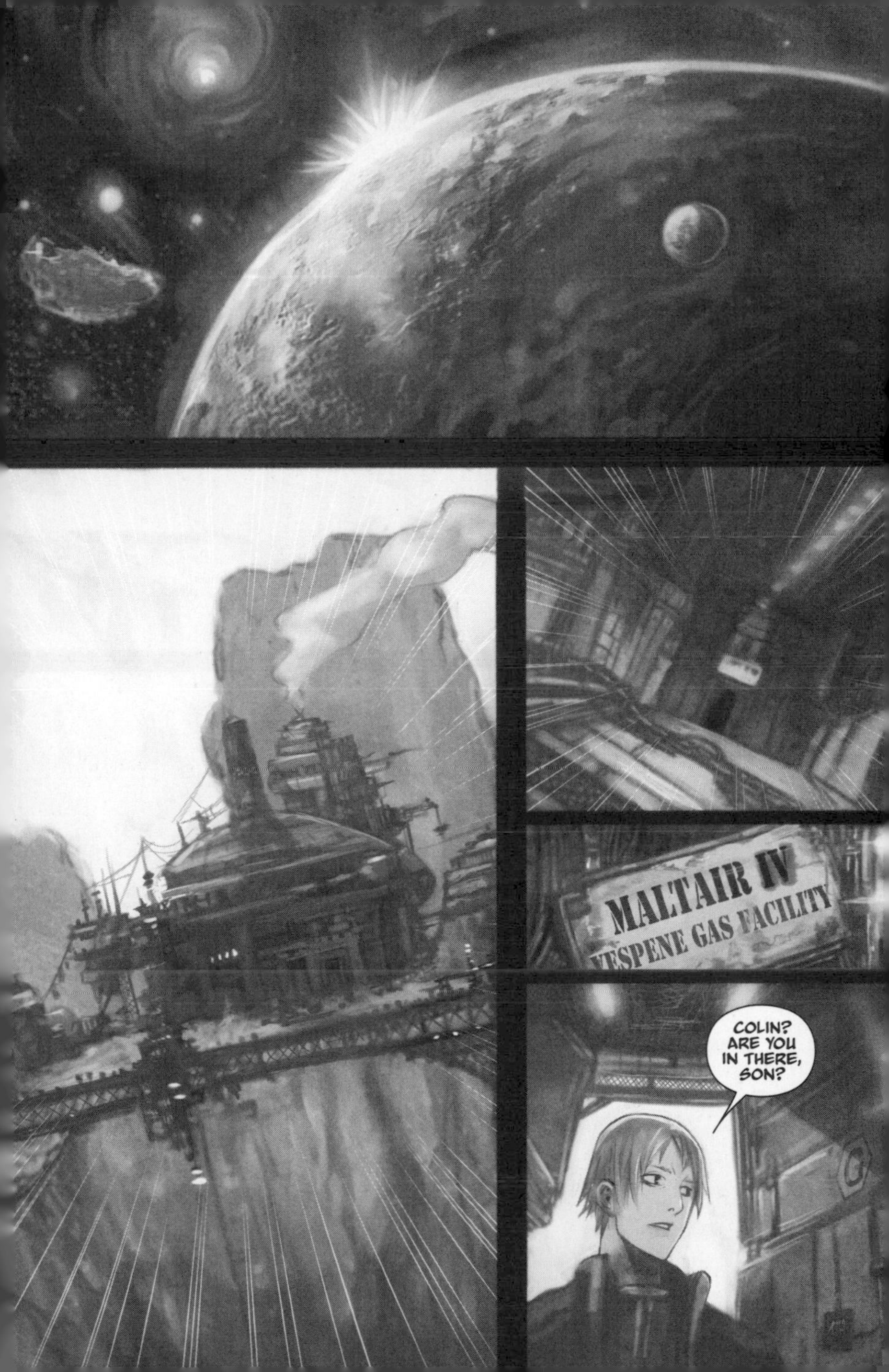
MALTAIR IV
VESPENE GAS FACILITY
COLIN? ARE YOU IN THERE, SON?

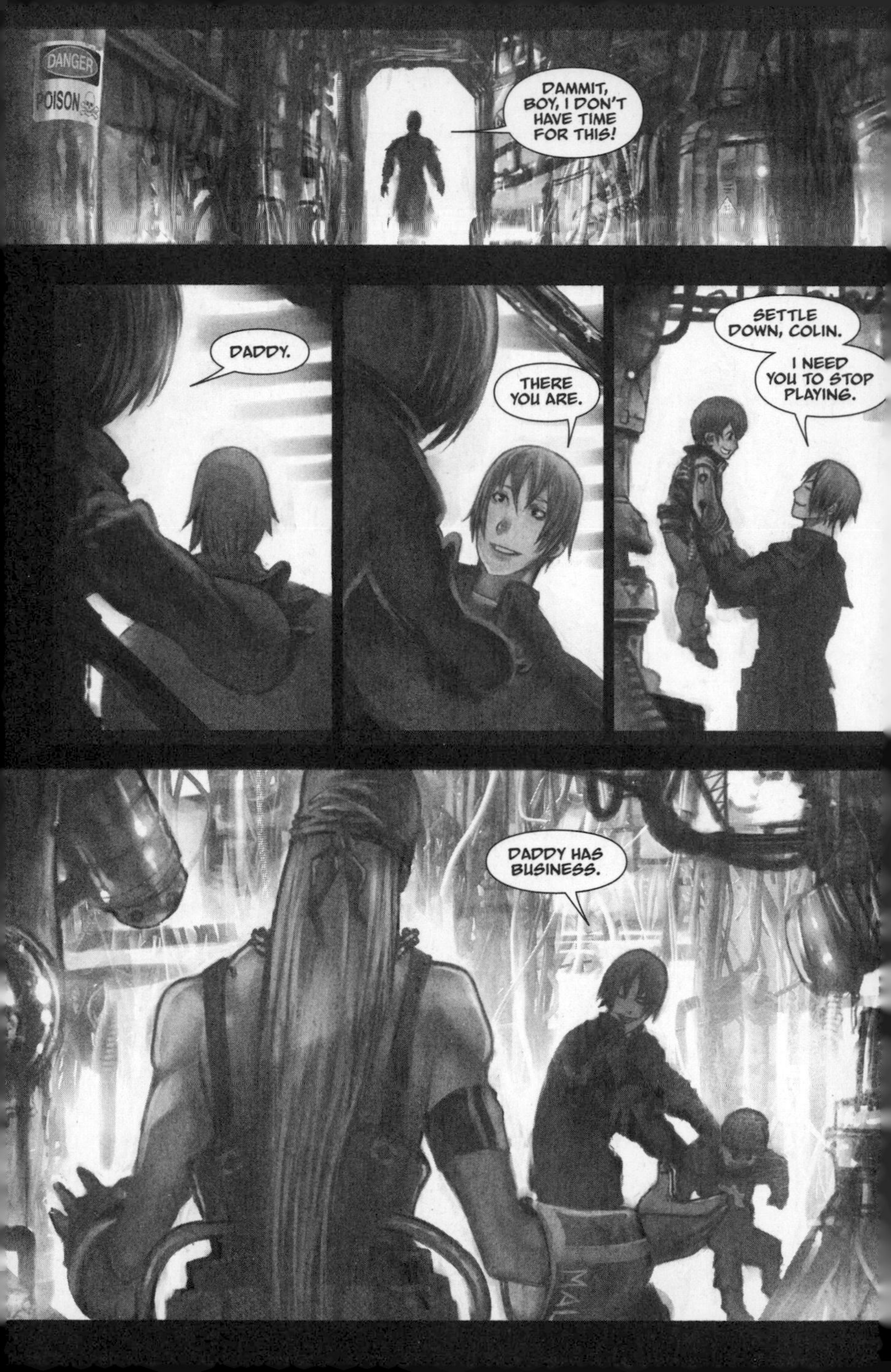
DANGER
POISON
DAMMIT, BOY, I DON'T HAVE TIME FOR THIS!
DADDY.
THERE YOU ARE.
SETTLE DOWN, COLIN.
I NEED YOU TO STOP PLAYING.
DADDY HAS BUSINESS.

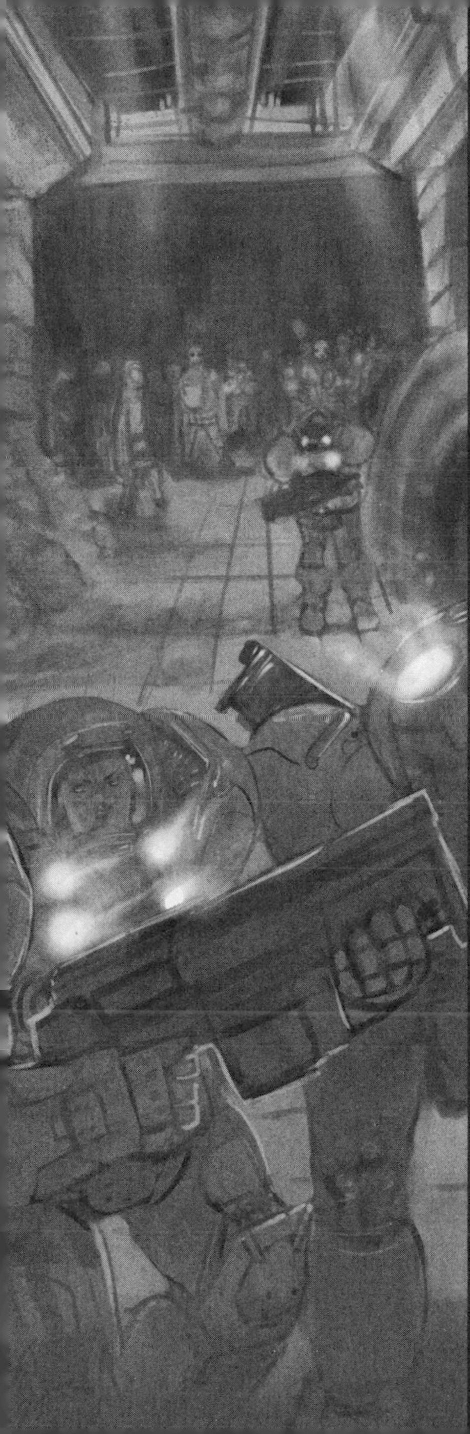

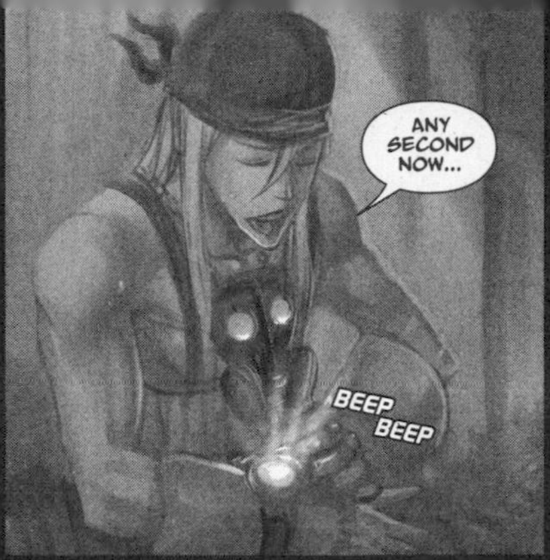
ANY SECOND NOW...
BEEP BEEP

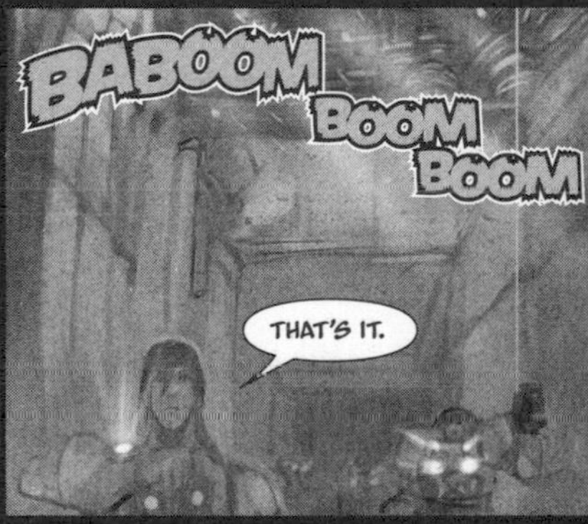
BABOOM BOOM BOOM
THAT'S IT.

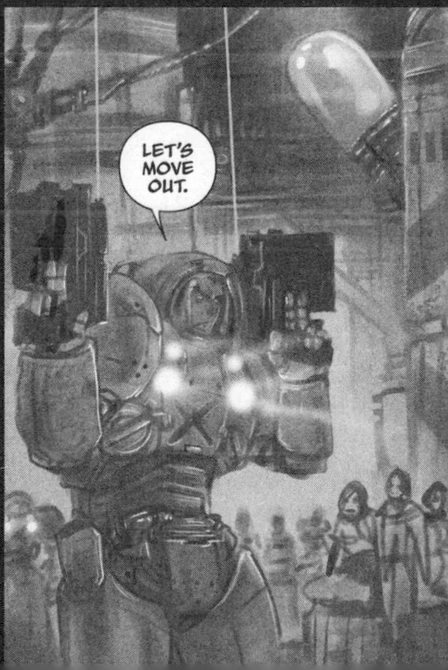
LET'S MOVE OUT.

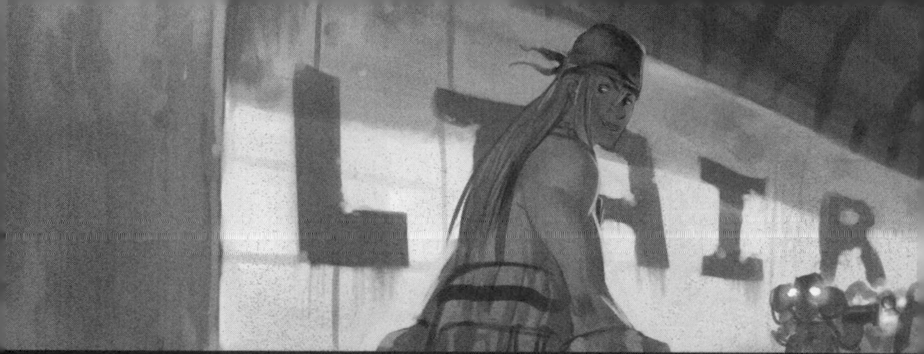

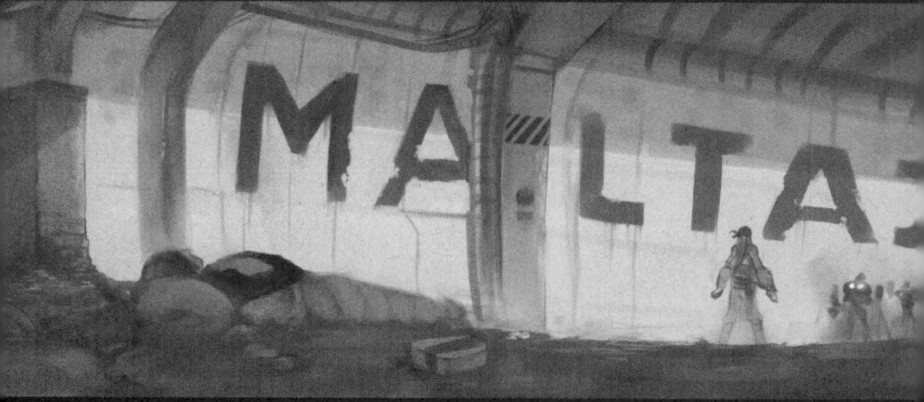
MALTA

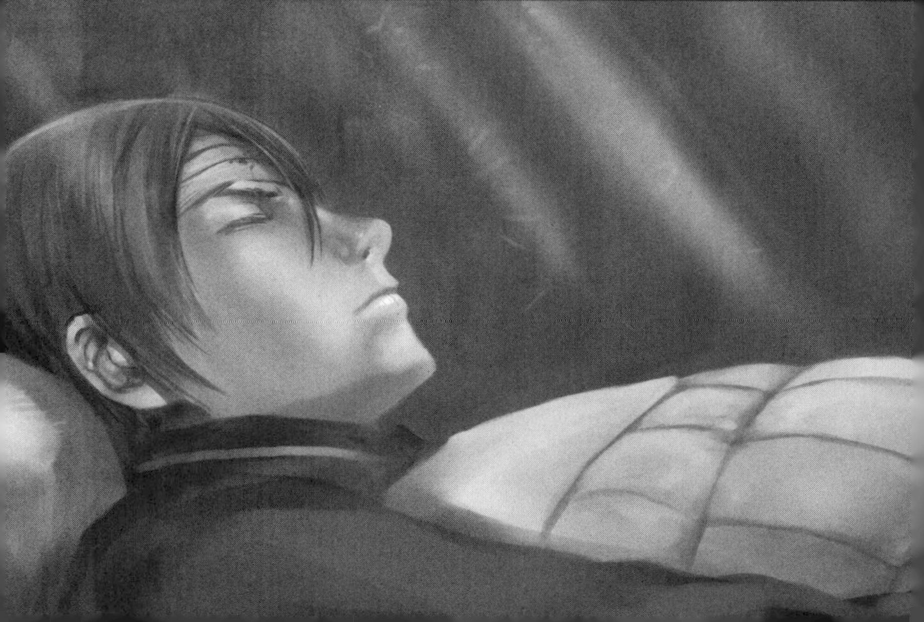

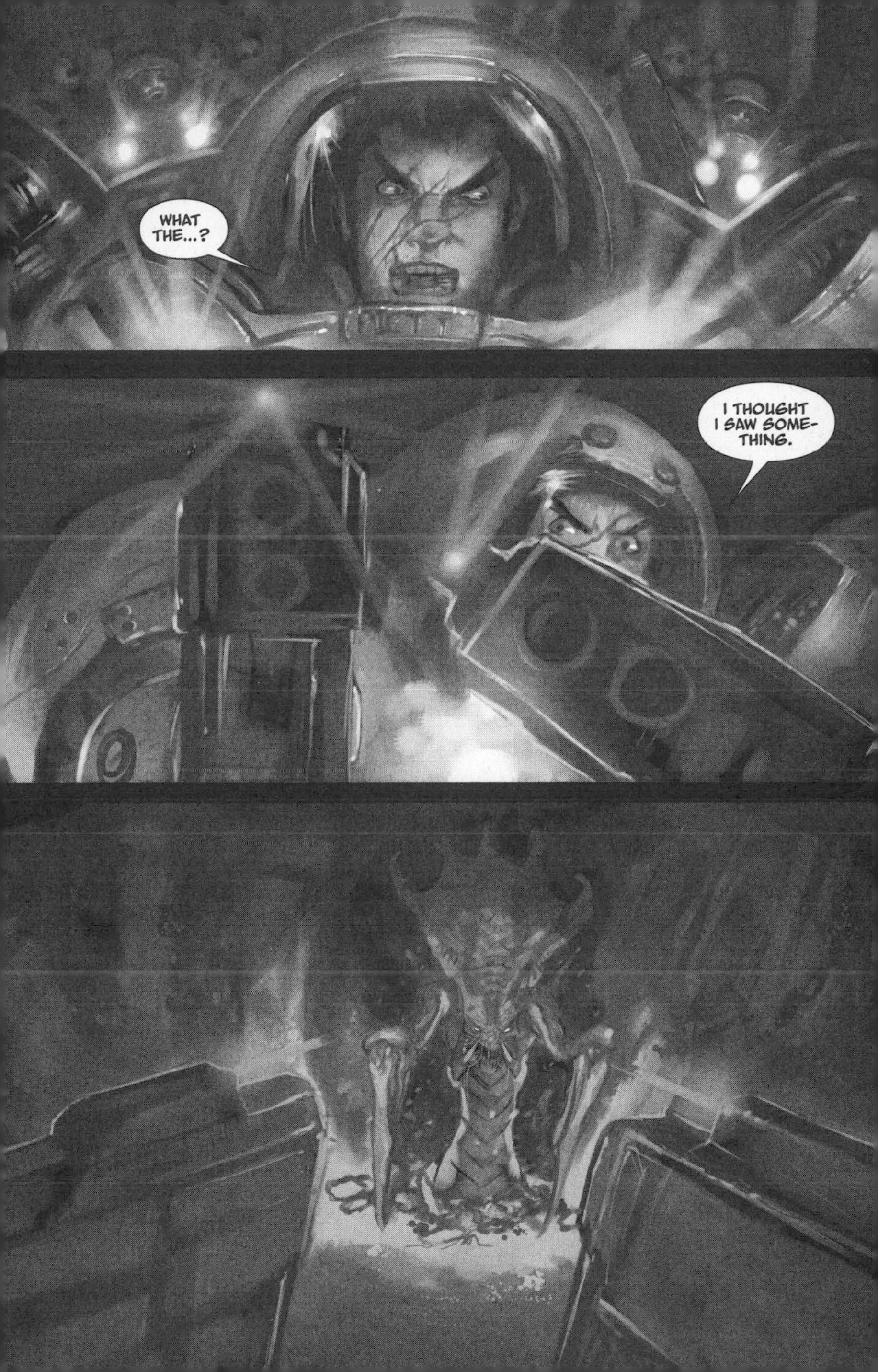
WHAT THE...?
I THOUGHT I SAW SOME-THING.

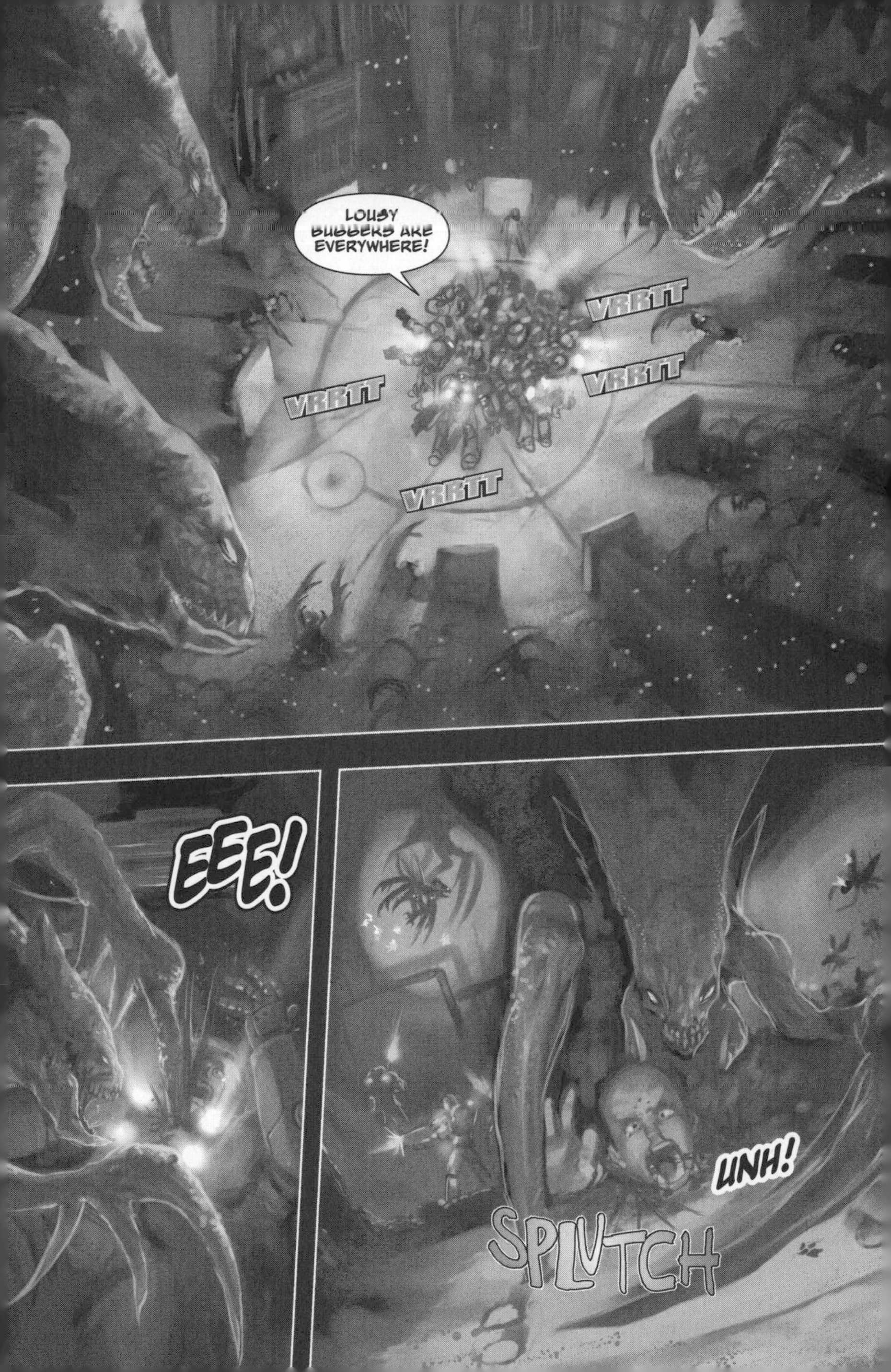
LOUSY BUGGERS ARE EVERYWHERE!
VRRTT
VRRTT
VRRTT
VRRTT
EEE!
UNH!
SPLUTCH

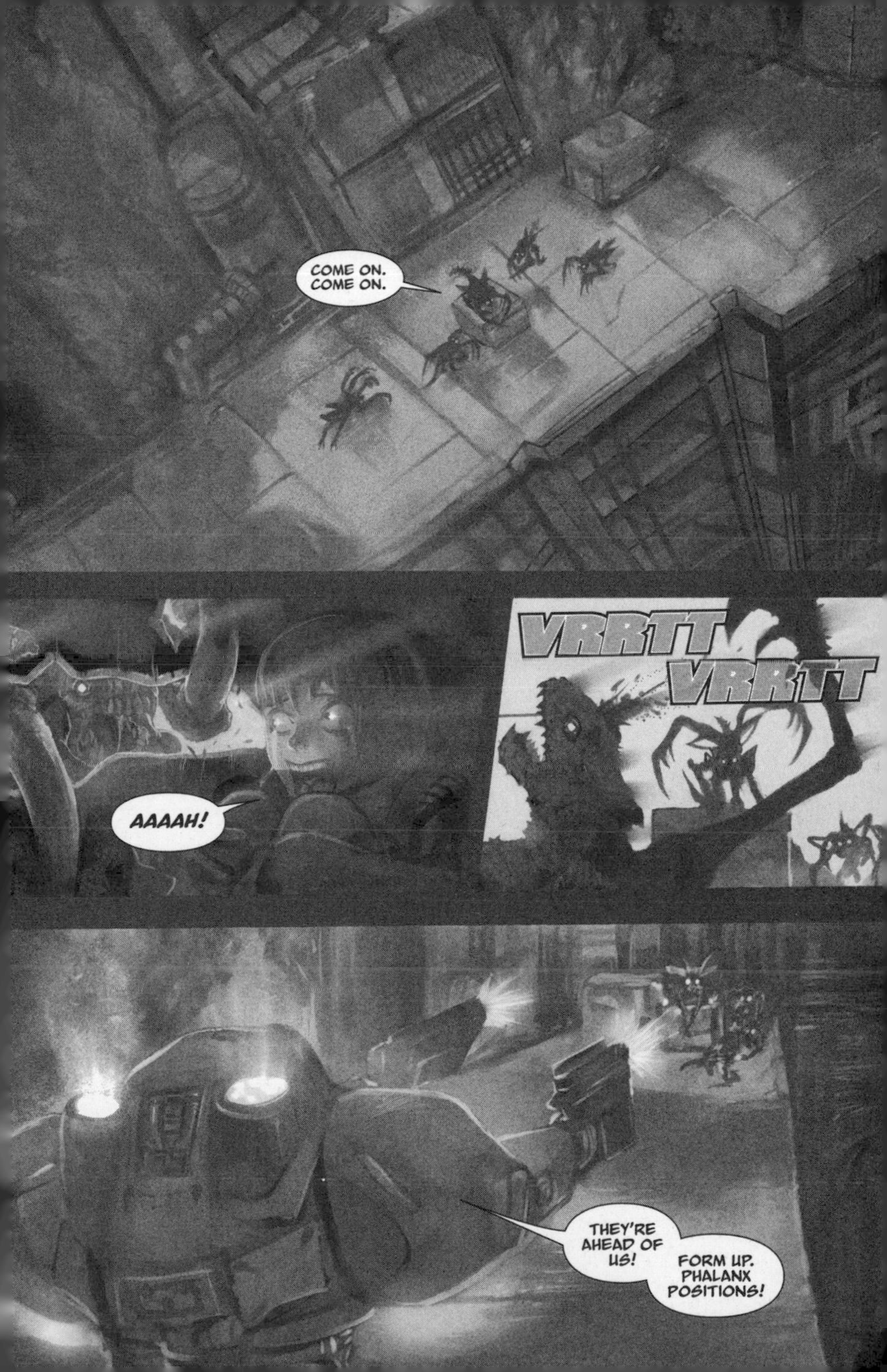
COME ON. COME ON.
AAAAH!
VRRTT VRRTT
THEY'RE AHEAD OF US!
FORM UP. PHALANX POSITIONS!

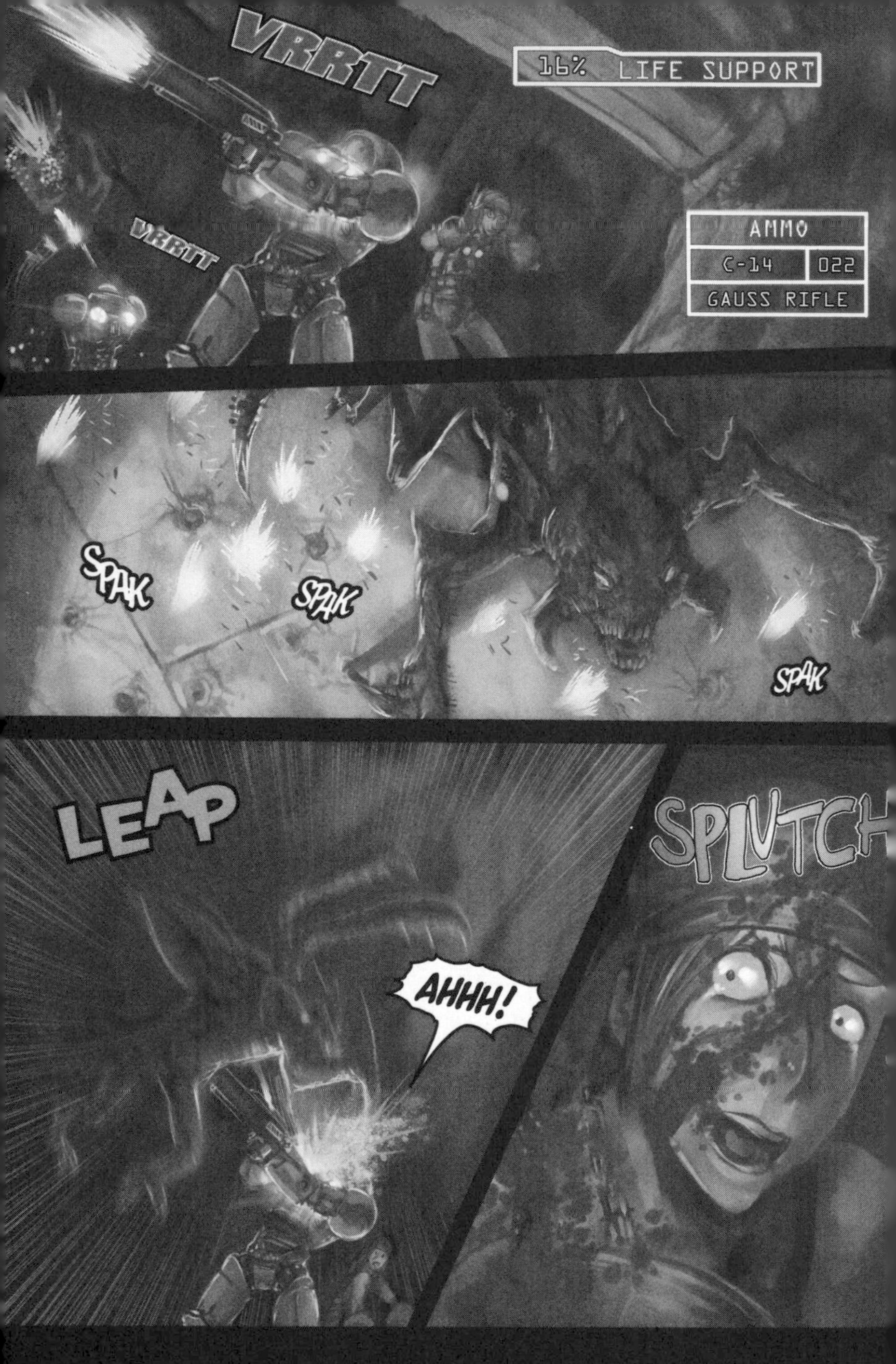
VRRTT
16% LIFE SUPPORT
VRRTT
AMMO
C-14
022
GAUSS RIFLE
SPAK
SPAK
SPAK
LEAP
AHHH!
SPLUTCH

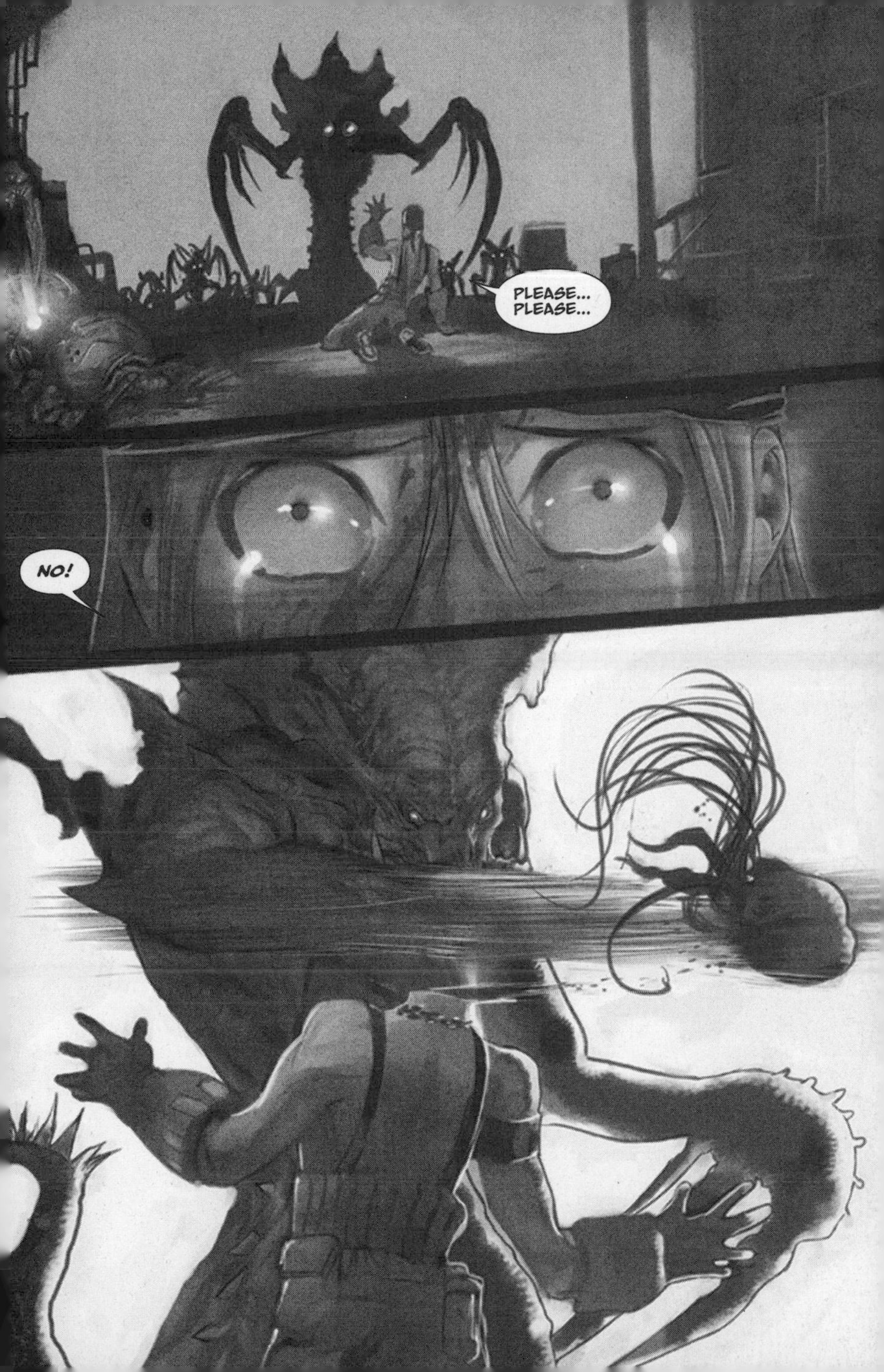
PLEASE...
PLEASE...
NO!

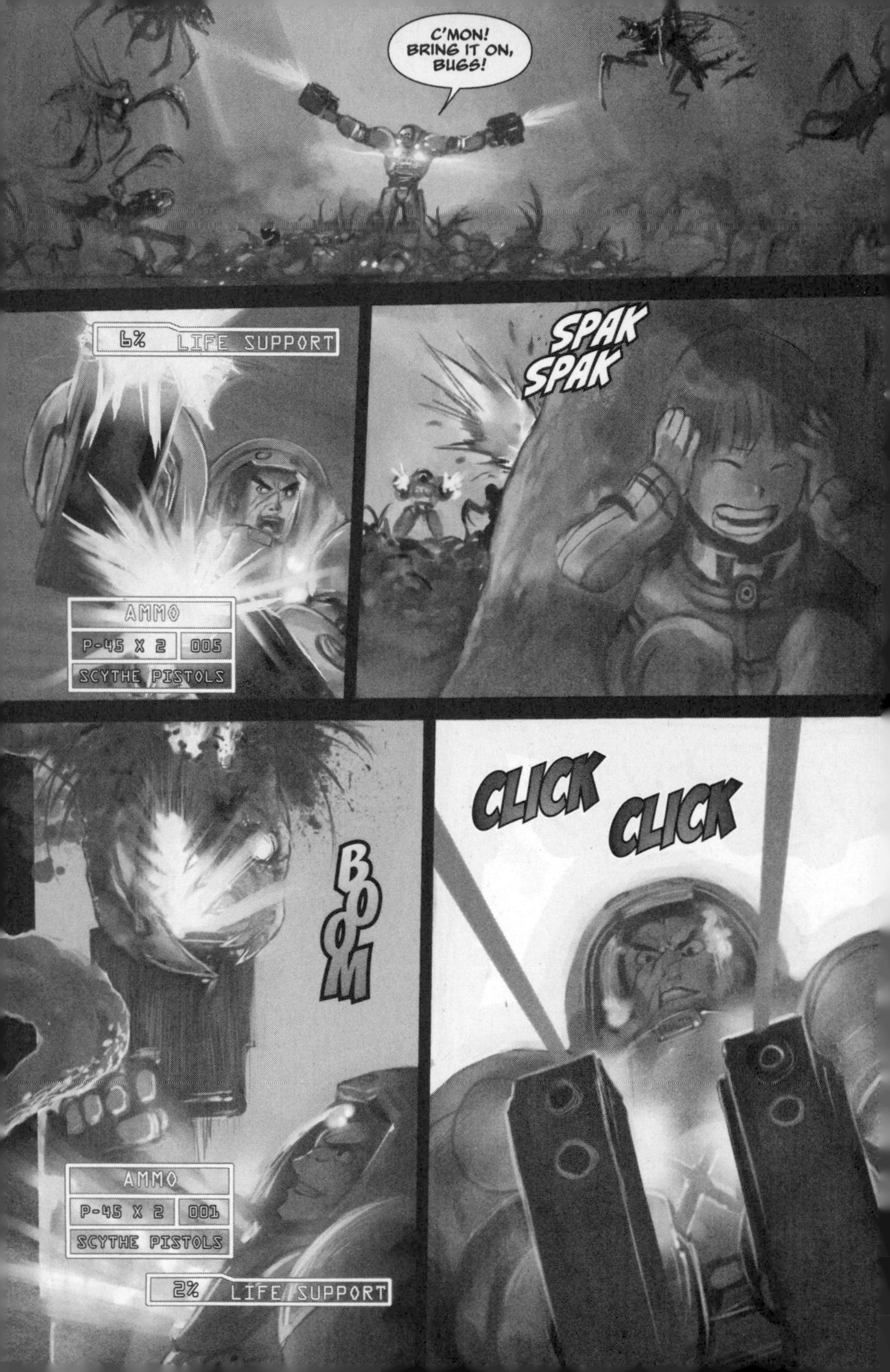
C'MON! BRING IT ON, BUGS!
6% LIFE SUPPORT
AMMO
P-45 X 2
005
SCYTHE PISTOLS
SPAK SPAK
BOOM
AMMO
P-45 X 2
001
SCYTHE PISTOLS
2% LIFE SUPPORT
CLICK CLICK

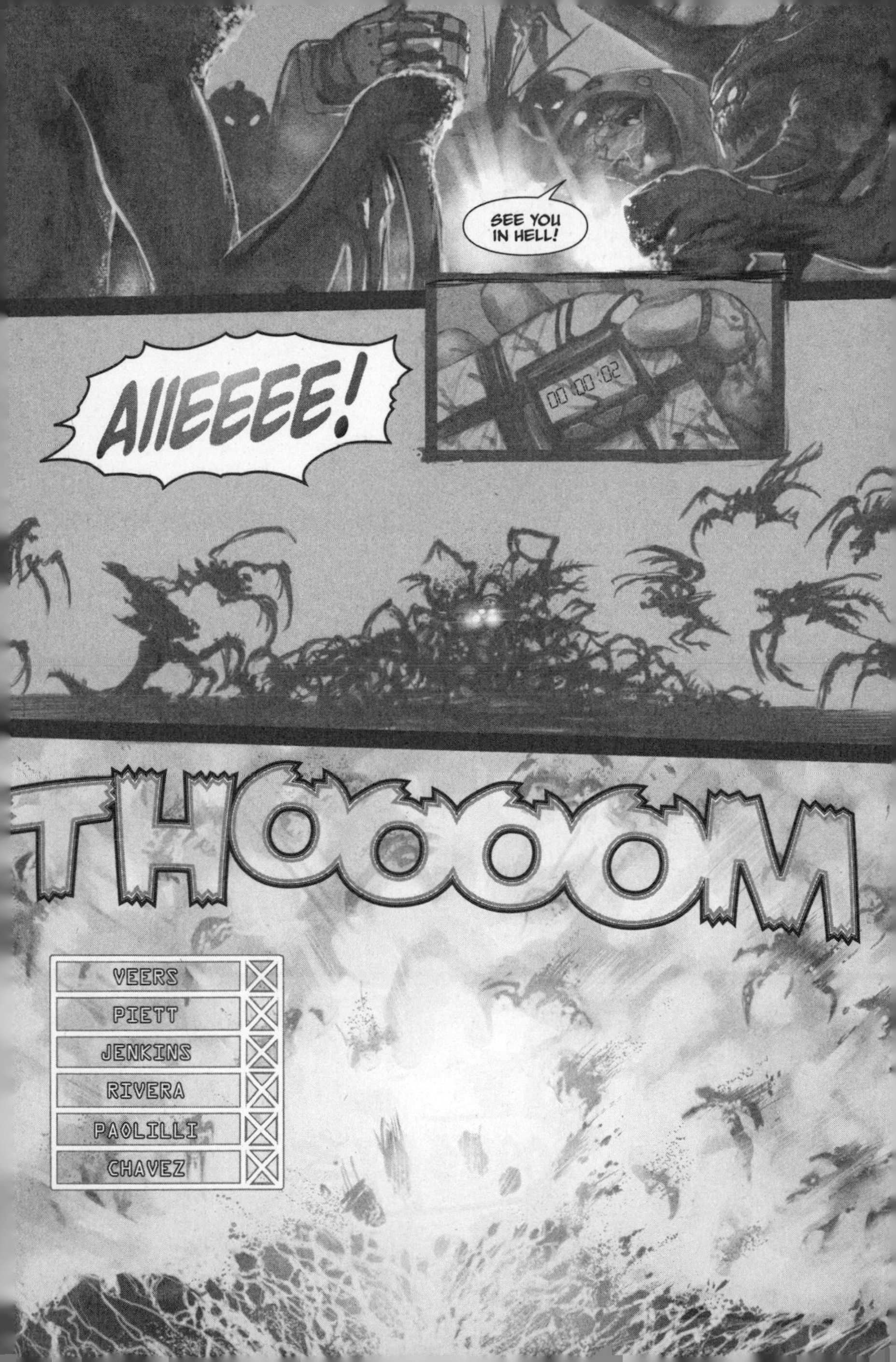
SEE YOU IN HELL!
AIIEEEE!
00:00:02
THOOOOM
VEERS
PIETT
JENKINS
RIVERA
PAOLILLI
CHAVEZ

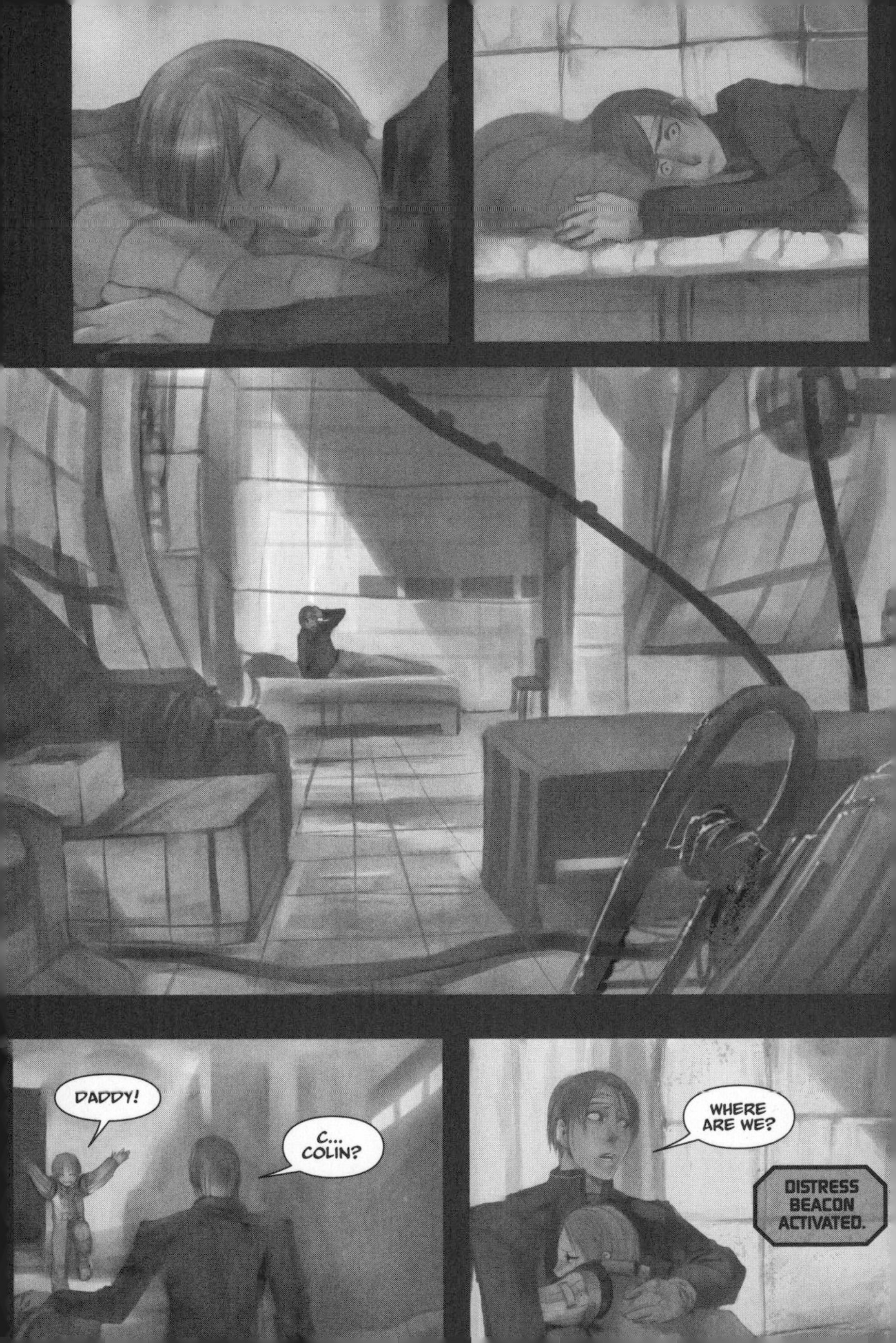
DADDY!
C... COLIN?
WHERE ARE WE?
DISTRESS BEACON ACTIVATED.

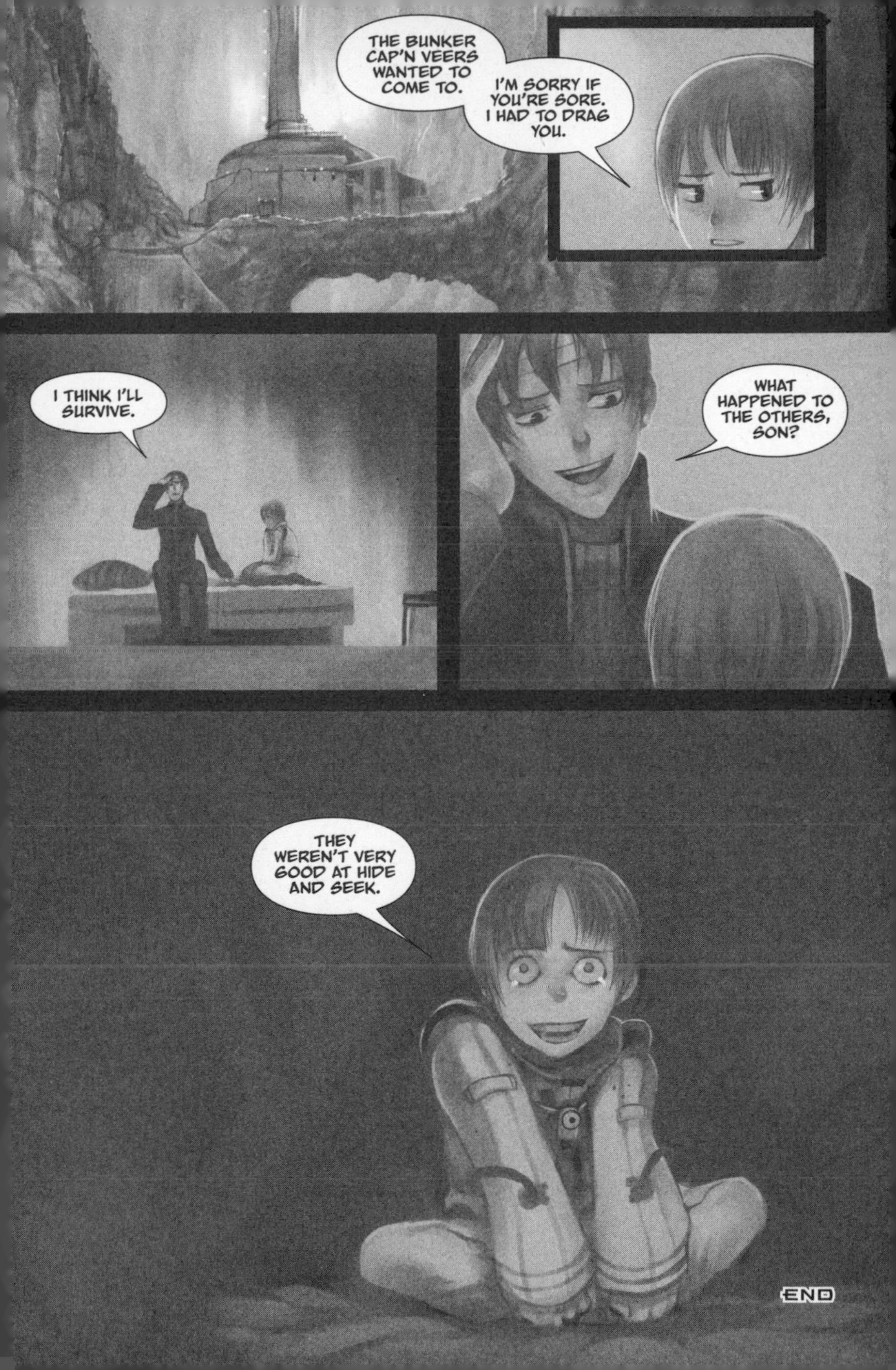
THE BUNKER CAP'N VEERS WANTED TO COME TO.
I'M SORRY IF YOU'RE SORE. I HAD TO DRAG YOU.
I THINK I'LL SURVIVE.
WHAT HAPPENED TO THE OTHERS, SON?
THEY WEREN'T VERY GOOD AT HIDE AND SEEK.
END

STARCRAFT

FRONTLINE
VOLUME 1

HEAVY ARMOR – PART 1

Written by Simon Furman

Pencils and Inks by Jesse Elliott

Tones by Chi Wang, Marcus Jones and JC Padilla

Letterer: Michael Paolilli

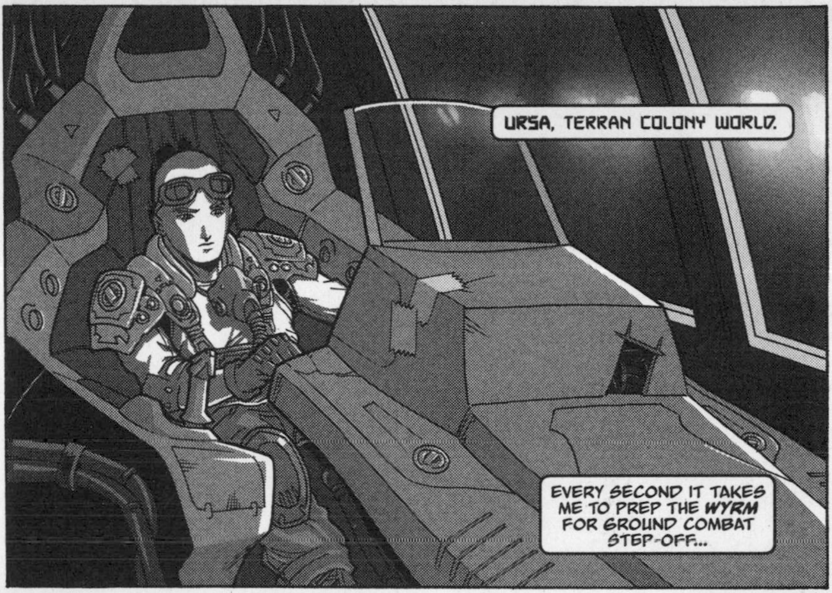
URSA, TERRAN COLONY WORLD.
EVERY SECOND IT TAKES ME TO PREP THE *WYRM* FOR GROUND COMBAT STEP-OFF...
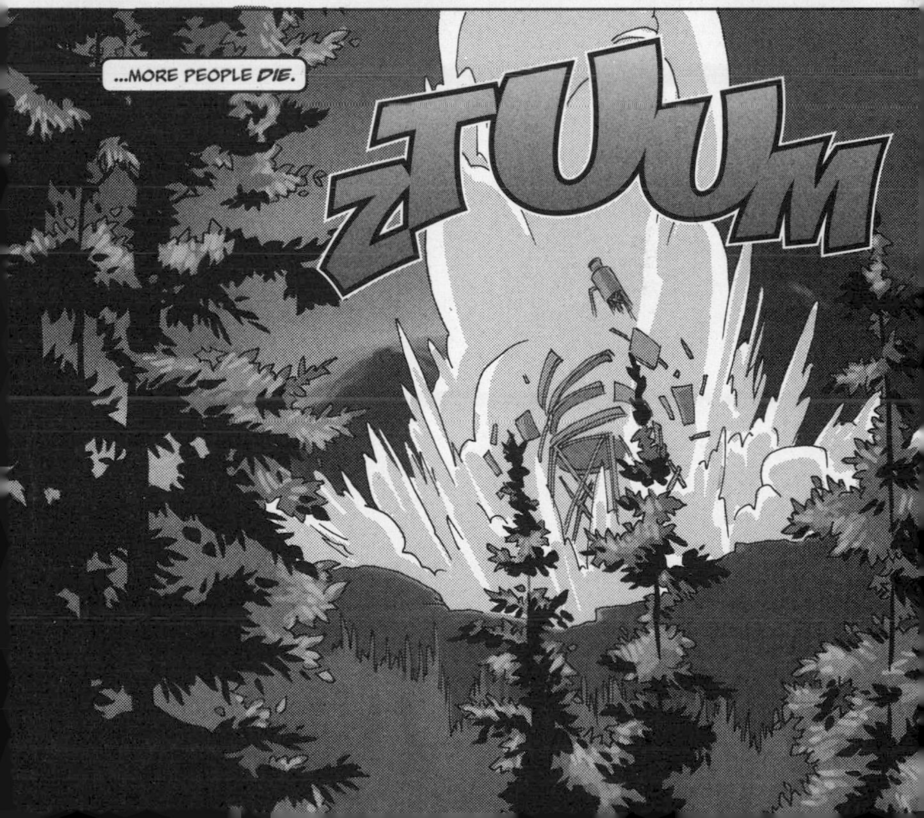
...MORE PEOPLE *DIE*.
ZTUUM

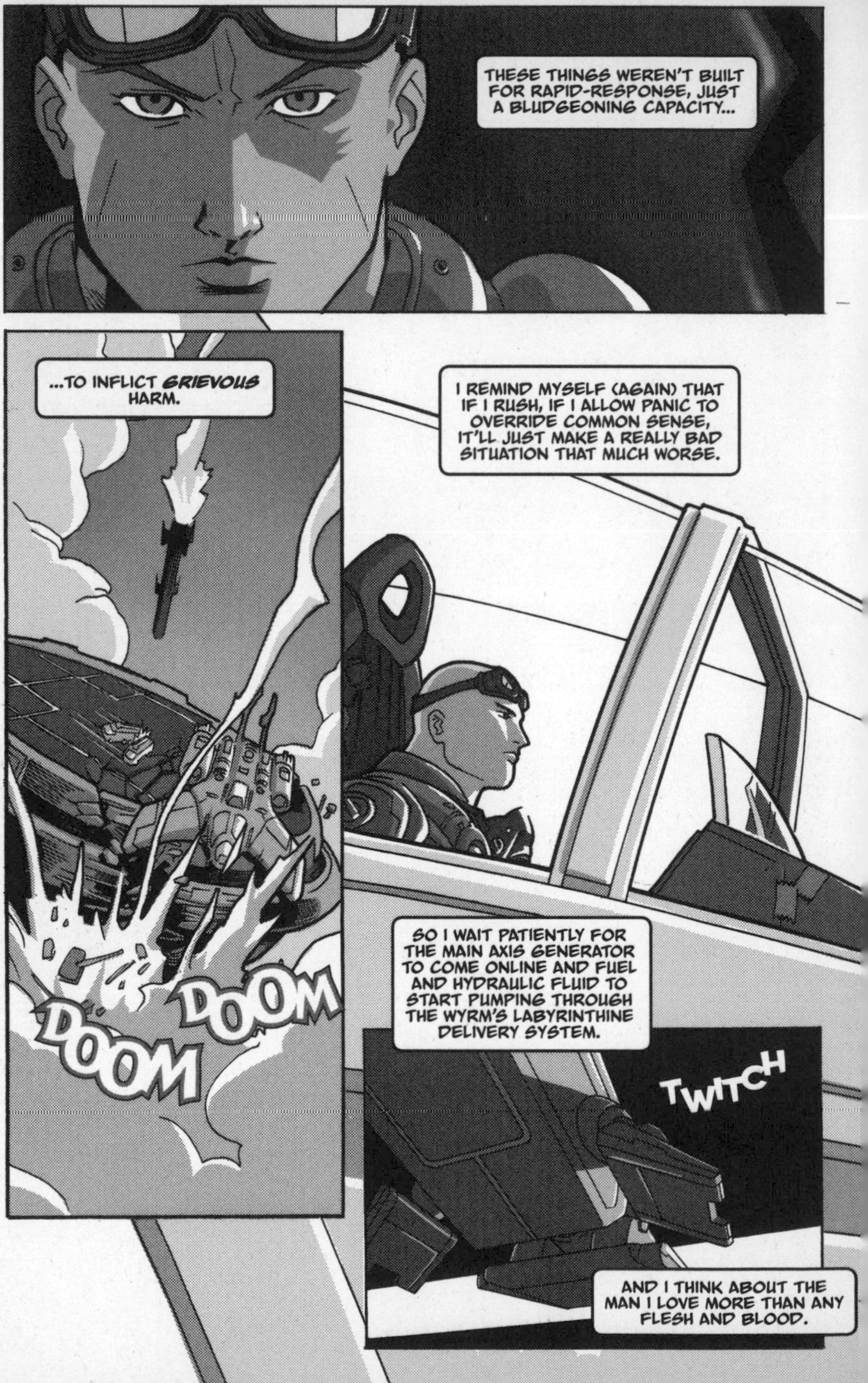
THESE THINGS WEREN'T BUILT FOR RAPID-RESPONSE, JUST A BLUDGEONING CAPACITY...
...TO INFLICT GRIEVOUS HARM.
DOOM
DOOM
I REMIND MYSELF (AGAIN) THAT IF I RUSH, IF I ALLOW PANIC TO OVERRIDE COMMON SENSE, IT'LL JUST MAKE A REALLY BAD SITUATION THAT MUCH WORSE.
SO I WAIT PATIENTLY FOR THE MAIN AXIS GENERATOR TO COME ONLINE AND FUEL AND HYDRAULIC FLUID TO START PUMPING THROUGH THE WYRM'S LABYRINTHINE DELIVERY SYSTEM.
TWITCH
AND I THINK ABOUT THE MAN I LOVE MORE THAN ANY FLESH AND BLOOD.

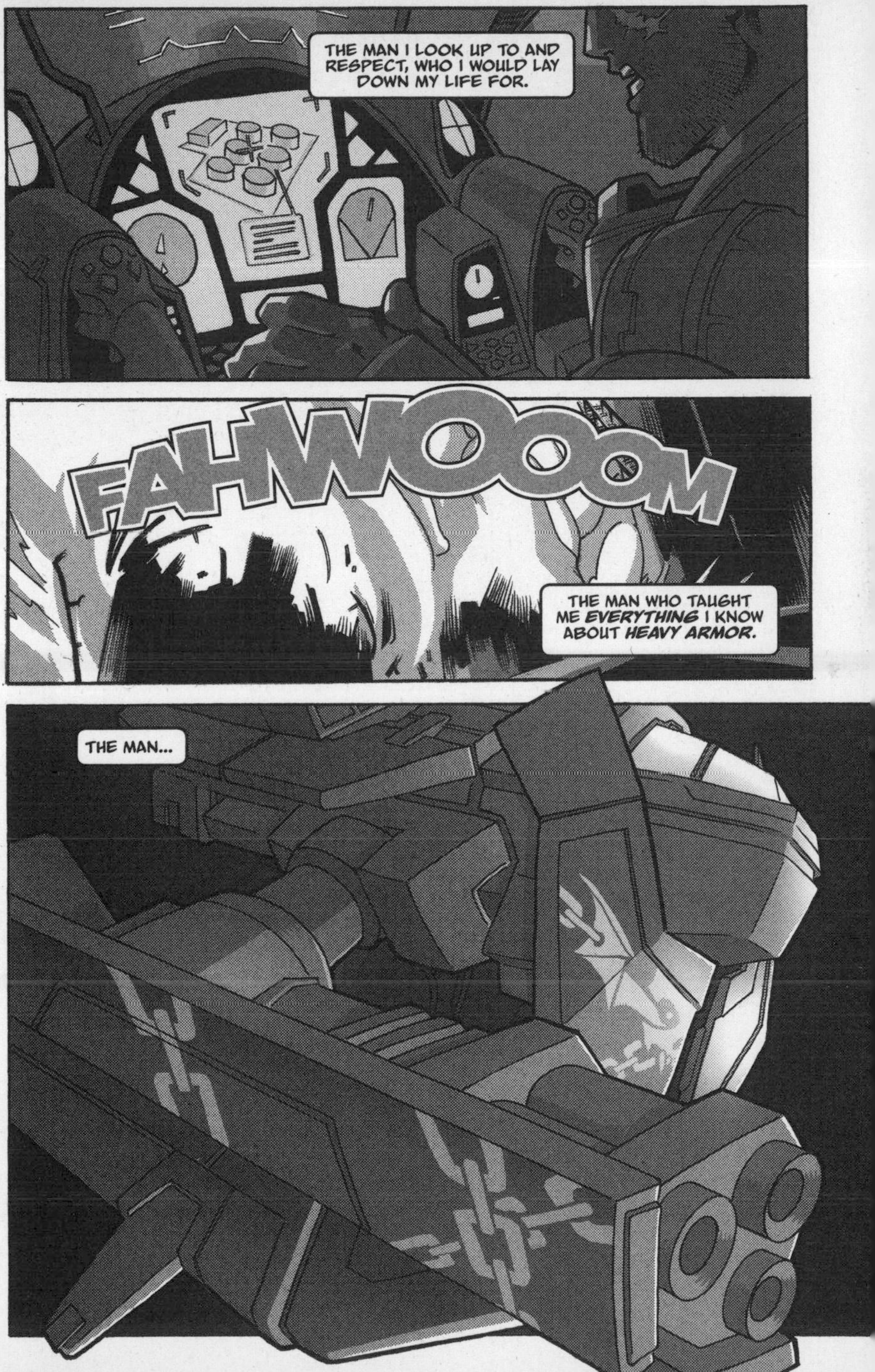
THE MAN I LOOK UP TO AND RESPECT, WHO I WOULD LAY DOWN MY LIFE FOR.
FAHWOOOM
THE MAN WHO TAUGHT ME EVERYTHING I KNOW ABOUT HEAVY ARMOR.
THE MAN...

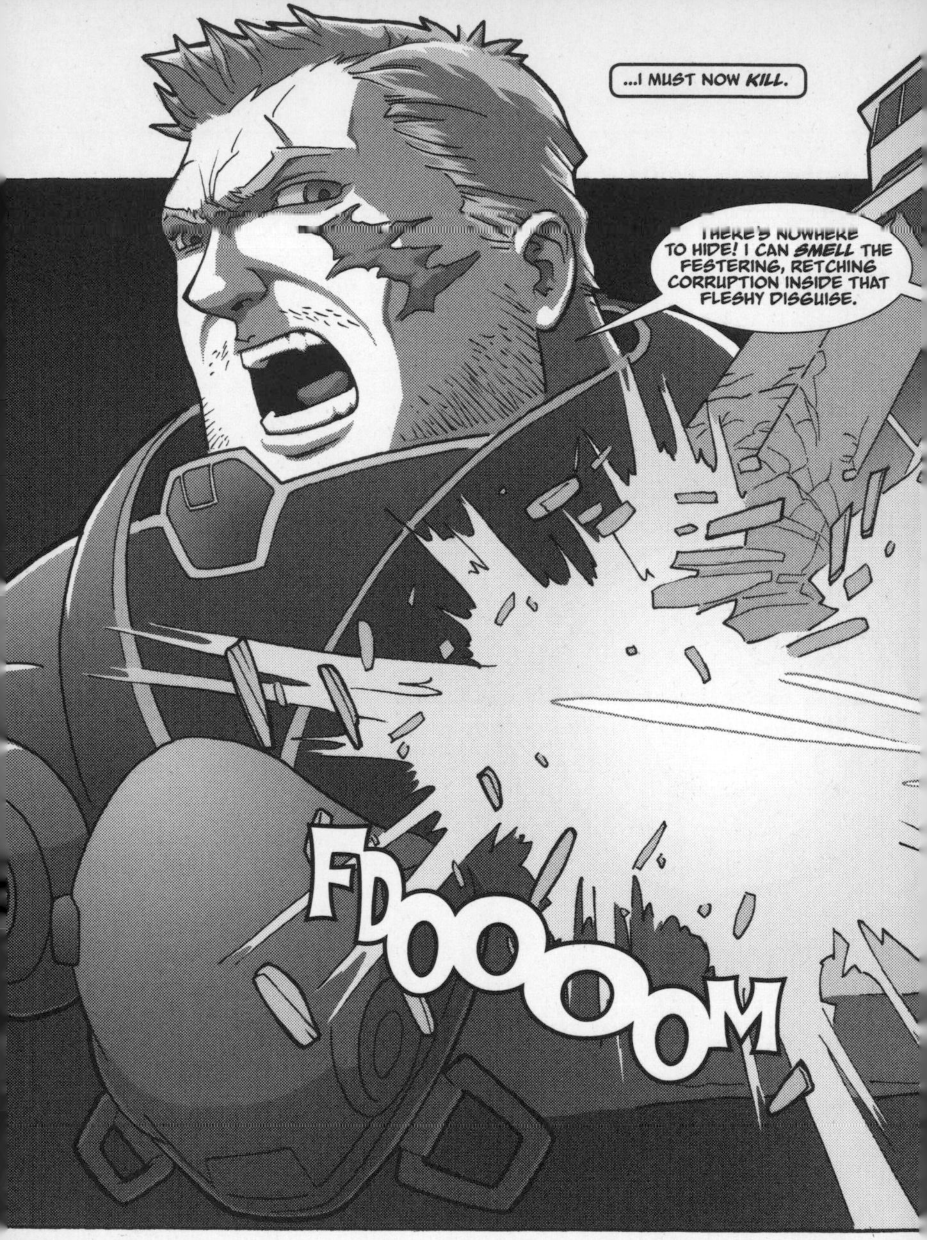
...I MUST NOW *KILL*.
THERE'S NOWHERE TO HIDE! I CAN *SMELL* THE FESTERING, RETCHING CORRUPTION INSIDE THAT FLESHY DISGUISE.
FDOOOOOM

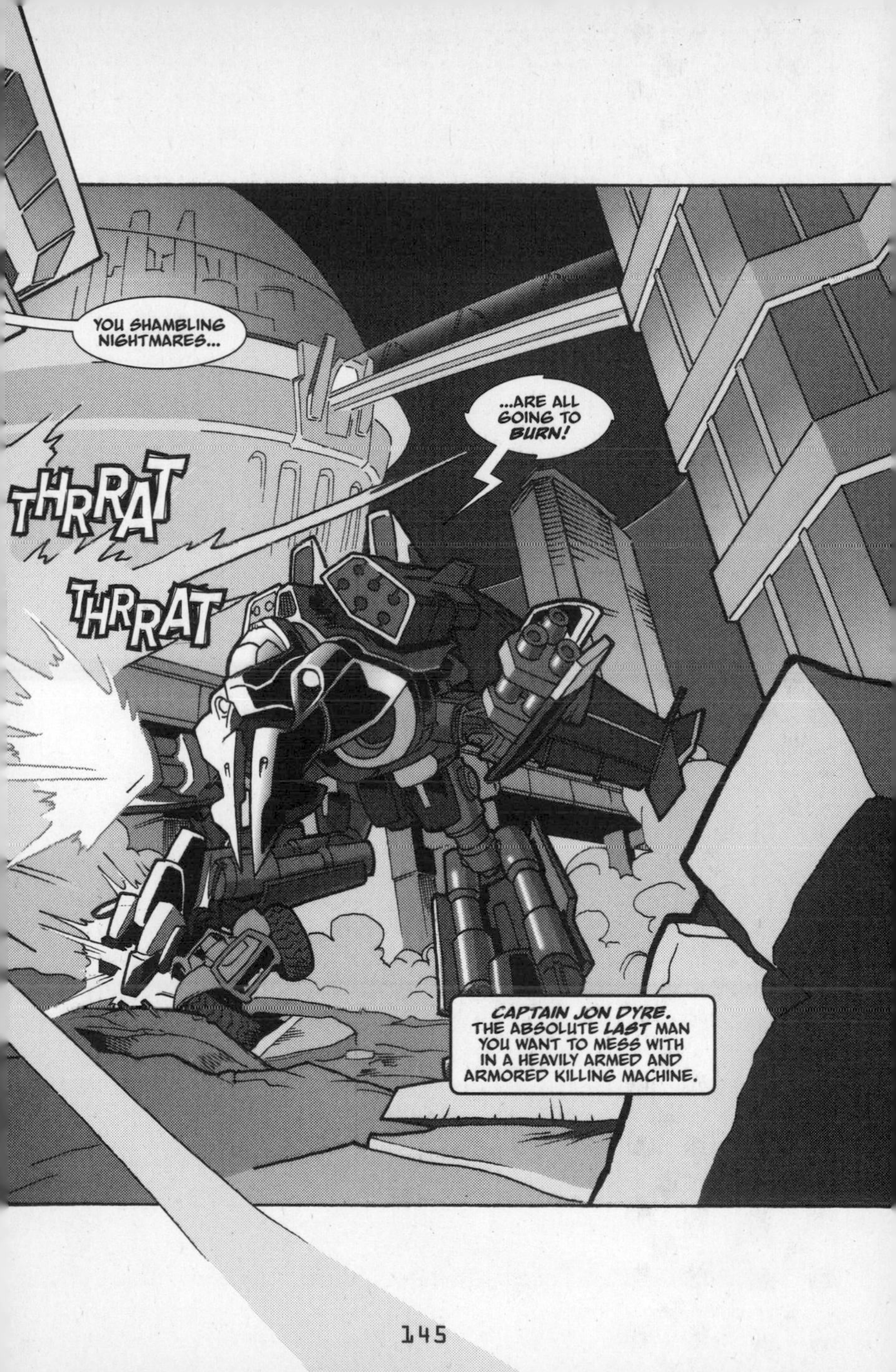
YOU SHAMBLING NIGHTMARES...
...ARE ALL GOING TO BURN!
THRRAT
THRRAT
CAPTAIN JON DYRE. THE ABSOLUTE LAST MAN YOU WANT TO MESS WITH IN A HEAVILY ARMED AND ARMORED KILLING MACHINE.

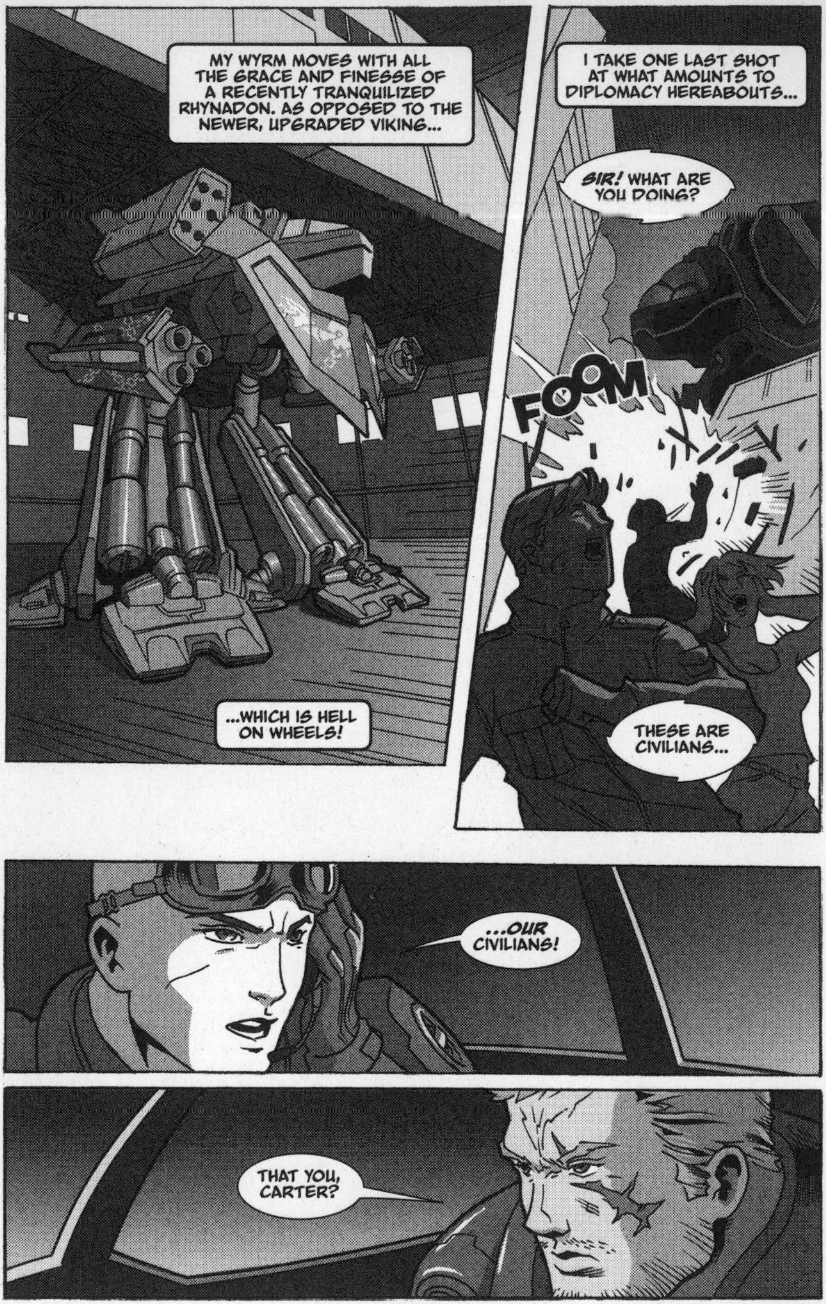
MY WYRM MOVES WITH ALL THE GRACE AND FINESSE OF A RECENTLY TRANQUILIZED RHYNADON. AS OPPOSED TO THE NEWER, UPGRADED VIKING...
...WHICH IS HELL ON WHEELS!
I TAKE ONE LAST SHOT AT WHAT AMOUNTS TO DIPLOMACY HEREABOUTS...
SIR! WHAT ARE YOU DOING?
FOOM
THESE ARE CIVILIANS...
...OUR CIVILIANS!
THAT YOU, CARTER?

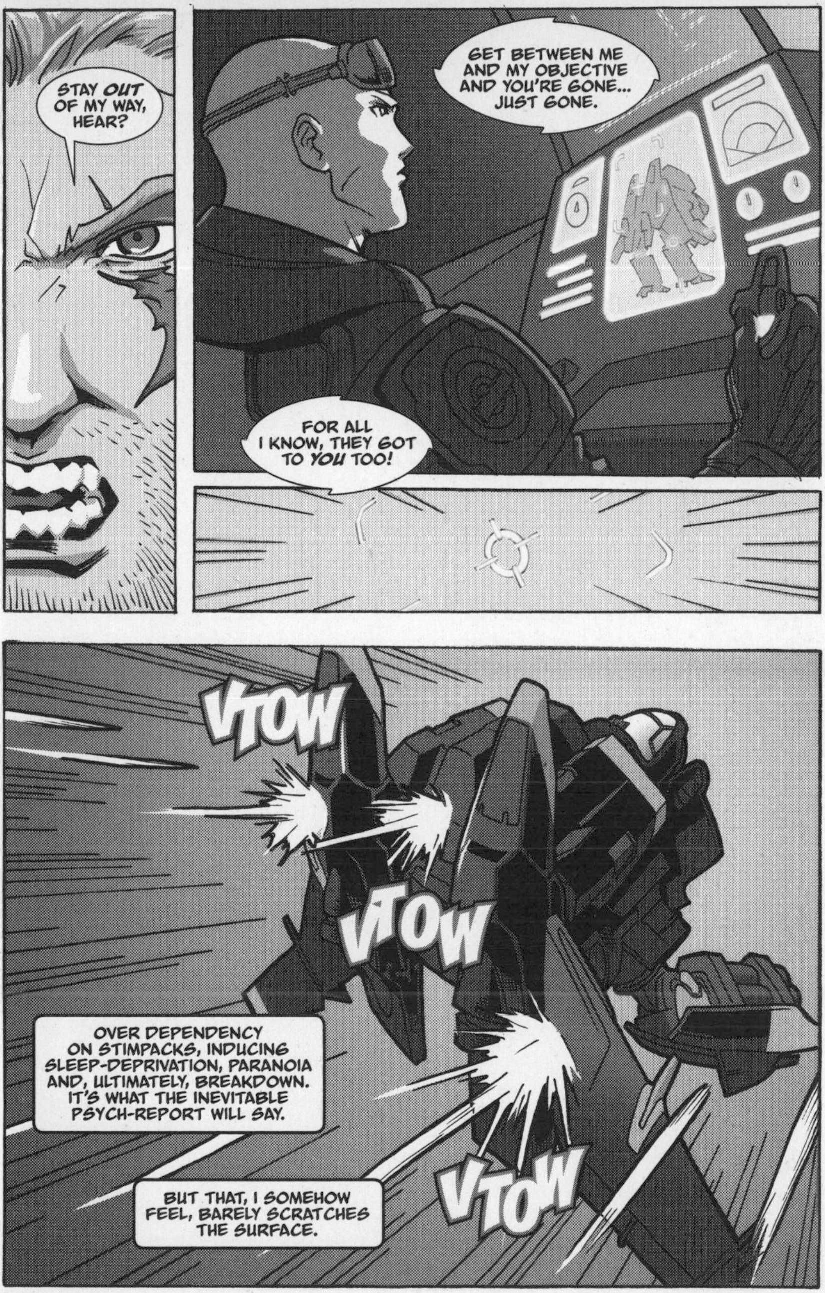
STAY *OUT* OF MY WAY, HEAR?
GET BETWEEN ME AND MY OBJECTIVE AND YOU'RE GONE... JUST GONE.
FOR ALL I KNOW, THEY GOT TO *YOU* TOO!
VTOW
VTOW
OVER DEPENDENCY ON STIMPACKS, INDUCING SLEEP-DEPRIVATION, PARANOIA AND, ULTIMATELY, BREAKDOWN. IT'S WHAT THE INEVITABLE PSYCH-REPORT WILL SAY.
VTOW
BUT THAT, I SOMEHOW FEEL, BARELY SCRATCHES THE SURFACE.

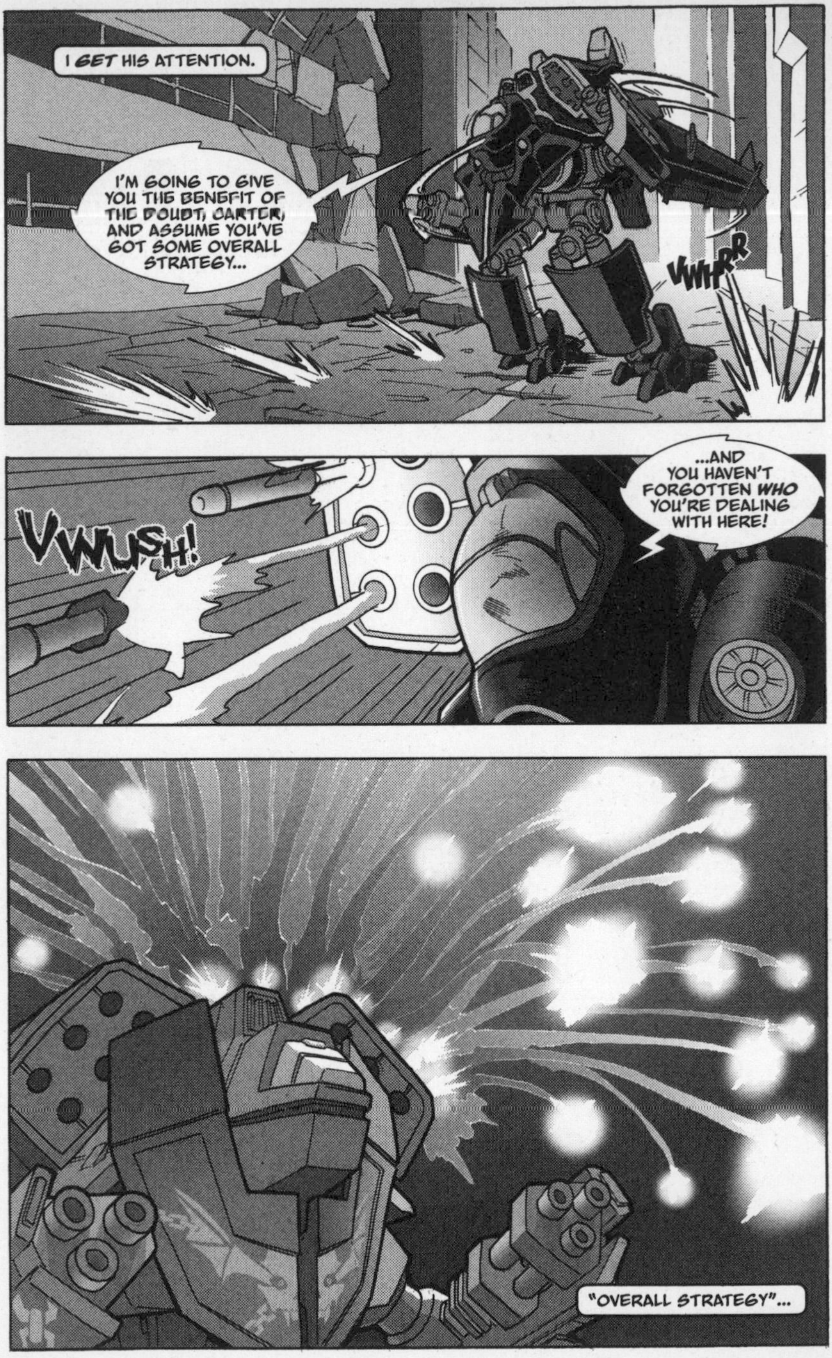
I GET HIS ATTENTION.
I'M GOING TO GIVE YOU THE BENEFIT OF THE DOUBT, CARTER, AND ASSUME YOU'VE GOT SOME OVERALL STRATEGY...
VWHRR
VWUSH!
...AND YOU HAVEN'T FORGOTTEN WHO YOU'RE DEALING WITH HERE!
"OVERALL STRATEGY"...

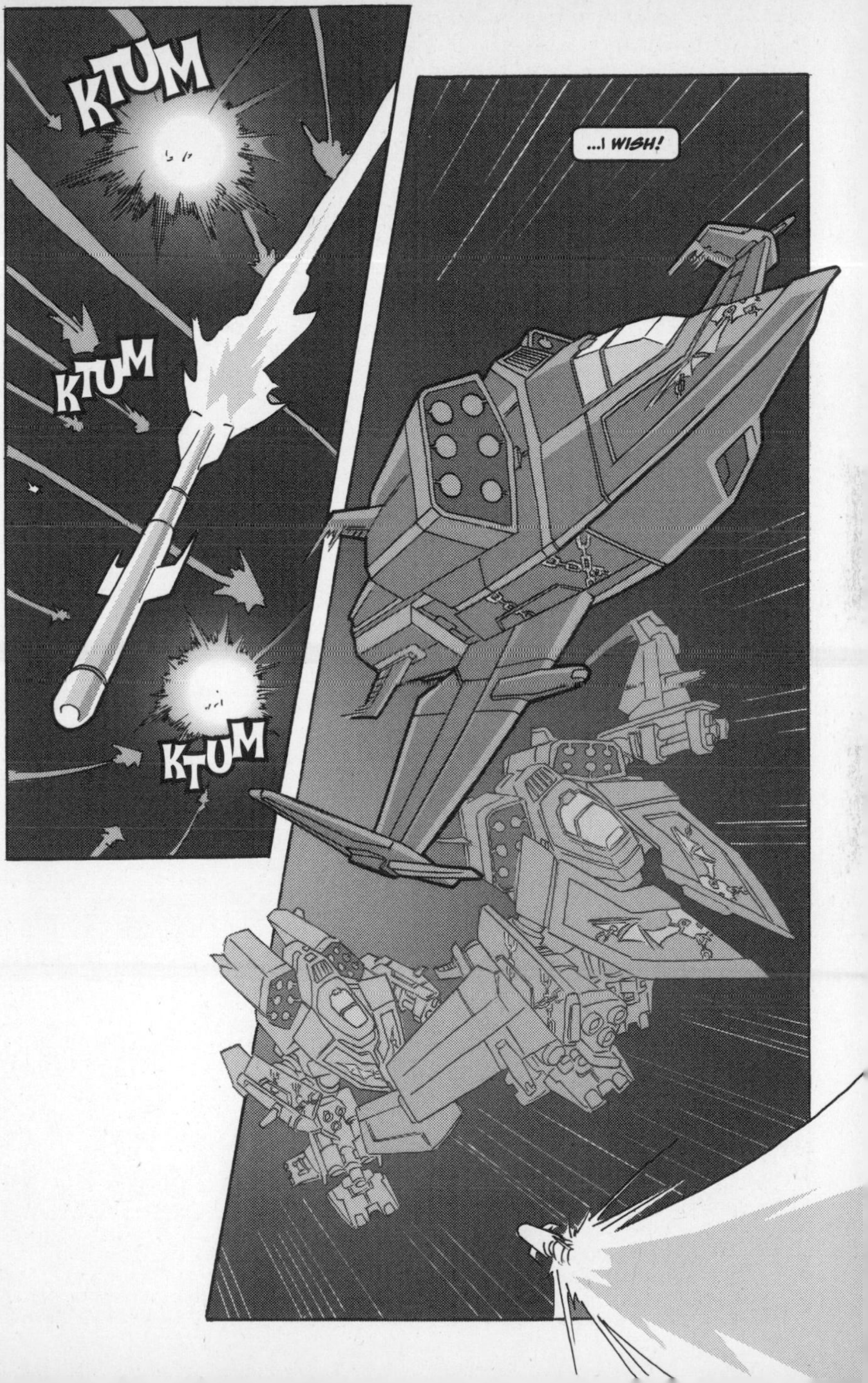
KTUM
KTUM
KTUM
...I WISH!

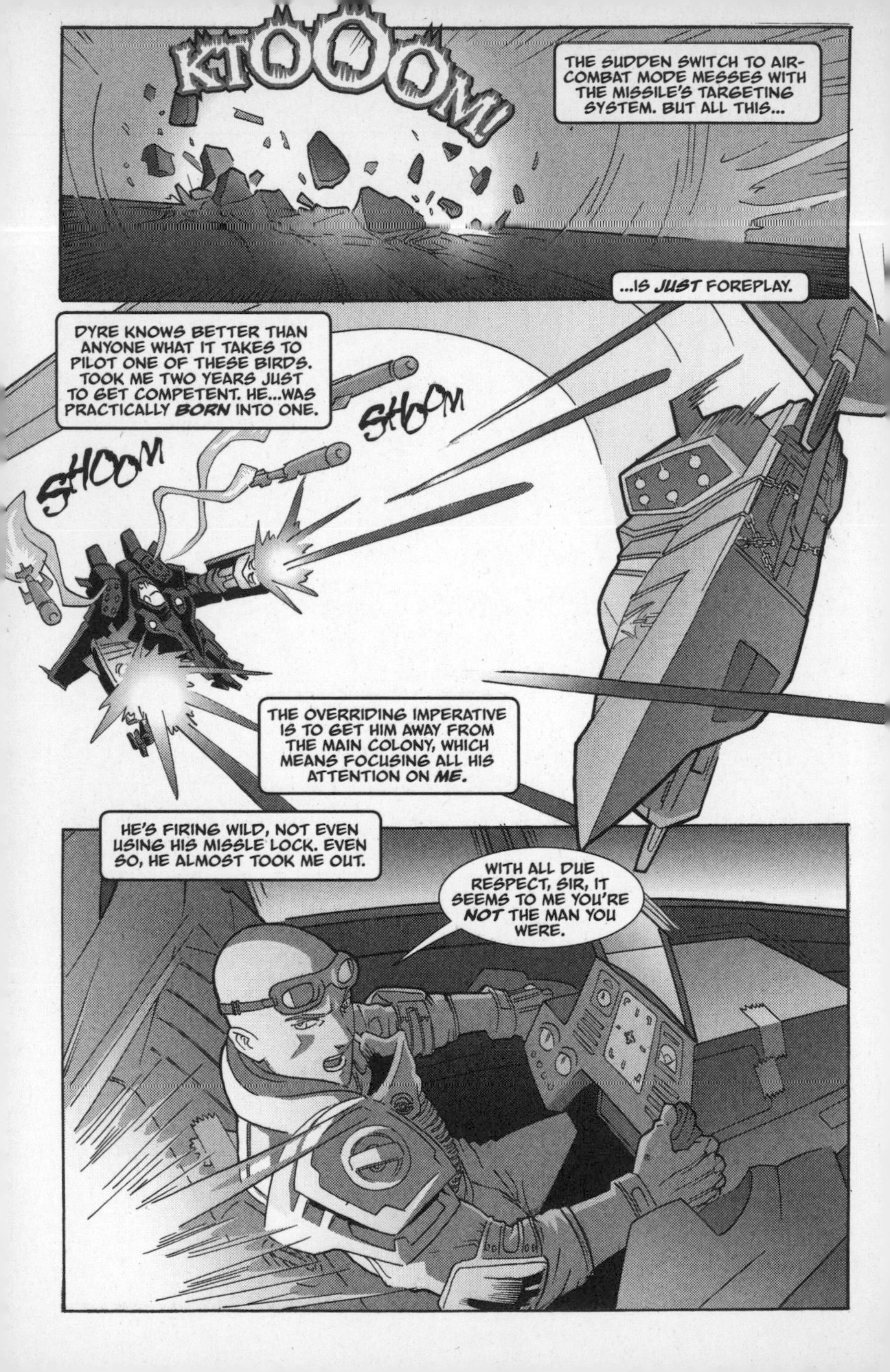
KTOOOOM!
THE SUDDEN SWITCH TO AIR-COMBAT MODE MESSES WITH THE MISSILE'S TARGETING SYSTEM. BUT ALL THIS...
...IS JUST FOREPLAY.
DYRE KNOWS BETTER THAN ANYONE WHAT IT TAKES TO PILOT ONE OF THESE BIRDS. TOOK ME TWO YEARS JUST TO GET COMPETENT. HE...WAS PRACTICALLY BORN INTO ONE.
SHOOM
SHOOM
THE OVERRIDING IMPERATIVE IS TO GET HIM AWAY FROM THE MAIN COLONY, WHICH MEANS FOCUSING ALL HIS ATTENTION ON ME.
HE'S FIRING WILD, NOT EVEN USING HIS MISSLE LOCK. EVEN SO, HE ALMOST TOOK ME OUT.
WITH ALL DUE RESPECT, SIR, IT SEEMS TO ME YOU'RE NOT THE MAN YOU WERE.

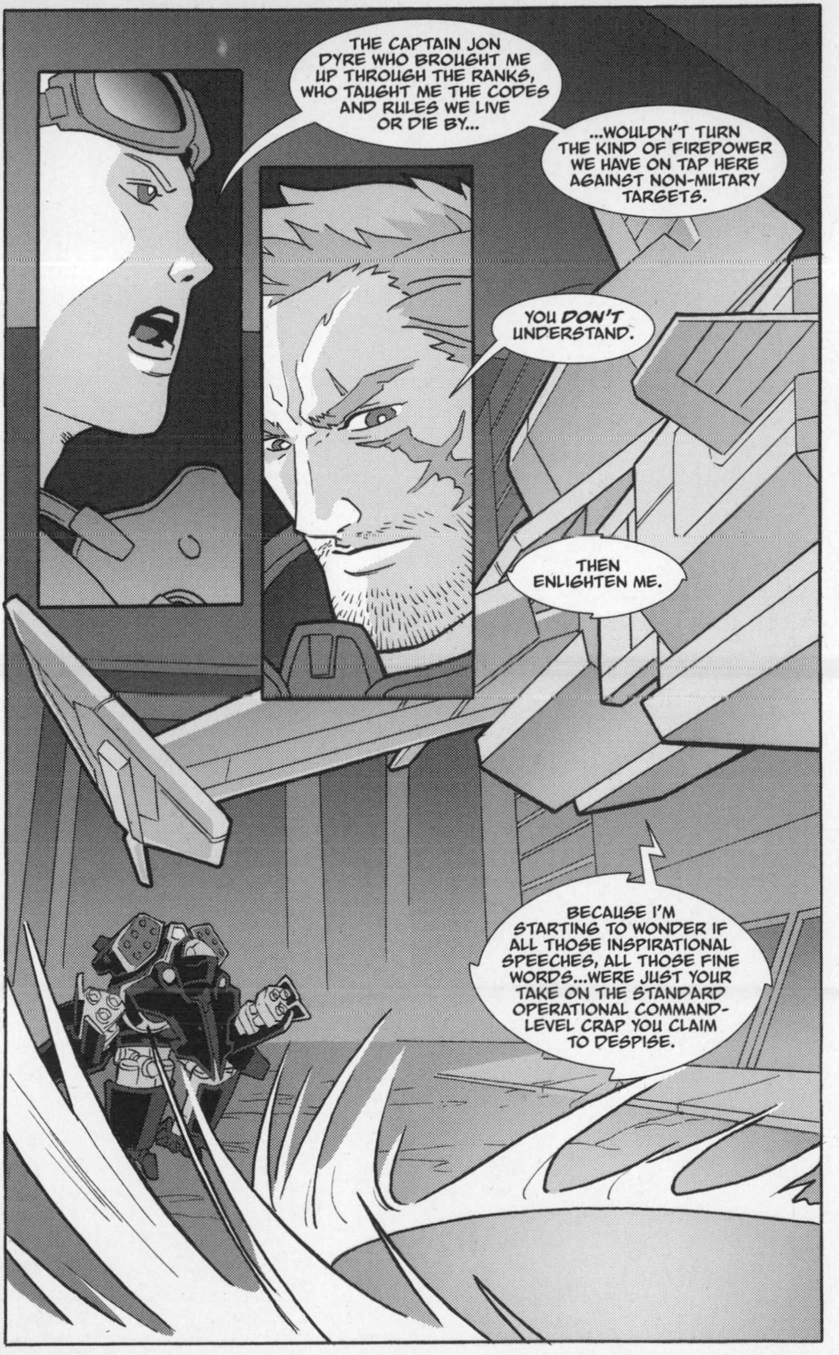
THE CAPTAIN JON DYRE WHO BROUGHT ME UP THROUGH THE RANKS, WHO TAUGHT ME THE CODES AND RULES WE LIVE OR DIE BY...
...WOULDN'T TURN THE KIND OF FIREPOWER WE HAVE ON TAP HERE AGAINST NON-MILTARY TARGETS.
YOU *DON'T* UNDERSTAND.
THEN ENLIGHTEN ME.
BECAUSE I'M STARTING TO WONDER IF ALL THOSE INSPIRATIONAL SPEECHES, ALL THOSE FINE WORDS...WERE JUST YOUR TAKE ON THE STANDARD OPERATIONAL COMMAND-LEVEL CRAP YOU CLAIM TO DESPISE.

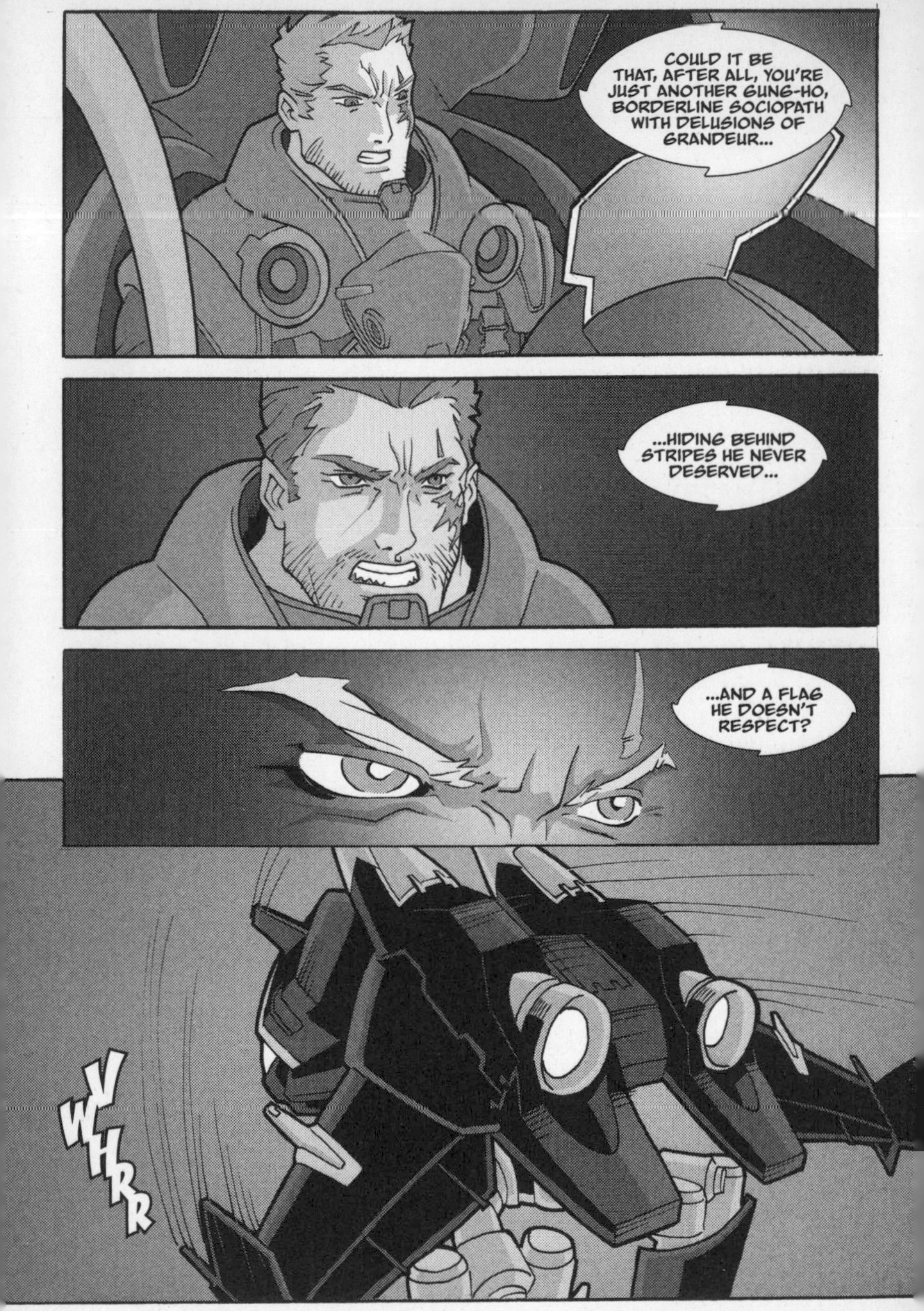
COULD IT BE THAT, AFTER ALL, YOU'RE JUST ANOTHER GUNG-HO, BORDERLINE SOCIOPATH WITH DELUSIONS OF GRANDEUR...
...HIDING BEHIND STRIPES HE NEVER DESERVED...
...AND A FLAG HE DOESN'T RESPECT?
WHRR

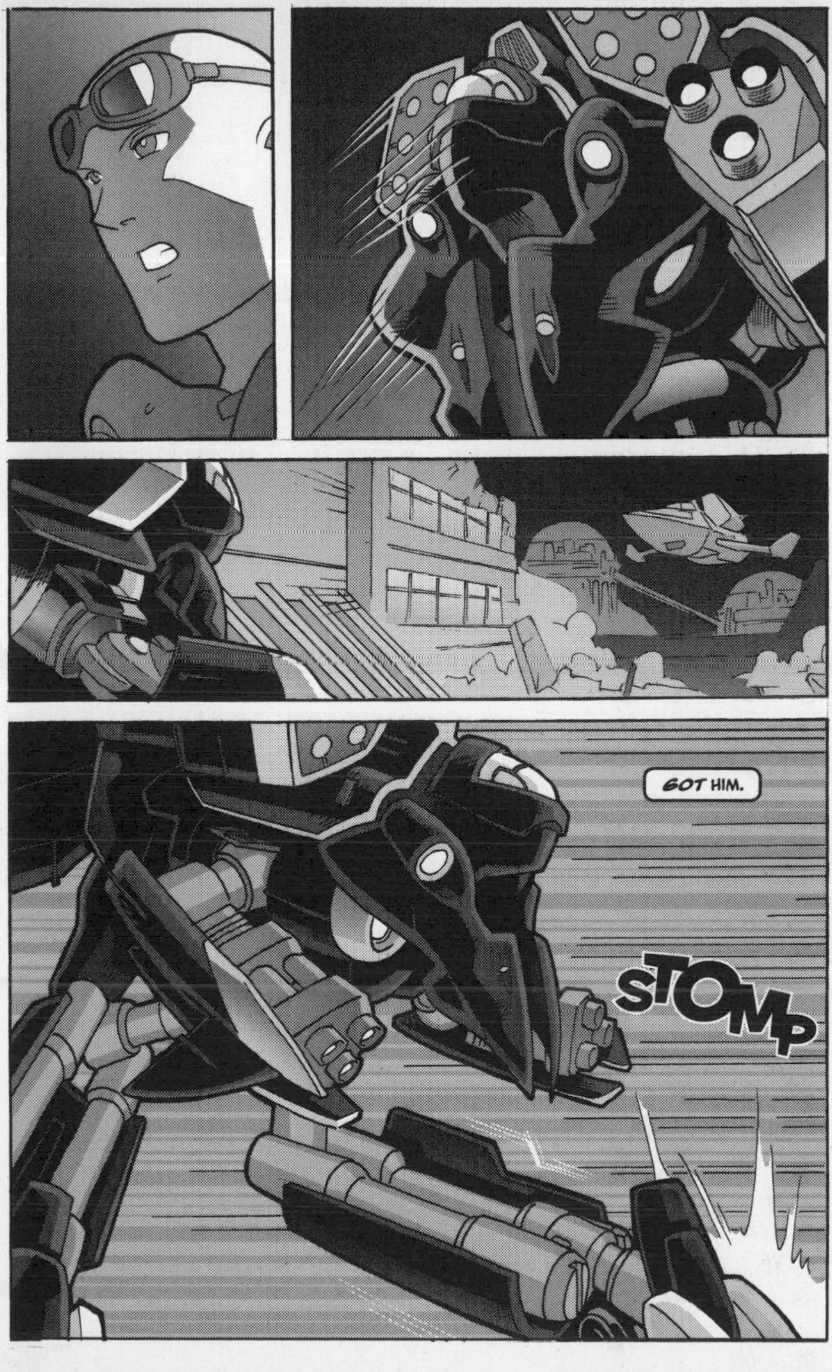
GOT HIM.
STOMP

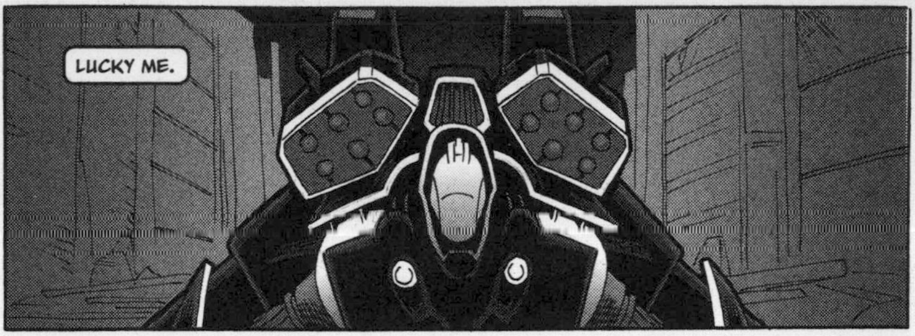
LUCKY ME.

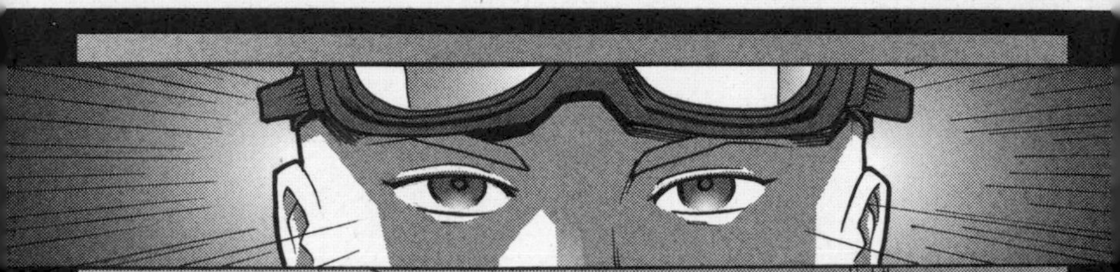

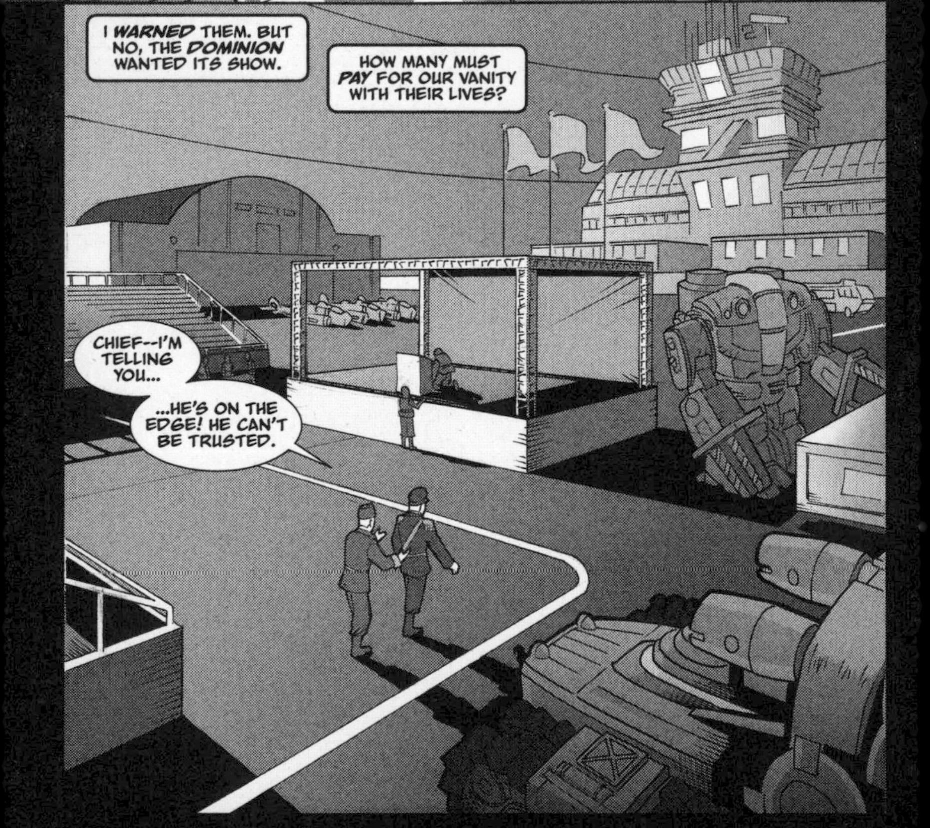
I WARNED THEM. BUT NO, THE DOMINION WANTED ITS SHOW.
HOW MANY MUST PAY FOR OUR VANITY WITH THEIR LIVES?
CHIEF--I'M TELLING YOU...
...HE'S ON THE EDGE! HE CAN'T BE TRUSTED.

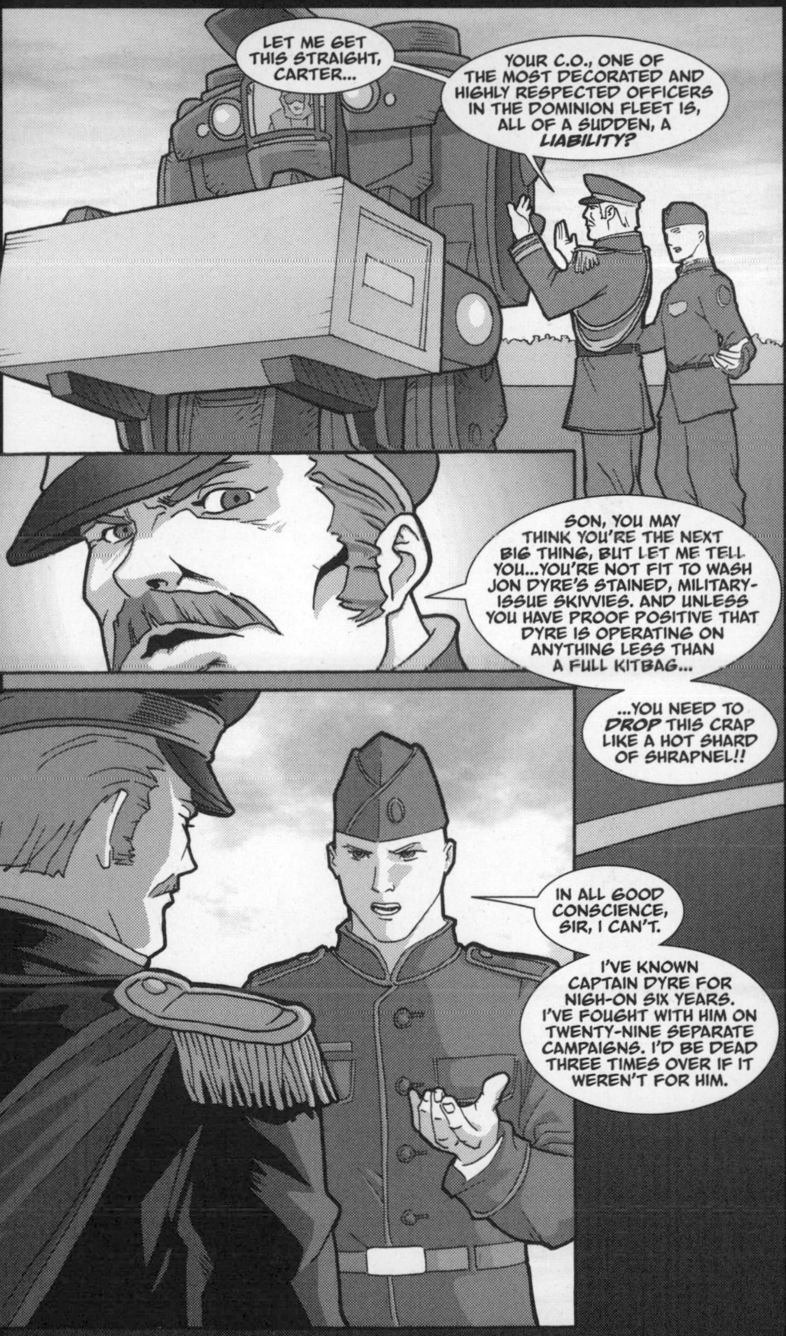

LET ME GET THIS STRAIGHT, CARTER...
YOUR C.O., ONE OF THE MOST DECORATED AND HIGHLY RESPECTED OFFICERS IN THE DOMINION FLEET IS, ALL OF A SUDDEN, A *LIABILITY?*
SON, YOU MAY THINK YOU'RE THE NEXT BIG THING, BUT LET ME TELL YOU...YOU'RE NOT FIT TO WASH JON DYRE'S STAINED, MILITARY-ISSUE SKIVVIES. AND UNLESS YOU HAVE PROOF POSITIVE THAT DYRE IS OPERATING ON ANYTHING LESS THAN A FULL KITBAG...
...YOU NEED TO *DROP* THIS CRAP LIKE A HOT SHARD OF SHRAPNEL!!
IN ALL GOOD CONSCIENCE, SIR, I CAN'T.
I'VE KNOWN CAPTAIN DYRE FOR NIGH-ON SIX YEARS. I'VE FOUGHT WITH HIM ON TWENTY-NINE SEPARATE CAMPAIGNS. I'D BE DEAD THREE TIMES OVER IF IT WEREN'T FOR HIM.

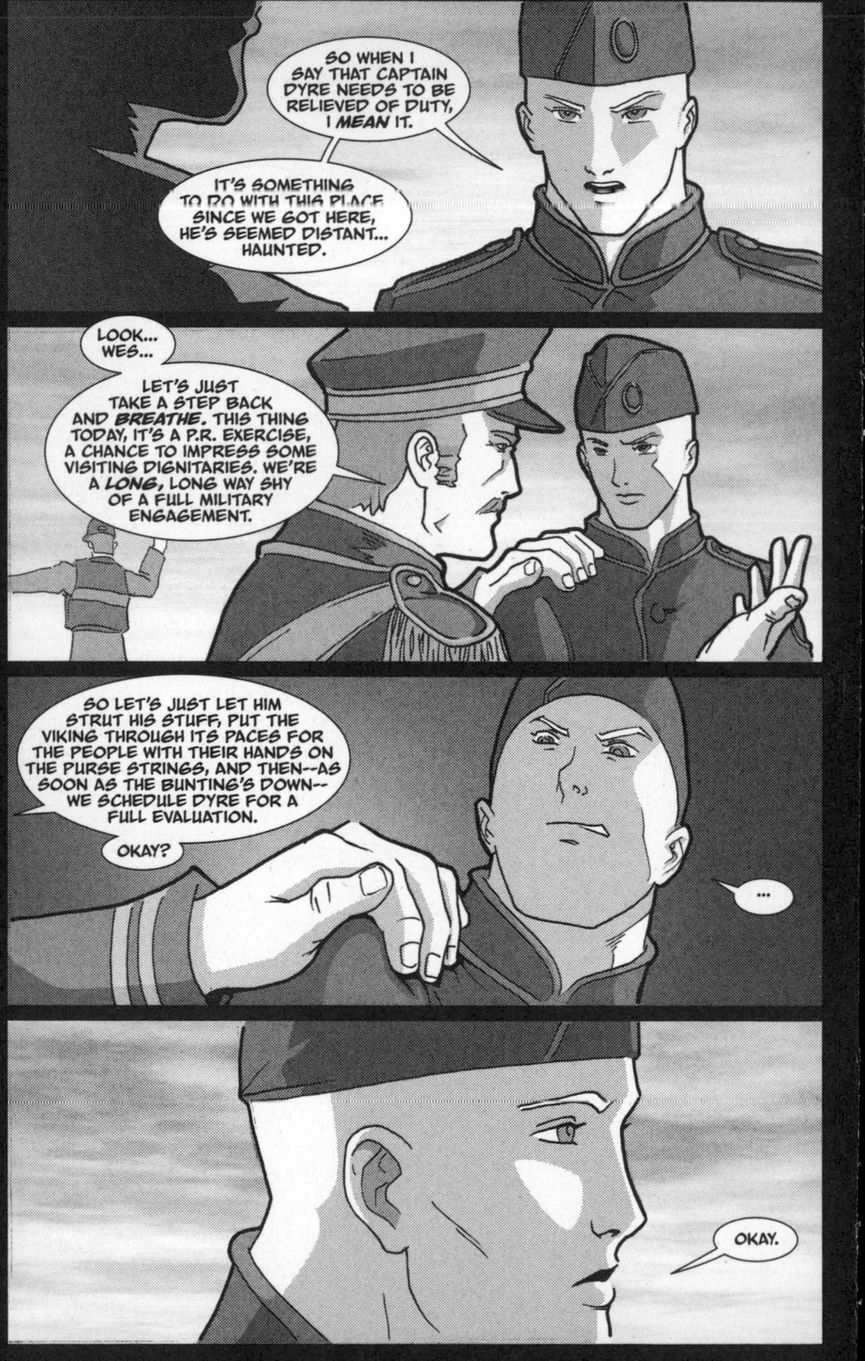
SO WHEN I SAY THAT CAPTAIN DYRE NEEDS TO BE RELIEVED OF DUTY, I MEAN IT.
IT'S SOMETHING TO DO WITH THIS PLACE. SINCE WE GOT HERE, HE'S SEEMED DISTANT... HAUNTED.
LOOK... WES...
LET'S JUST TAKE A STEP BACK AND BREATHE. THIS THING TODAY, IT'S A P.R. EXERCISE, A CHANCE TO IMPRESS SOME VISITING DIGNITARIES. WE'RE A LONG, LONG WAY SHY OF A FULL MILITARY ENGAGEMENT.
SO LET'S JUST LET HIM STRUT HIS STUFF, PUT THE VIKING THROUGH ITS PACES FOR THE PEOPLE WITH THEIR HANDS ON THE PURSE STRINGS, AND THEN--AS SOON AS THE BUNTING'S DOWN--WE SCHEDULE DYRE FOR A FULL EVALUATION.
OKAY?
...
OKAY.

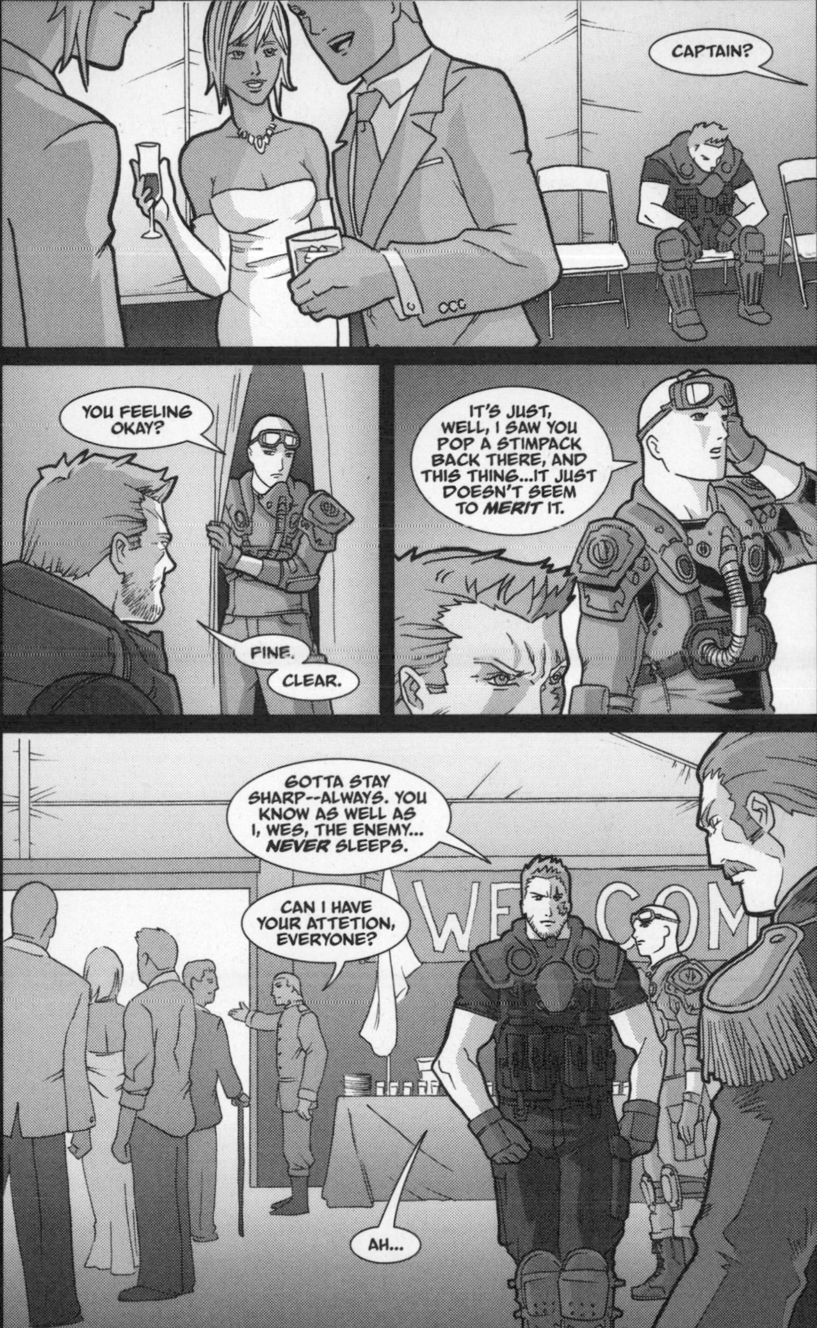
CAPTAIN?
YOU FEELING OKAY?
FINE.
CLEAR.
IT'S JUST, WELL, I SAW YOU POP A STIMPACK BACK THERE, AND THIS THING...IT JUST DOESN'T SEEM TO *MERIT* IT.
GOTTA STAY SHARP--ALWAYS. YOU KNOW AS WELL AS I, WES, THE ENEMY... *NEVER* SLEEPS.
CAN I HAVE YOUR ATTETION, EVERYONE?
AH...

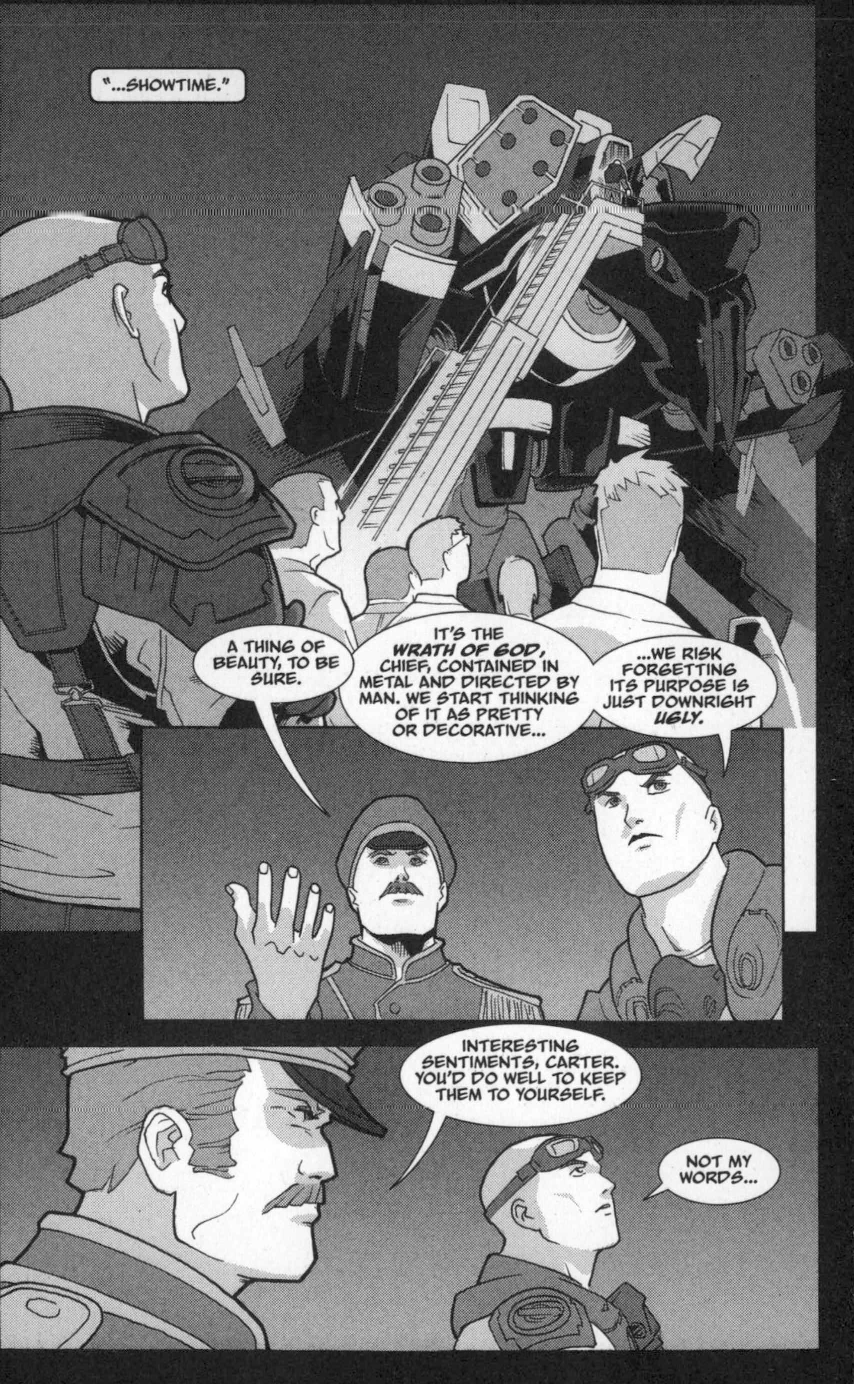
"...SHOWTIME."
A THING OF BEAUTY, TO BE SURE.
IT'S THE WRATH OF GOD, CHIEF, CONTAINED IN METAL AND DIRECTED BY MAN. WE START THINKING OF IT AS PRETTY OR DECORATIVE...
...WE RISK FORGETTING ITS PURPOSE IS JUST DOWNRIGHT UGLY.
INTERESTING SENTIMENTS, CARTER. YOU'D DO WELL TO KEEP THEM TO YOURSELF.
NOT MY WORDS...

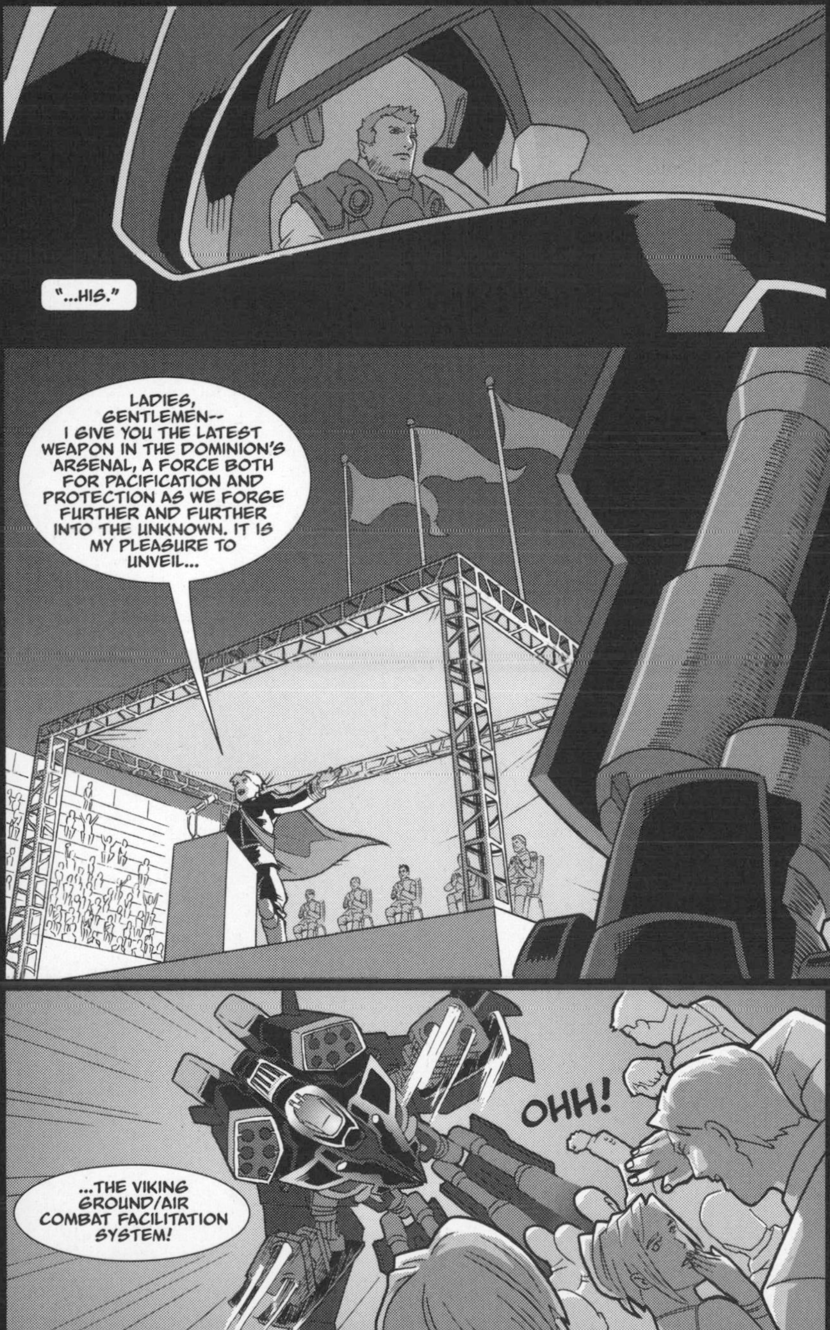
"...HIS."
LADIES, GENTLEMEN-- I GIVE YOU THE LATEST WEAPON IN THE DOMINION'S ARSENAL, A FORCE BOTH FOR PACIFICATION AND PROTECTION AS WE FORGE FURTHER AND FURTHER INTO THE UNKNOWN. IT IS MY PLEASURE TO UNVEIL...
OHH!
...THE VIKING GROUND/AIR COMBAT FACILITATION SYSTEM!

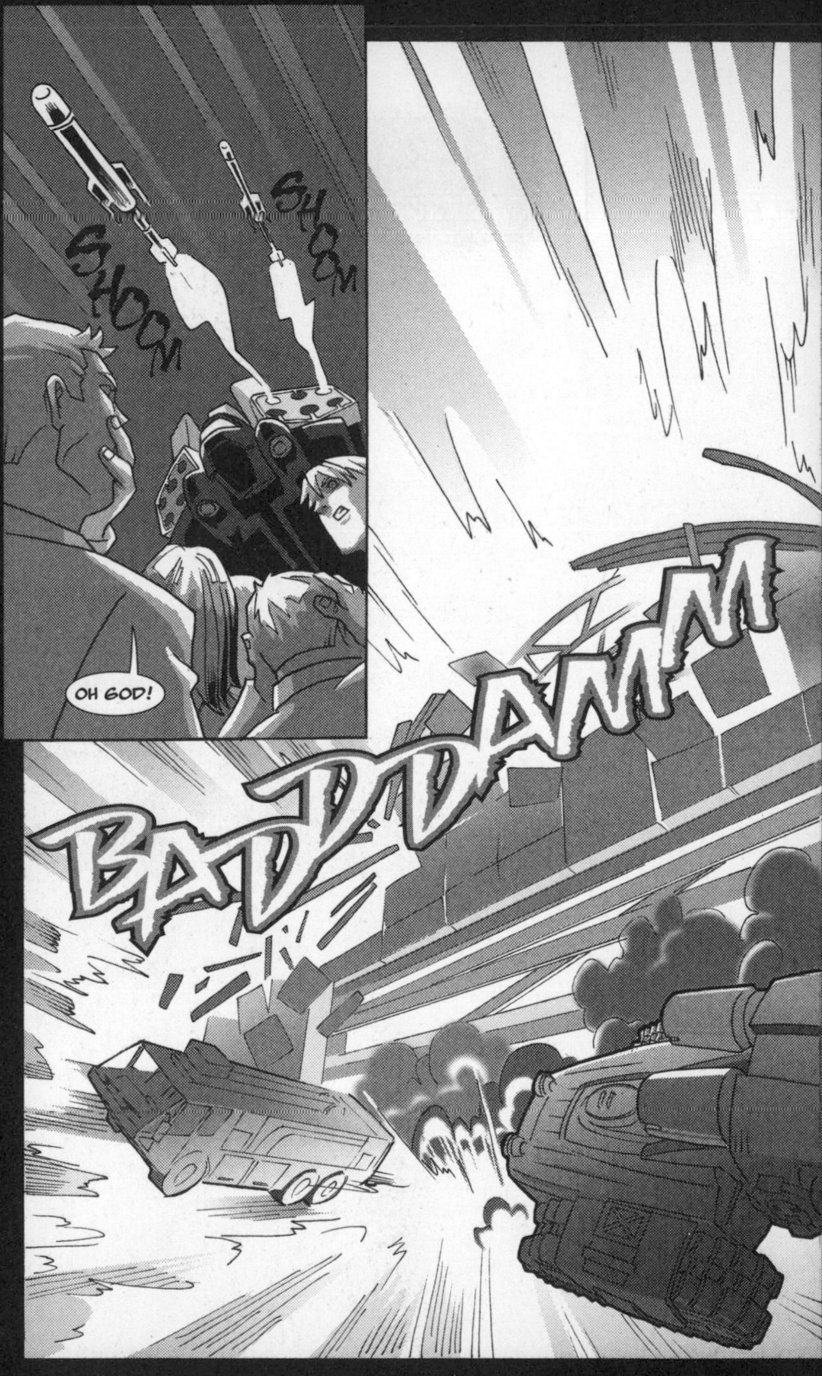
SHOOM
SHOOM
OH GOD!
BADDAMM

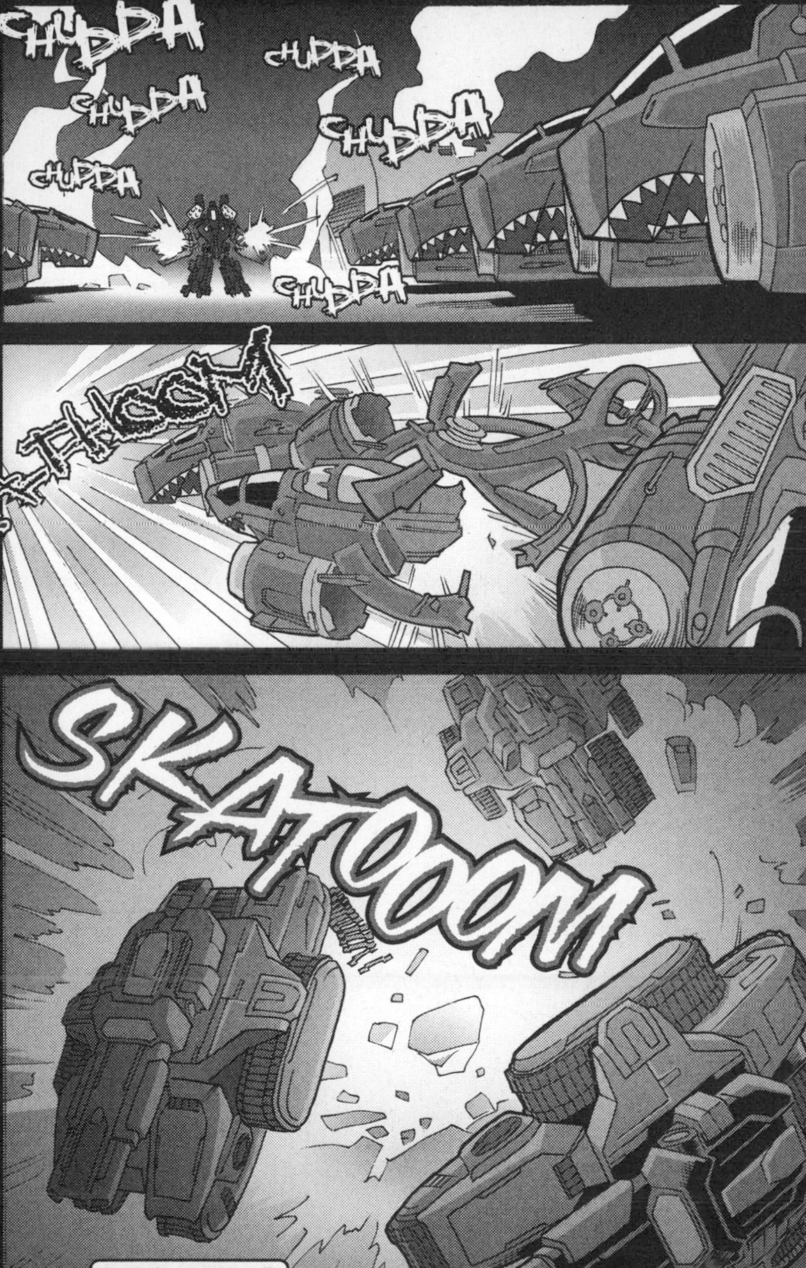
CHUDDA
CHUDDA
CHUDDA
CHUDDA
CHUDDA
CHUDDA
KA-THOOM
SKATOOOM
"WHAT'S HE DOING?"

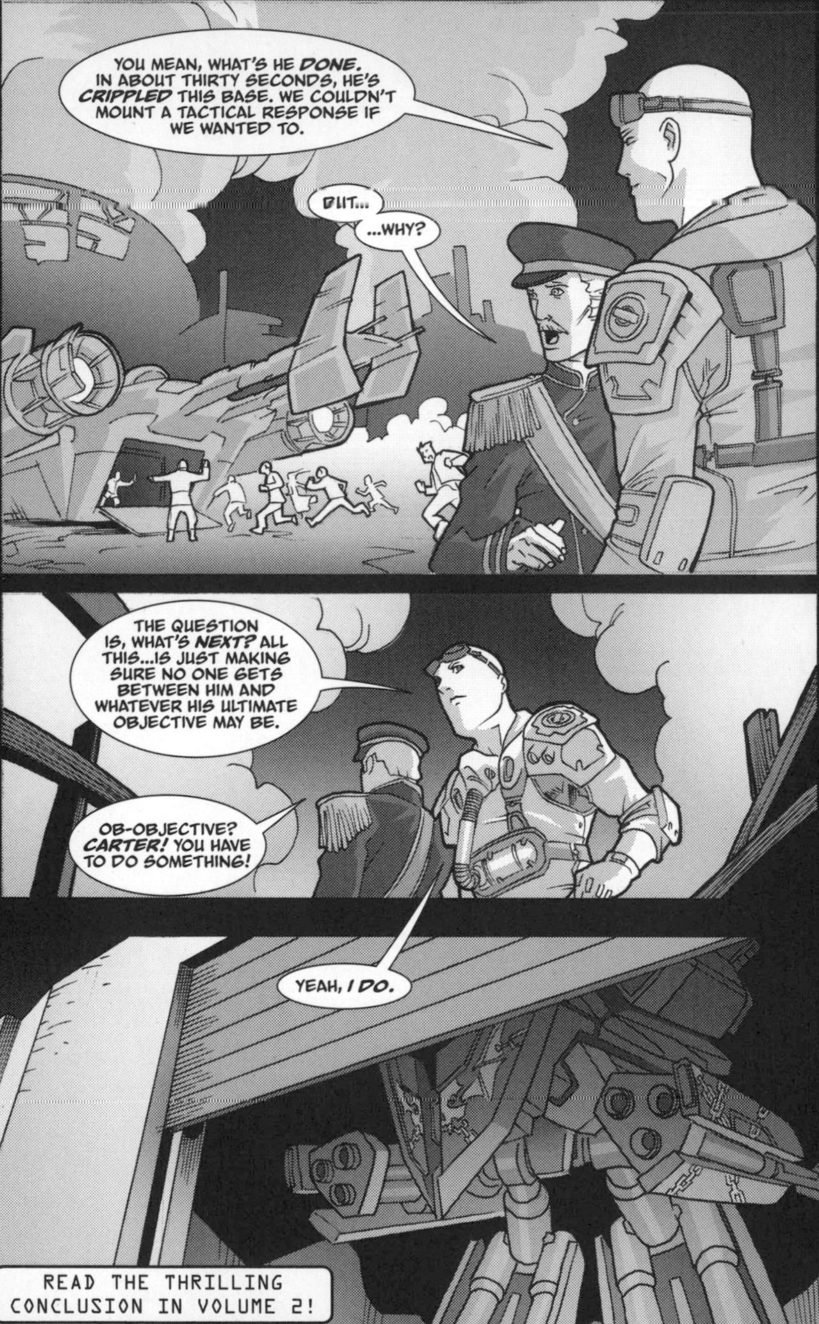

YOU MEAN, WHAT'S HE DONE. IN ABOUT THIRTY SECONDS, HE'S CRIPPLED THIS BASE. WE COULDN'T MOUNT A TACTICAL RESPONSE IF WE WANTED TO.
BUT...
...WHY?
THE QUESTION IS, WHAT'S NEXT? ALL THIS...IS JUST MAKING SURE NO ONE GETS BETWEEN HIM AND WHATEVER HIS ULTIMATE OBJECTIVE MAY BE.
OB-OBJECTIVE? CARTER! YOU HAVE TO DO SOMETHING!
YEAH, I DO.
READ THE THRILLING CONCLUSION IN VOLUME 2!

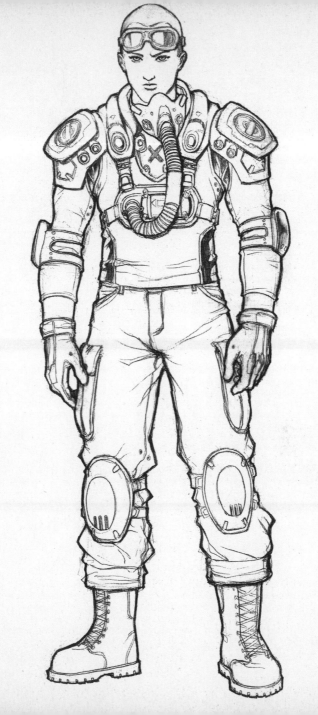

RICHARD A. KNAAK

Richard A. Knaak is the *New York Times* bestselling fantasy author of 27 novels and over a dozen short pieces, including *The Legend of Huma, Night of Blood* for *Dragonlance* and the *War of the Ancients* trilogy for *Warcraft*. In addition to the TOKYOPOP series *Warcraft: The Sunwell Trilogy*, he is the author of its forthcoming sequel trilogy, *Warcraft: Dragons of Outland*. Richard also has a serialized story being featured in *Warcraft: Legends*, an anthology series also published by TOKYOPOP. To find out more about Richard's projects, visit his website at www.sff.net/people/knaak.

SIMON FURMAN

Simon Furman is a writer for comic books and TV animation, his name inextricably linked to *Transformers*, the 80s toy phenomenon. He has written for *Transformers: Infiltration/Escalation/Devastation, Beast Wars: The Gathering/The Ascending, Transformers: Spotlight* and *Transformers UK*. Other comic book credits include *Dragon's Claws, Death's Head, Alpha Flight, Turok, She-Hulk, Robocop* and *What If?* In the TV animation field, Furman has written for shows such as *Beast Wars, Roswell Conspiracies, Dan Dare, X-Men: Evolution, Alien Racers* and *A.T.O.M.* Furman's recent/current writing work includes *Terminator 2 — Infinity, Ronan, Death's Head 3.0, Teenage Mutant Ninja Turtles,* and *Torchwood.* He is also the author of *Transformers: The Ultimate Guide*, a lavish twentieth anniversary hardcover, *You Can Draw Transformers* and a *Doctor Who* audio adventure (The Axis of Insanity).

PAUL BENJAMIN

Paul Benjamin is a writer, editor, supermodel and video game producer whose TOKYOPOP manga series include *Pantheon High* and *Star Trek: The Manga*. Paul has written *Marvel Adventures Hulk* and *Spider-Man Family* for Marvel and has developed comics-to-film projects for Hollywood. He's edited graphic novels for Humanoids/DC Comics and is writing and producing video games, including *The Incredible Hulk DS* for Sega. And, of course, everyone in the world is familiar with Paul's long list of credits as a supermodel. For more info, go to http://www.thepaulbenjamin.com

DAVE SHRAMEK

Dave Shramek is a game designer and writer in Austin, Texas. As is so often the case, he settled there after graduating from the University of Texas with a degree in Radio, Television and Film. Much to the delight of his parents, he was able to turn this normally unemployable degree into an actual profession with regular employment opportunities in the game development rich environment of Austin. He currently resides there with his ambitions of global dominance and an unhealthy addiction to Tex-Mex.

JOSH ELDER

Josh Elder is the handsome and brilliant writer of *Mail Order Ninja*, which he's pretty sure has been acclaimed by some critic, somewhere. A graduate of Northwestern University with a degree in Film, Joshua currently resides in the quaint, little Midwestern town of Chicago, Illinois. An avid StarCraft player, Josh is thrilled to have upcoming stories in *StarCraft: Frontline* volumes 2 & 3. But Josh also played football, so he isn't a total dork. But he also played Dungeons & Dragons. So yeah, he kind of is a total dork.

ARTISTS:

NAOHIRO WASHIO

Born 1972 in Niigata Prefecture, Japan, Naohiro **Washio** is a well known mecha designer and accomplished graphic artist. He has worked on mech designs for anime such as *Stellvia* and *Fafner of the Azure,* as well as the TOKYOPOP's manga *The Third.* A fan of funk music and sci-fi dramas, Washio also manages to find time between working on giant robots and motorcycles to watch his favorite anime, *The Powerpuff Girls*.

JESSE ELLIOTT

Jesse Elliott was born in S. Korea, but has lived most of his life in New Orleans, LA. He began drawing at a very young age and started collecting comic books as a child, which further fueled his interest in art. He discovered anime and manga while attending college at the University of New Orleans, where he received a degree in Fine Arts. Upon graduating, Jesse spent many successful years as the manager of a video-game store, but left to pursue a career in illustration. More of his work can be seen online at jelli76.deviantart.com.

HECTOR SEVILLA

Hector hails from Chihuahua, Mexico. He is a huge fan of *StarCraft*, and never imagined he would ever help create a part of the *StarCraft* universe. He thanks Kathy Schilling, Paul Morrissey and Blizzard for the wonderful opportunity. In addition to creating *Lullaby* and working on *Leviticus Cross* and Konami's *Lunar Knights*, Hector is developing a new property called *DrawSkill* for TOKYOPOP's Pilot Program. You can take a sneak peek at *DrawSkill* at http://elsevilla.deviantart.com

RAMANDA KAMARGA

Like a superhero, **Ramanda** holds a regular job during the day, and draws comics at night. An avid gamer, he divides his free time between his wife and his PSP. Ramanda's previous works include *GI Joe: Sigma Six, Bristol Board Jungle* and TOKYOPOP's *Psy*Comm* volumes 2 & 3.

The battle is finally over. And you, dear readers, hold the fruits of a major victory in your hands: The very first **StarCraft** manga **ever** published! I certainly hope you enjoyed the spoils of this initial skirmish, because the war has only just begun. In addition to two more volumes of **StarCraft: Frontline**, readers will soon be treated to a whole new **StarCraft** series called **Ghost Academy,** written by Keith R.A. DeCandido!

Of course, victory requires camaraderie and teamwork. And all the soldiers here at TOKYOPOP would be lost without Blizzard Entertainment's leadership. Their support, guidance and creative brainstorming have been **invaluable.** In particular, I'd like to thank Jason Bischoff, Brian Hsieh, Gina Pippin, Cory Jones, Mick Neilson, and the "general" himself—Chris Metzen. Luckily, Metzen's not afraid to be a grunt, since it looks like he might contribute a Jim Raynor story for **StarCraft: Frontline** volume 3!

Speaking of the grunts, I'd very much like to pin medals on all of writers, artists, inkers and toners who fought valiantly in the trenches. They faced insurmountable odds and an ever-looming deadline to D-Day. Luckily, there were no casualties—only a few cramped drawing hands and several sleepless nights. Time to take some R & R, boys! You deserved it! Now that the boys are resting, there's one very special woman that was our secret weapon: Rie Shiramizu. An agent in our Japanese office, Rie coordinated our attack plans with artist Washio. Without her translation skills and editorial expertise, we would not have been able to send Washio's amazing art off to war.

Lastly, and most importantly, I'd like to thank all of the fans who entered the fray by picking up this first volume of **StarCraft: Frontline!** If you enjoyed these stories, please tell your friends to enlist! And don't forget to pick up the first volume of our other new Blizzard series, **Warcraft: Legends,** available in stores now. If you're curious, there's a preview of it on the following pages! And don't forget to pick up **StarCraft: Frontline** volume 2, available November 2008!

Paul Morrissey
Editor

STARCRAFT

FRONTLINE

IN THE NEXT VOLUME...

You've just read four tales of valor, greed, sacrifice and duty... but still you look toward the future, fixing your eyes upon further *StarCraft* adventures that await you on the near horizon...

Carter's exciting showdown with his former mentor concludes in *Heavy Armor – Part 2*...

The sadistic Dr. Burgess, from "Why We Fight," gets his bloody hands on Muadun, a recently captured protoss High Templar...

Reporter Nora Colby embeds herself with Terran Marines and sees the shocking horrors of war first-hand...

The protoss begin experimenting with zerg creep...with fascinating results...

On a fringe planet, Kel-Morians uncover a deserted compound that appears to be haunted...

So suit up in your marine armor, get on the FRONTLINE, and prepare yourself for another intense barrage of *StarCraft* stories!

STARCRAFT: FRONTLINE VOLUME 2

COMING NOVEMBER 2008

WARCRAFT® LEGENDS™

VOLUME ONE

SNEAK PEEK

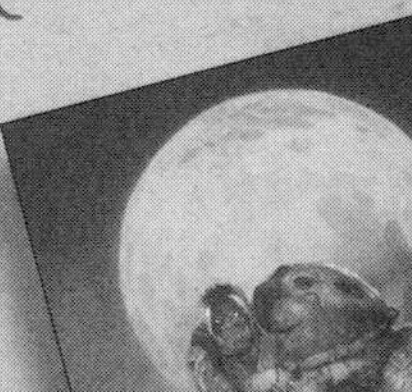

Halsand is a poor farmer struggling to make a living for his wife and three children. With a mangy ox, a rusty plow and a house falling down around him, Halsand's dreams of a brighter future are now tarnished by poverty.

When a party of warriors come to Halsand's farm seeking shelter and a hot meal, they tell him of their plans to drive the Scourge out of Andorhal and reclaim the city for the Alliance. Inspired by their noble cause, Halsand informs them that he knows a shortcut to their rendezvous point at Chillwind Camp, and volunteers to lead them there. For the first time in years, Halsand's heart is filled not with sadness and despair, but with hope for the future...

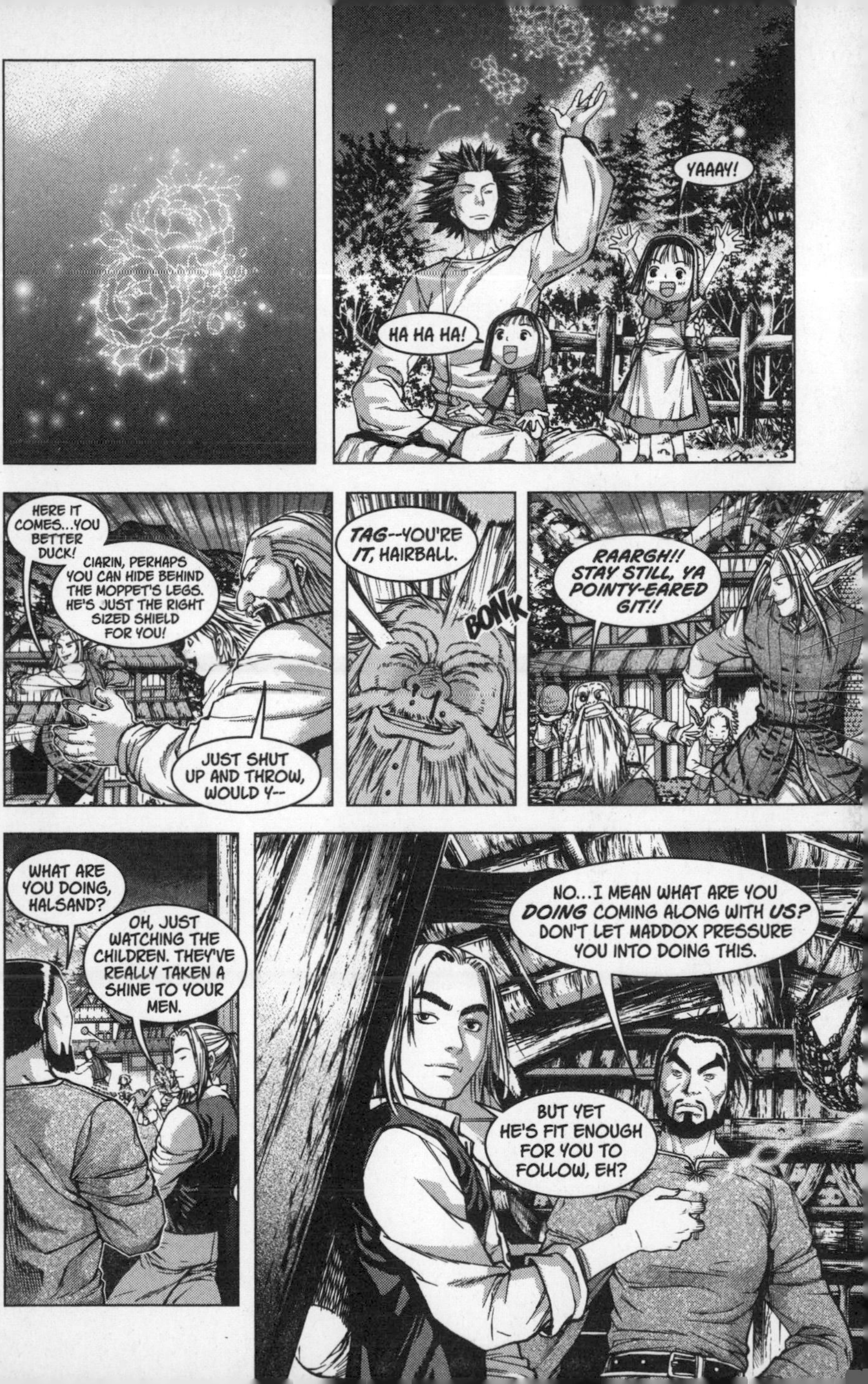
YAAAY!
HA HA HA!
HERE IT COMES...YOU BETTER DUCK!
CIARIN, PERHAPS YOU CAN HIDE BEHIND THE MOPPET'S LEGS. HE'S JUST THE RIGHT SIZED SHIELD FOR YOU!
JUST SHUT UP AND THROW, WOULD Y--
TAG--YOU'RE IT, HAIRBALL.
BONK
RAARGH!! STAY STILL, YA POINTY-EARED GIT!!
WHAT ARE YOU DOING, HALSAND?
OH, JUST WATCHING THE CHILDREN. THEY'VE REALLY TAKEN A SHINE TO YOUR MEN.
NO...I MEAN WHAT ARE YOU DOING COMING ALONG WITH US? DON'T LET MADDOX PRESSURE YOU INTO DOING THIS.
BUT YET HE'S FIT ENOUGH FOR YOU TO FOLLOW, EH?

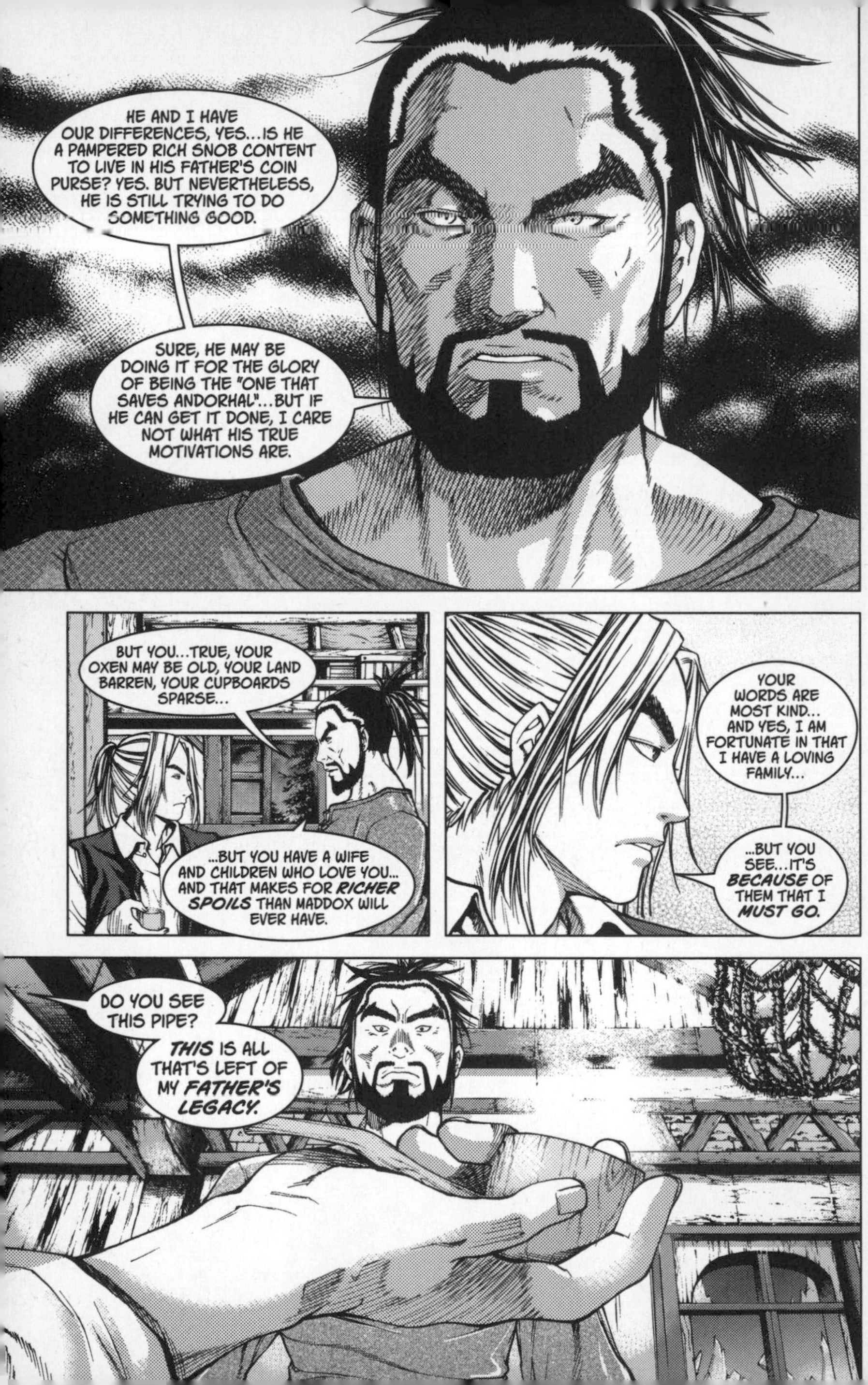
HE AND I HAVE OUR DIFFERENCES, YES…IS HE A PAMPERED RICH SNOB CONTENT TO LIVE IN HIS FATHER'S COIN PURSE? YES. BUT NEVERTHELESS, HE IS STILL TRYING TO DO SOMETHING GOOD.
SURE, HE MAY BE DOING IT FOR THE GLORY OF BEING THE "ONE THAT SAVES ANDORHAL"…BUT IF HE CAN GET IT DONE, I CARE NOT WHAT HIS TRUE MOTIVATIONS ARE.
BUT YOU…TRUE, YOUR OXEN MAY BE OLD, YOUR LAND BARREN, YOUR CUPBOARDS SPARSE…
...BUT YOU HAVE A WIFE AND CHILDREN WHO LOVE YOU… AND THAT MAKES FOR *RICHER SPOILS* THAN MADDOX WILL EVER HAVE.
YOUR WORDS ARE MOST KIND… AND YES, I AM FORTUNATE IN THAT I HAVE A LOVING FAMILY…
...BUT YOU SEE…IT'S *BECAUSE* OF THEM THAT I *MUST GO.*
DO YOU SEE THIS PIPE?
THIS IS ALL THAT'S LEFT OF MY *FATHER'S LEGACY.*

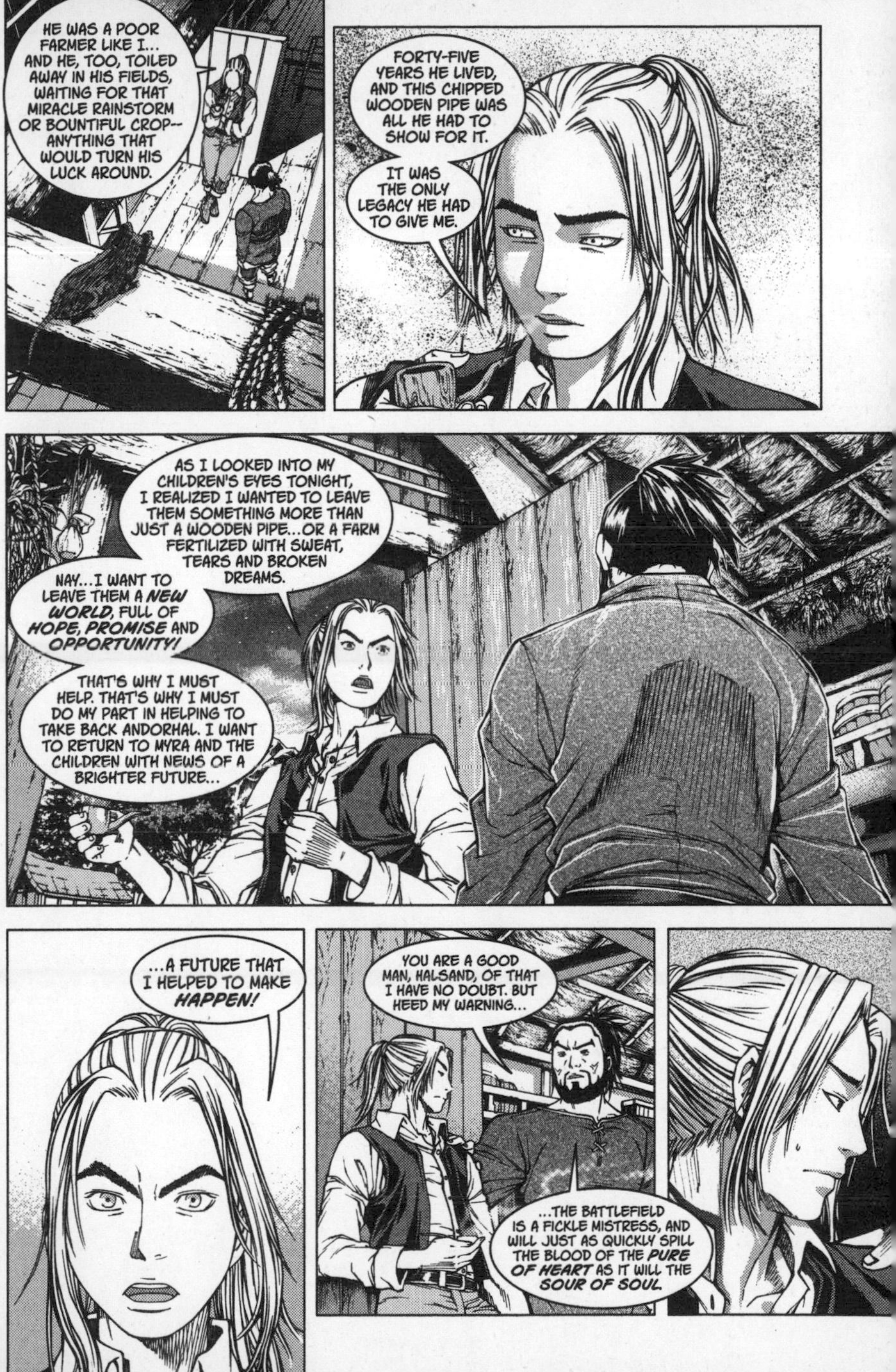
HE WAS A POOR FARMER LIKE I... AND HE, TOO, TOILED AWAY IN HIS FIELDS, WAITING FOR THAT MIRACLE RAINSTORM OR BOUNTIFUL CROP--ANYTHING THAT WOULD TURN HIS LUCK AROUND.
FORTY-FIVE YEARS HE LIVED, AND THIS CHIPPED WOODEN PIPE WAS ALL HE HAD TO SHOW FOR IT.
IT WAS THE ONLY LEGACY HE HAD TO GIVE ME.
AS I LOOKED INTO MY CHILDREN'S EYES TONIGHT, I REALIZED I WANTED TO LEAVE THEM SOMETHING MORE THAN JUST A WOODEN PIPE...OR A FARM FERTILIZED WITH SWEAT, TEARS AND BROKEN DREAMS.
NAY...I WANT TO LEAVE THEM A ***NEW WORLD***, FULL OF ***HOPE, PROMISE*** AND ***OPPORTUNITY!***
THAT'S WHY I MUST HELP. THAT'S WHY I MUST DO MY PART IN HELPING TO TAKE BACK ANDORHAL. I WANT TO RETURN TO MYRA AND THE CHILDREN WITH NEWS OF A BRIGHTER FUTURE...
...A FUTURE THAT I HELPED TO MAKE ***HAPPEN!***
YOU ARE A GOOD MAN, HALSAND, OF THAT I HAVE NO DOUBT. BUT HEED MY WARNING...
...THE BATTLEFIELD IS A FICKLE MISTRESS, AND WILL JUST AS QUICKLY SPILL THE BLOOD OF THE ***PURE OF HEART*** AS IT WILL THE ***SOUR OF SOUL.***

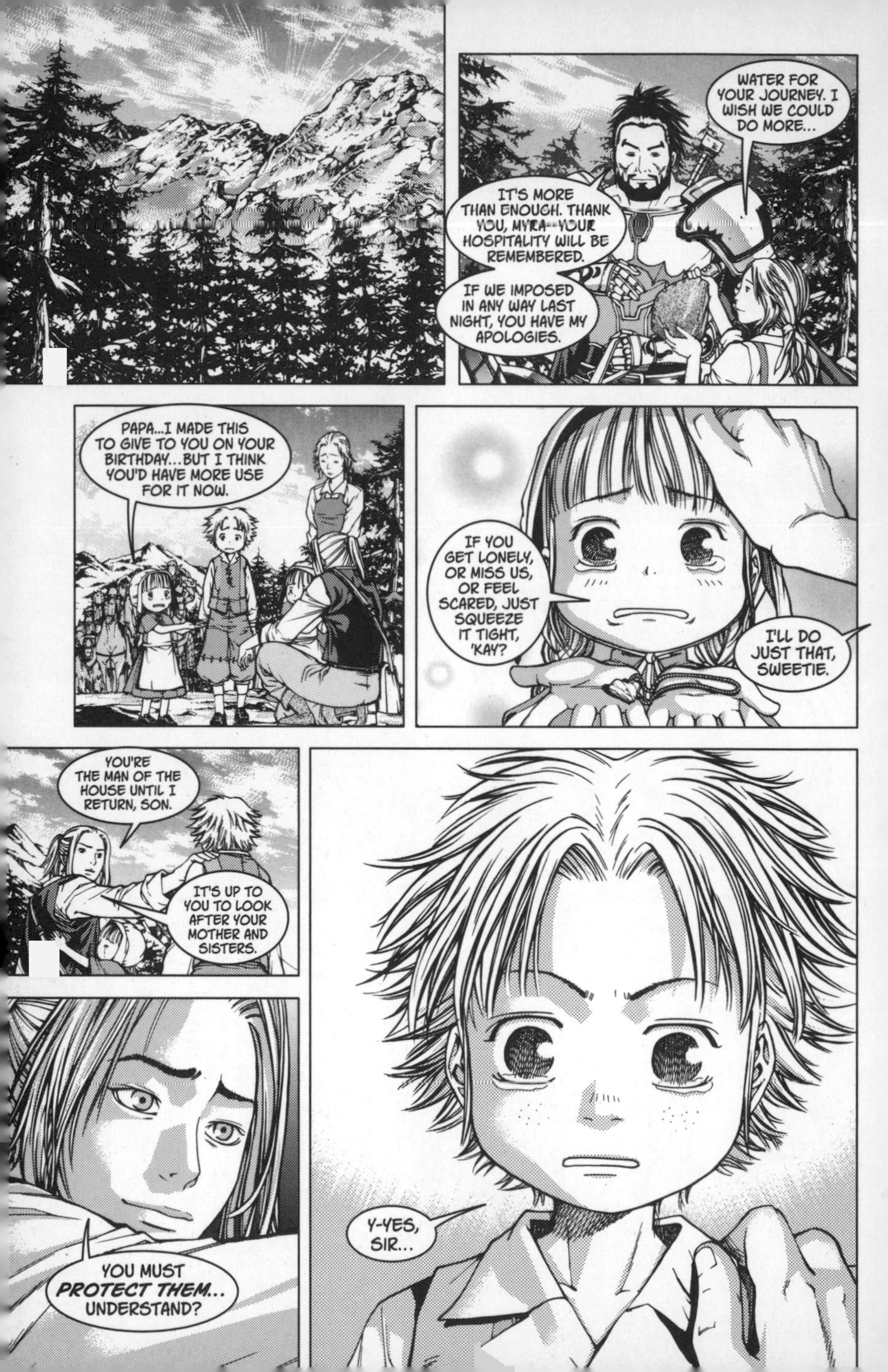
WATER FOR YOUR JOURNEY. I WISH WE COULD DO MORE...
IT'S MORE THAN ENOUGH. THANK YOU, MYRA--YOUR HOSPITALITY WILL BE REMEMBERED.
IF WE IMPOSED IN ANY WAY LAST NIGHT, YOU HAVE MY APOLOGIES.
PAPA...I MADE THIS TO GIVE TO YOU ON YOUR BIRTHDAY...BUT I THINK YOU'D HAVE MORE USE FOR IT NOW.
IF YOU GET LONELY, OR MISS US, OR FEEL SCARED, JUST SQUEEZE IT TIGHT, 'KAY?
I'LL DO JUST THAT, SWEETIE.
YOU'RE THE MAN OF THE HOUSE UNTIL I RETURN, SON.
IT'S UP TO YOU TO LOOK AFTER YOUR MOTHER AND SISTERS.
YOU MUST *PROTECT THEM...* UNDERSTAND?
Y-YES, SIR...

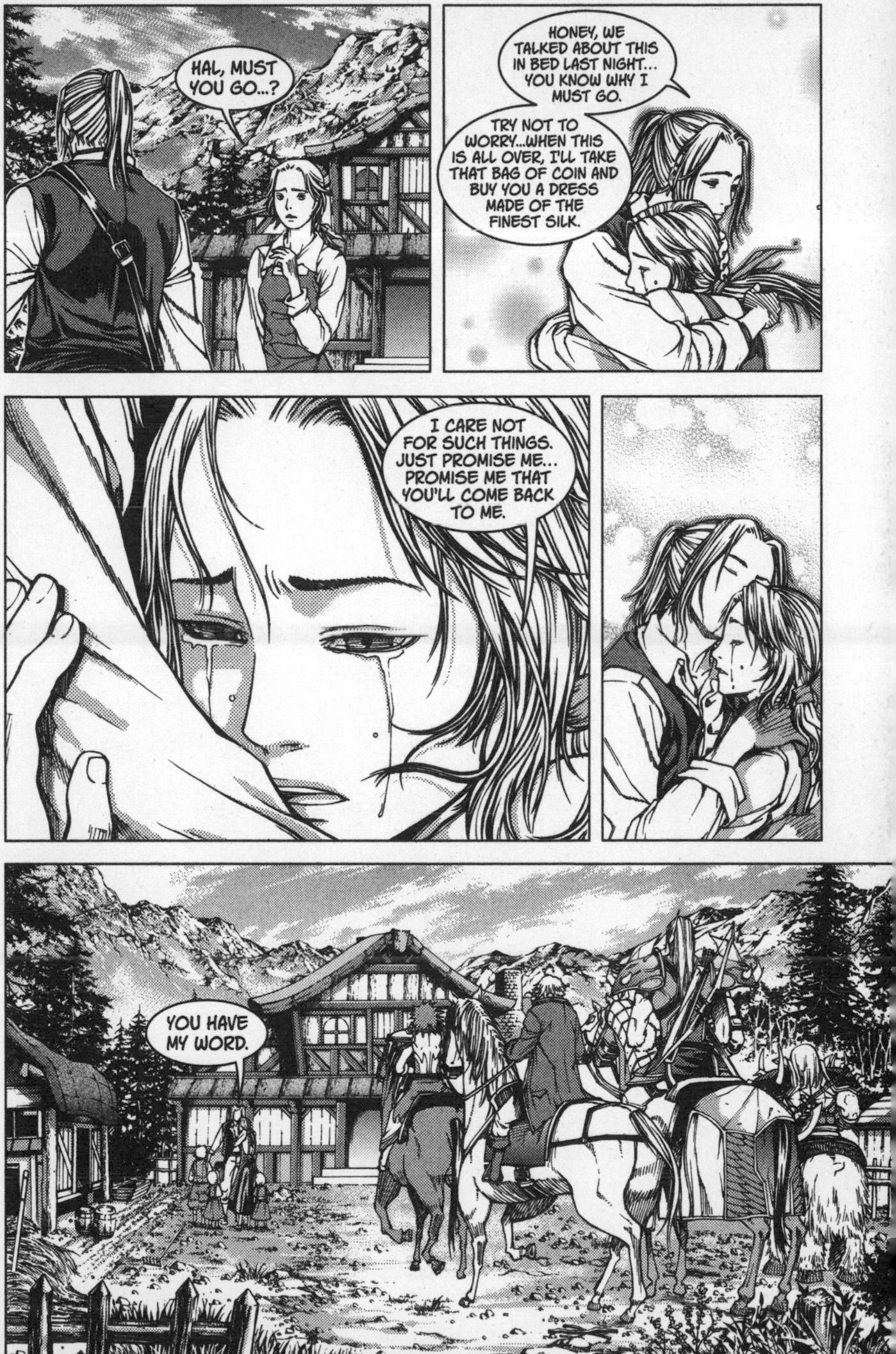
HAL, MUST YOU GO...?
HONEY, WE TALKED ABOUT THIS IN BED LAST NIGHT... YOU KNOW WHY I MUST GO.
TRY NOT TO WORRY...WHEN THIS IS ALL OVER, I'LL TAKE THAT BAG OF COIN AND BUY YOU A DRESS MADE OF THE FINEST SILK.
I CARE NOT FOR SUCH THINGS. JUST PROMISE ME... PROMISE ME THAT YOU'LL COME BACK TO ME.
YOU HAVE MY WORD.

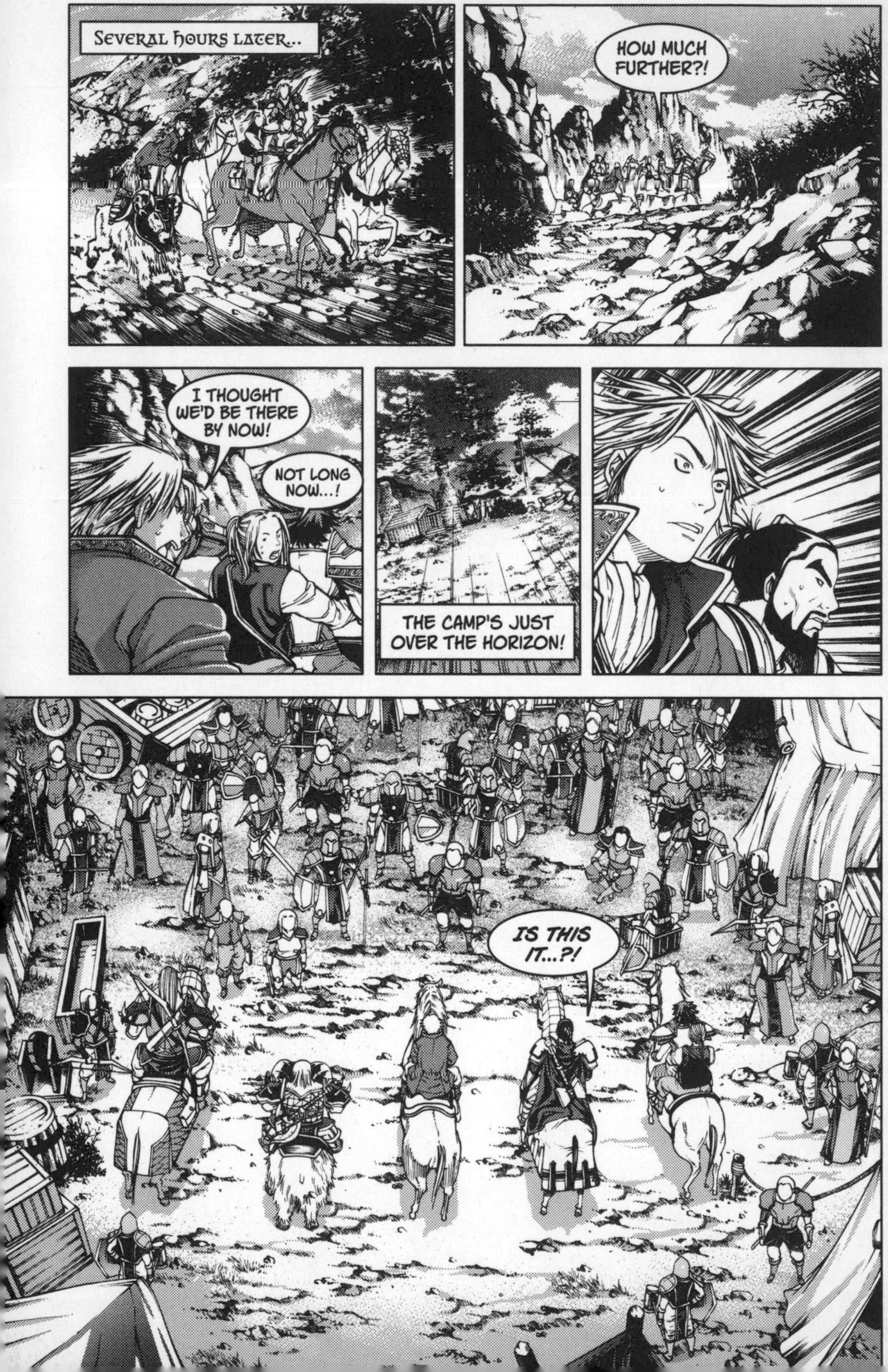
SEVERAL HOURS LATER...
HOW MUCH FURTHER?!
I THOUGHT WE'D BE THERE BY NOW!
NOT LONG NOW...!
THE CAMP'S JUST OVER THE HORIZON!
IS THIS IT...?!

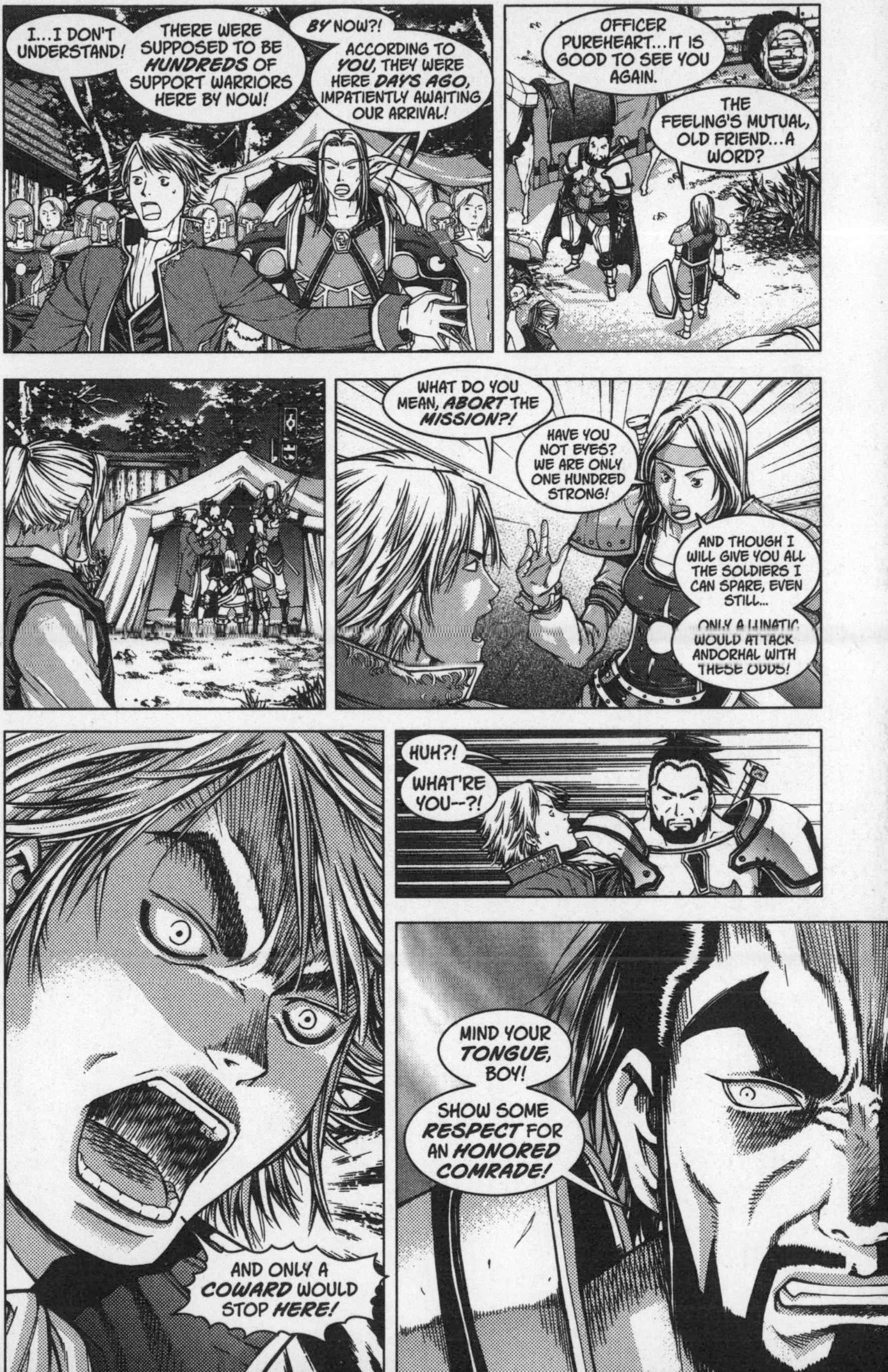
I...I DON'T UNDERSTAND!
THERE WERE SUPPOSED TO BE HUNDREDS OF SUPPORT WARRIORS HERE BY NOW!
BY NOW?!
ACCORDING TO YOU, THEY WERE HERE DAYS AGO, IMPATIENTLY AWAITING OUR ARRIVAL!
OFFICER PUREHEART...IT IS GOOD TO SEE YOU AGAIN.
THE FEELING'S MUTUAL, OLD FRIEND...A WORD?
WHAT DO YOU MEAN, ABORT THE MISSION?!
HAVE YOU NOT EYES? WE ARE ONLY ONE HUNDRED STRONG!
AND THOUGH I WILL GIVE YOU ALL THE SOLDIERS I CAN SPARE, EVEN STILL...
ONLY A LUNATIC WOULD ATTACK ANDORHAL WITH THESE ODDS!
AND ONLY A COWARD WOULD STOP HERE!
HUH?!
WHAT'RE YOU--?!
MIND YOUR TONGUE, BOY!
SHOW SOME RESPECT FOR AN HONORED COMRADE!

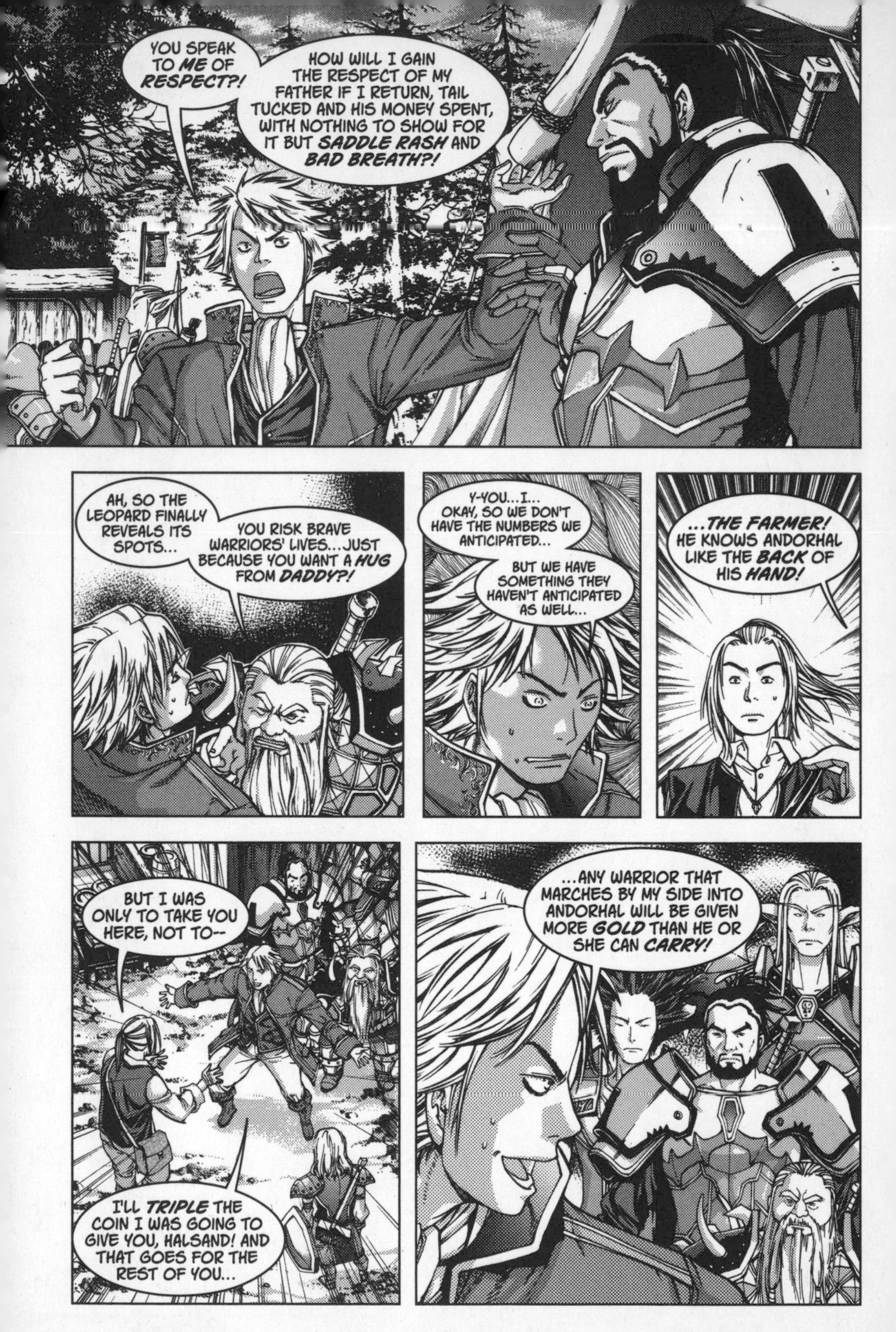
YOU SPEAK TO ME OF RESPECT?!
HOW WILL I GAIN THE RESPECT OF MY FATHER IF I RETURN, TAIL TUCKED AND HIS MONEY SPENT, WITH NOTHING TO SHOW FOR IT BUT SADDLE RASH AND BAD BREATH?!
AH, SO THE LEOPARD FINALLY REVEALS ITS SPOTS...
YOU RISK BRAVE WARRIORS' LIVES...JUST BECAUSE YOU WANT A HUG FROM DADDY?!
Y-YOU...I... OKAY, SO WE DON'T HAVE THE NUMBERS WE ANTICIPATED...
BUT WE HAVE SOMETHING THEY HAVEN'T ANTICIPATED AS WELL...
...THE FARMER! HE KNOWS ANDORHAL LIKE THE BACK OF HIS HAND!
BUT I WAS ONLY TO TAKE YOU HERE, NOT TO--
I'LL TRIPLE THE COIN I WAS GOING TO GIVE YOU, HALSAND! AND THAT GOES FOR THE REST OF YOU...
...ANY WARRIOR THAT MARCHES BY MY SIDE INTO ANDORHAL WILL BE GIVEN MORE GOLD THAN HE OR SHE CAN CARRY!

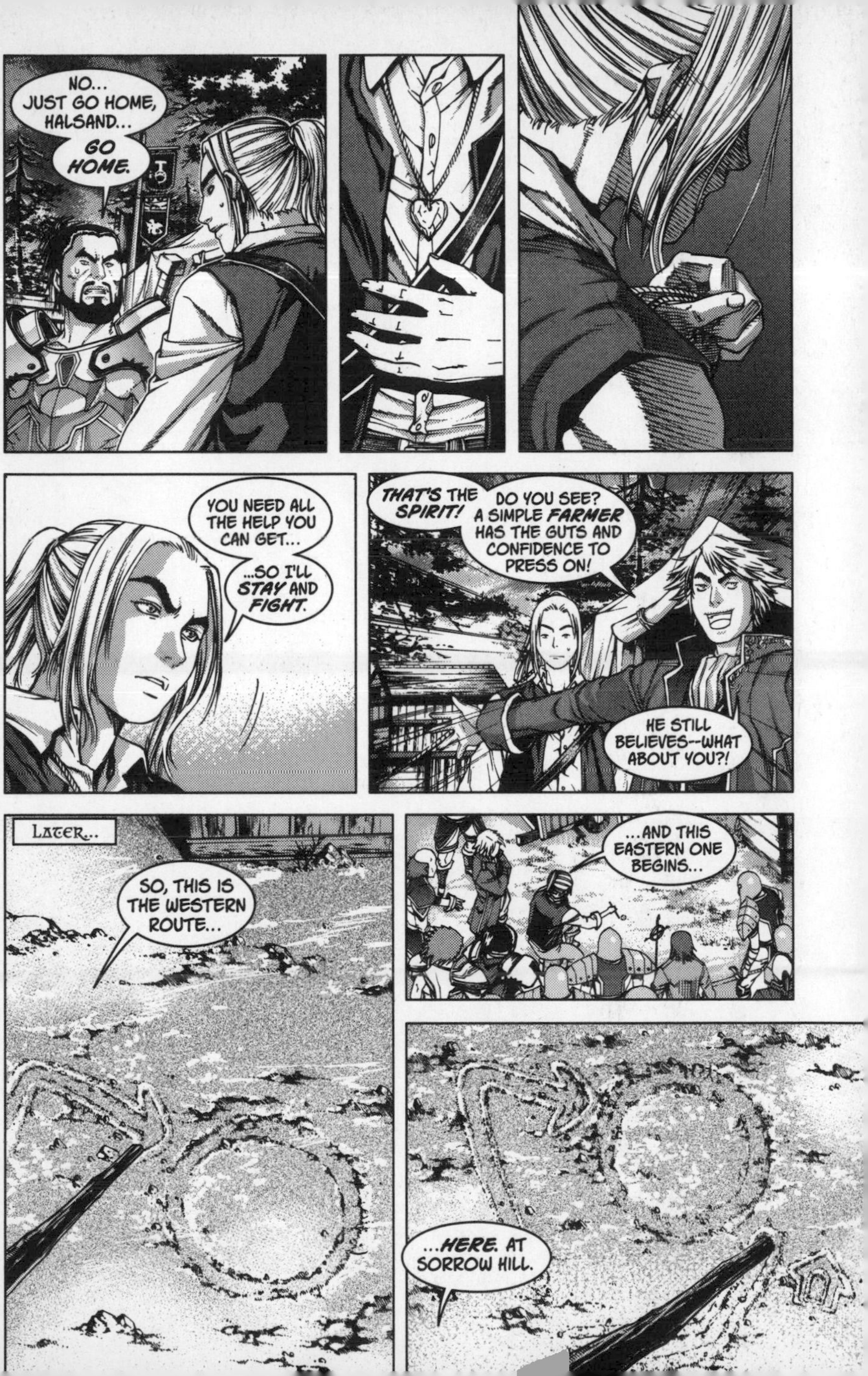
NO... JUST GO HOME, HALSAND...
GO HOME.
YOU NEED ALL THE HELP YOU CAN GET...
...SO I'LL STAY AND FIGHT.
THAT'S THE SPIRIT!
DO YOU SEE? A SIMPLE FARMER HAS THE GUTS AND CONFIDENCE TO PRESS ON!
HE STILL BELIEVES--WHAT ABOUT YOU?!
LATER...
SO, THIS IS THE WESTERN ROUTE...
...AND THIS EASTERN ONE BEGINS...
...HERE. AT SORROW HILL.

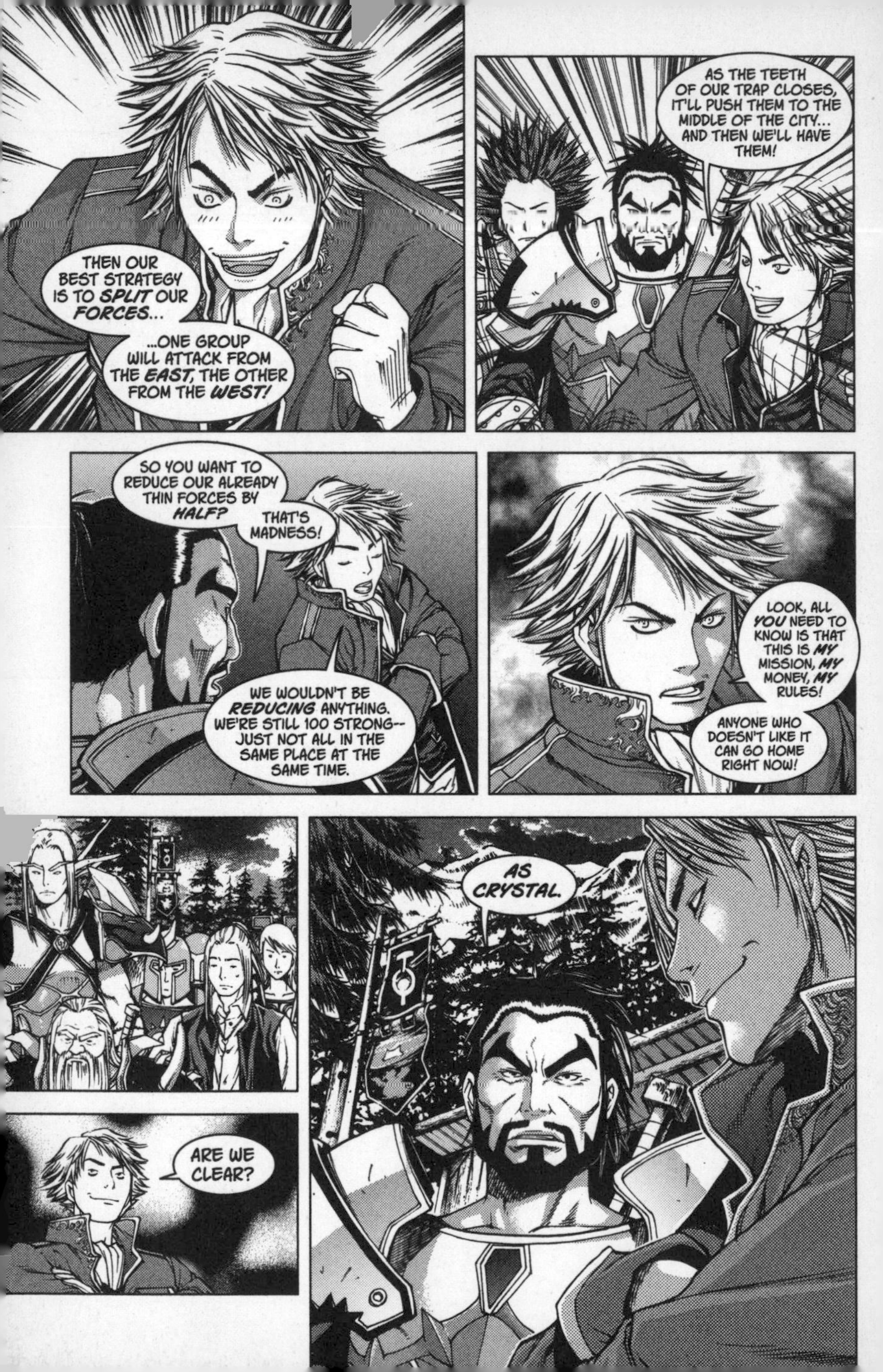
THEN OUR BEST STRATEGY IS TO SPLIT OUR FORCES...
...ONE GROUP WILL ATTACK FROM THE EAST, THE OTHER FROM THE WEST!
AS THE TEETH OF OUR TRAP CLOSES, IT'LL PUSH THEM TO THE MIDDLE OF THE CITY... AND THEN WE'LL HAVE THEM!
SO YOU WANT TO REDUCE OUR ALREADY THIN FORCES BY HALF?
THAT'S MADNESS!
WE WOULDN'T BE REDUCING ANYTHING. WE'RE STILL 100 STRONG-- JUST NOT ALL IN THE SAME PLACE AT THE SAME TIME.
LOOK, ALL YOU NEED TO KNOW IS THAT THIS IS MY MISSION, MY MONEY, MY RULES!
ANYONE WHO DOESN'T LIKE IT CAN GO HOME RIGHT NOW!
ARE WE CLEAR?
AS CRYSTAL.

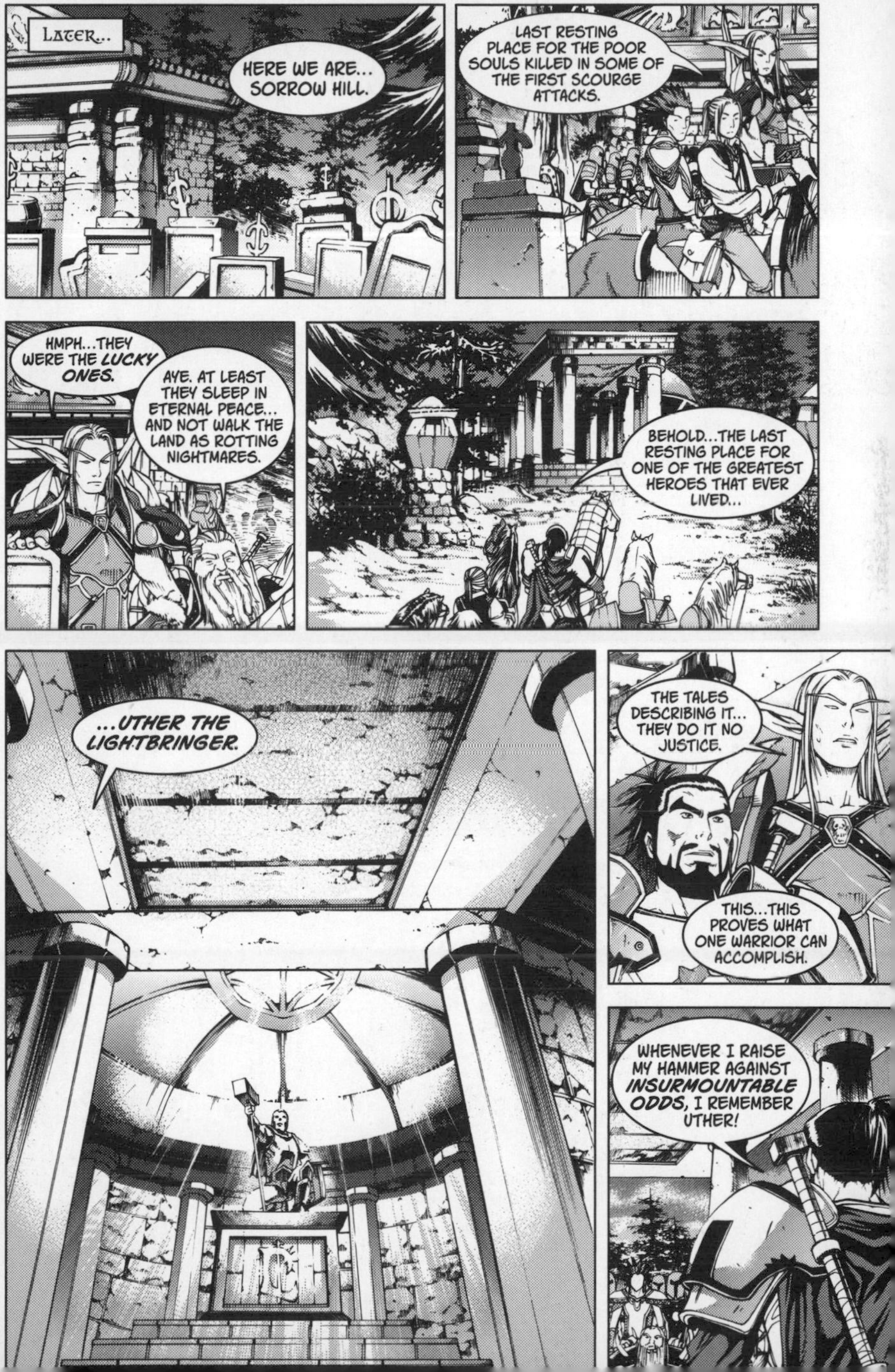
LATER...
HERE WE ARE... SORROW HILL.
LAST RESTING PLACE FOR THE POOR SOULS KILLED IN SOME OF THE FIRST SCOURGE ATTACKS.
HMPH...THEY WERE THE *LUCKY ONES.*
AYE. AT LEAST THEY SLEEP IN ETERNAL PEACE... AND NOT WALK THE LAND AS ROTTING NIGHTMARES.
BEHOLD...THE LAST RESTING PLACE FOR ONE OF THE GREATEST HEROES THAT EVER LIVED...
...UTHER THE LIGHTBRINGER.
THE TALES DESCRIBING IT... THEY DO IT NO JUSTICE.
THIS...THIS PROVES WHAT ONE WARRIOR CAN ACCOMPLISH.
WHENEVER I RAISE MY HAMMER AGAINST *INSURMOUNTABLE ODDS*, I REMEMBER UTHER!

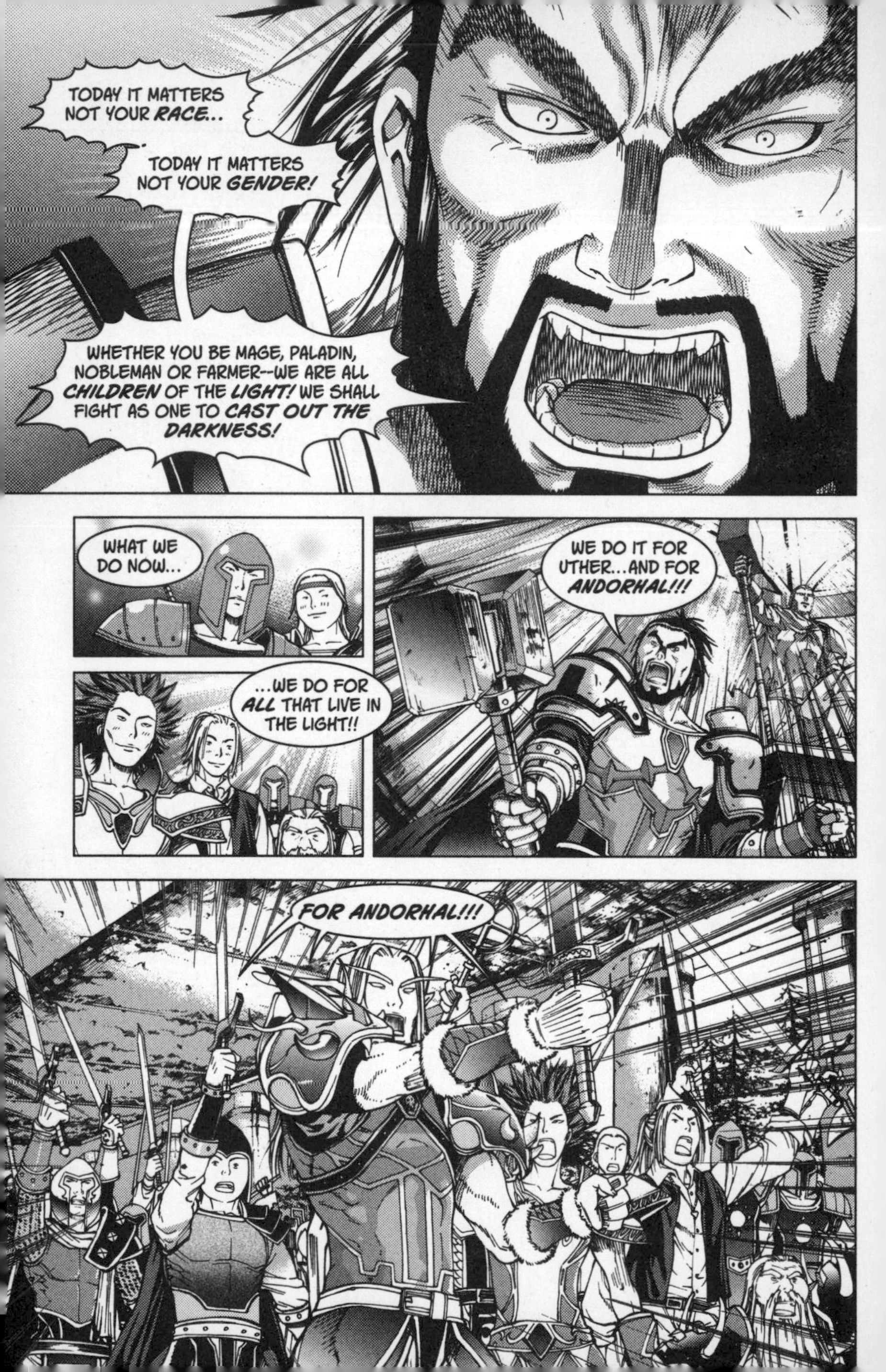
TODAY IT MATTERS NOT YOUR *RACE...*
TODAY IT MATTERS NOT YOUR *GENDER!*
WHETHER YOU BE MAGE, PALADIN, NOBLEMAN OR FARMER--WE ARE ALL *CHILDREN* OF THE *LIGHT!* WE SHALL FIGHT AS ONE TO *CAST OUT THE DARKNESS!*
WHAT WE DO NOW...
...WE DO FOR *ALL* THAT LIVE IN THE LIGHT!!
WE DO IT FOR UTHER...AND FOR *ANDORHAL!!!*
FOR ANDORHAL!!!

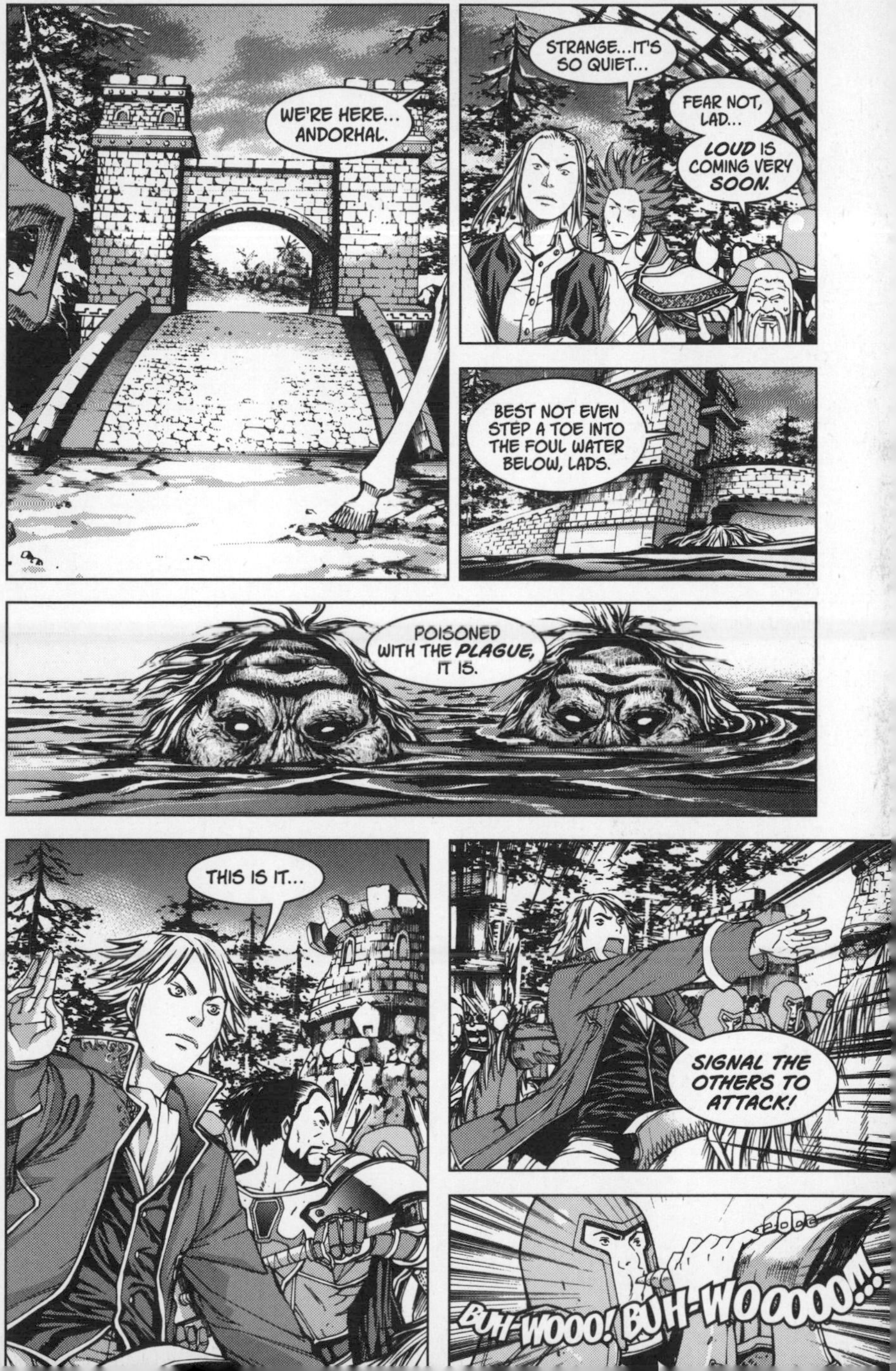
WE'RE HERE... ANDORHAL.
STRANGE...IT'S SO QUIET...
FEAR NOT, LAD... *LOUD* IS COMING VERY *SOON.*
BEST NOT EVEN STEP A TOE INTO THE FOUL WATER BELOW, LADS.
POISONED WITH THE *PLAGUE,* IT IS.
THIS IS IT...
SIGNAL THE OTHERS TO ATTACK!
BUH-WOOO! BUH-WOOOOO!!...

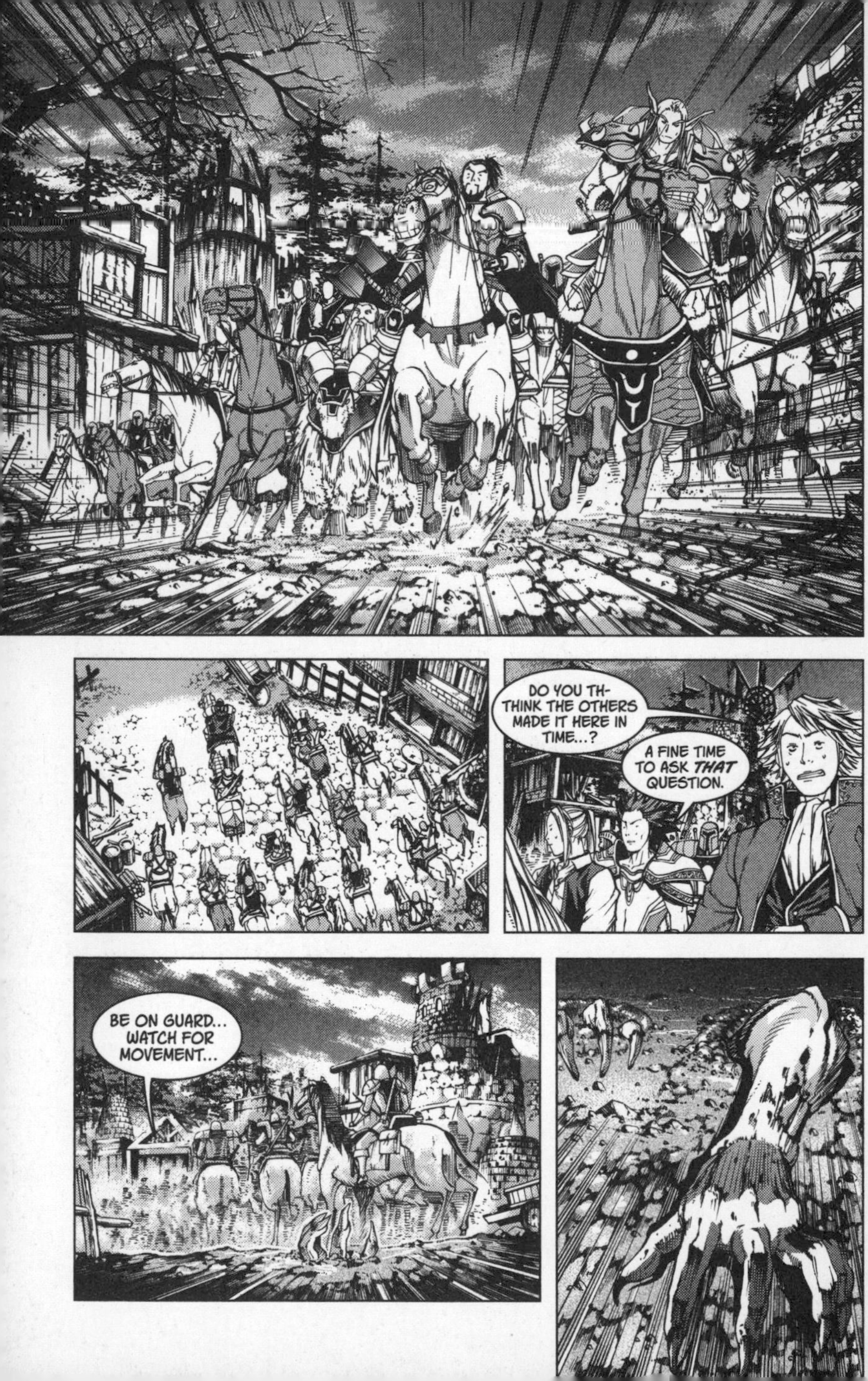
DO YOU TH-THINK THE OTHERS MADE IT HERE IN TIME...?
A FINE TIME TO ASK *THAT* QUESTION.
BE ON GUARD... WATCH FOR MOVEMENT...

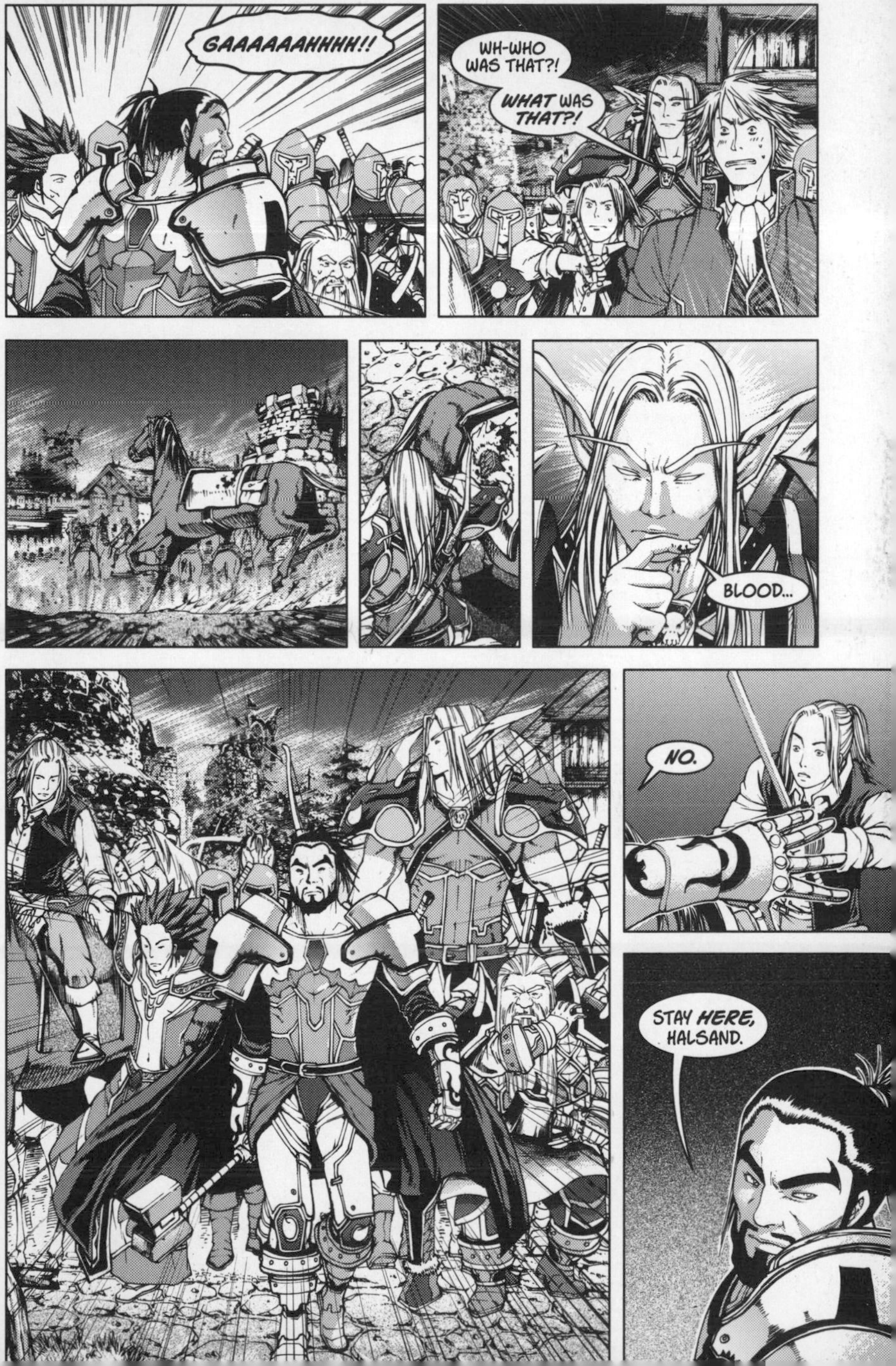
GAAAAAAHHHH!!
WH-WHO WAS THAT?!
WHAT WAS THAT?!
BLOOD...
NO.
STAY HERE, HALSAND.

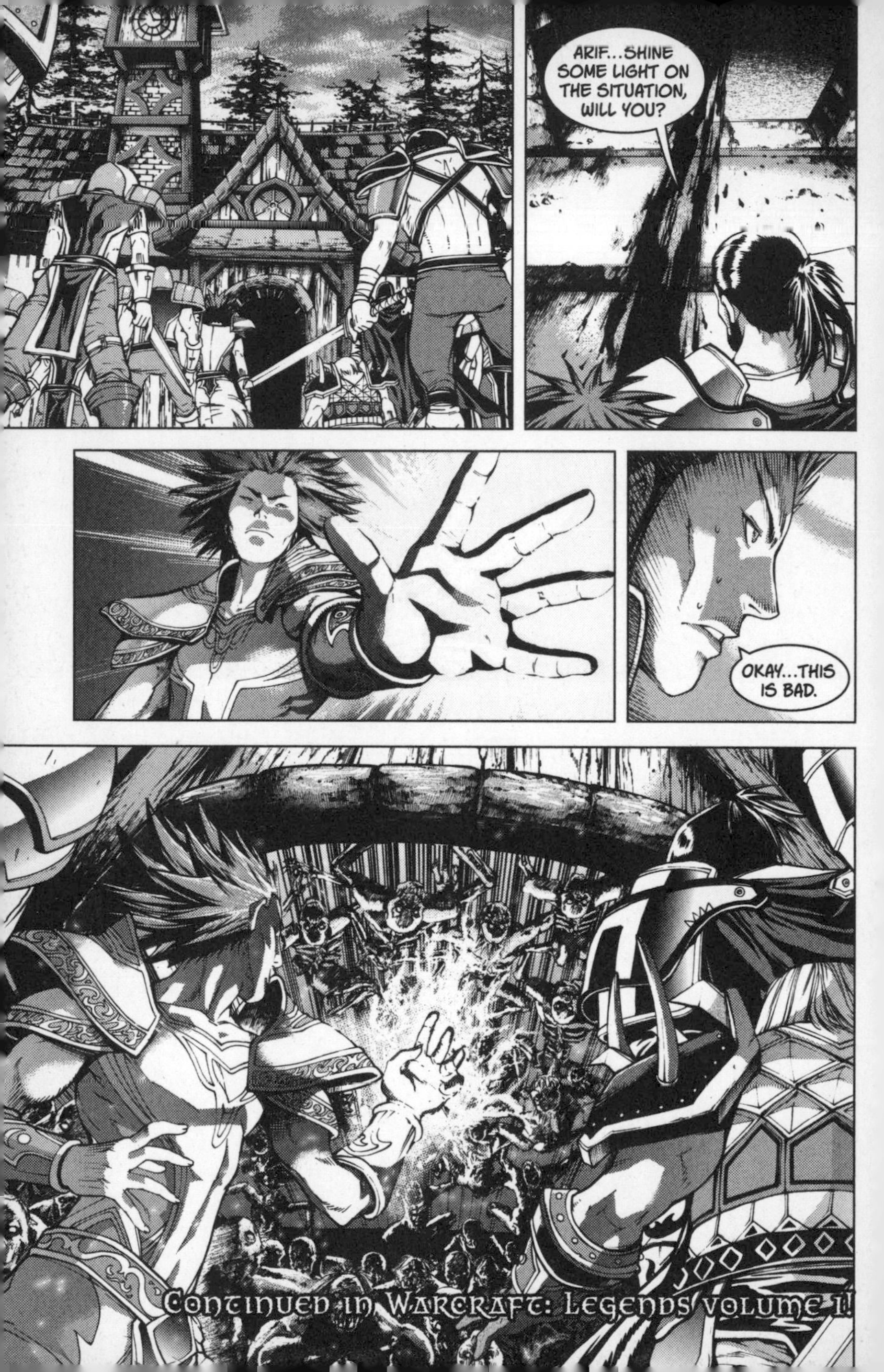
ARIF...SHINE SOME LIGHT ON THE SITUATION, WILL YOU?
OKAY...THIS IS BAD.
Continued in Warcraft: Legends volume 1!

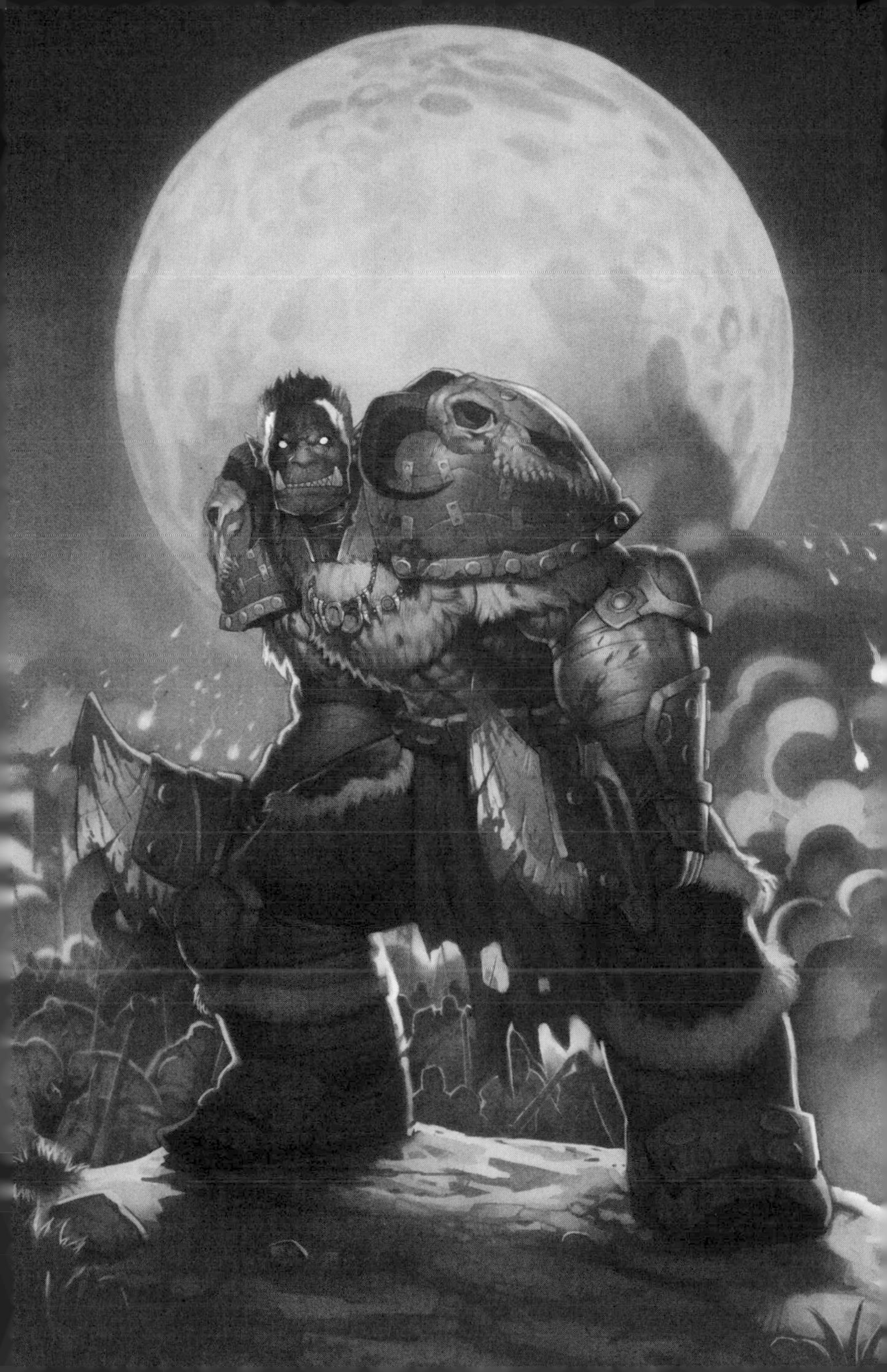

WARCRAFT: LEGENDS / STARCRAFT: FRONTLINE

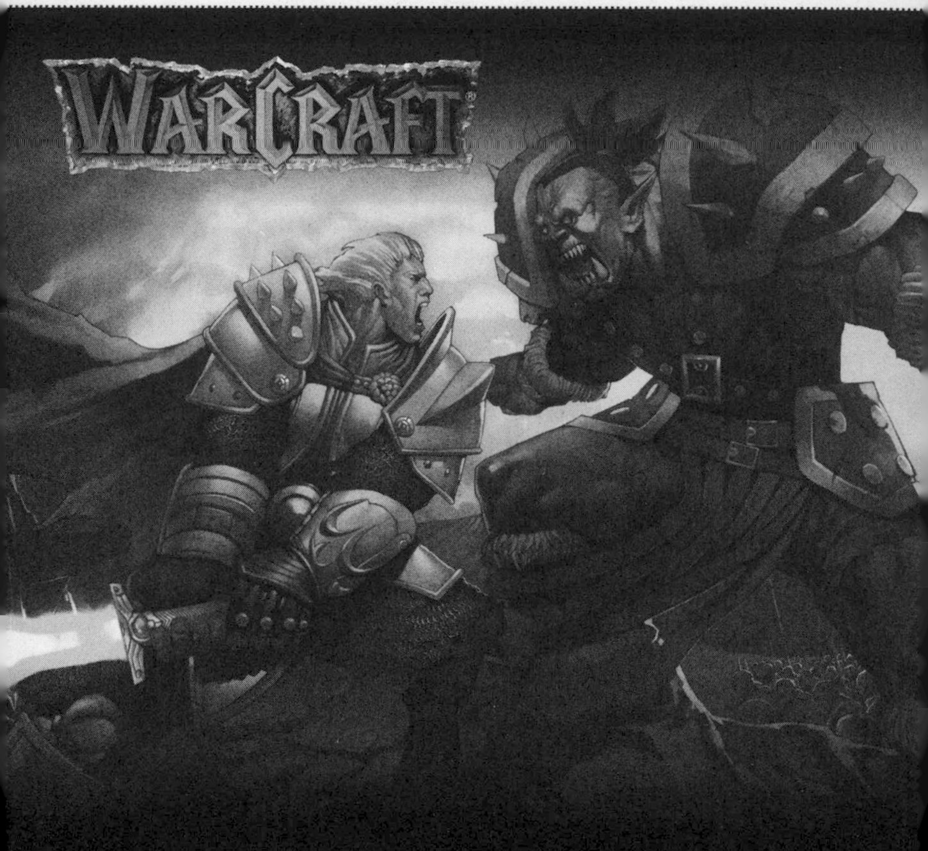
WARCRAFT

NEW MANGA BASED ON THE BESTSELLING VIDEO GAMES

Warcraft: Legends *Volume 1*

Check out www.TOKYOPOP.com/WARCRAFT
for exclusive news, updates and free downloadable art.

BUY IT AT WWW.TOKYOPOP.COM/SHOP

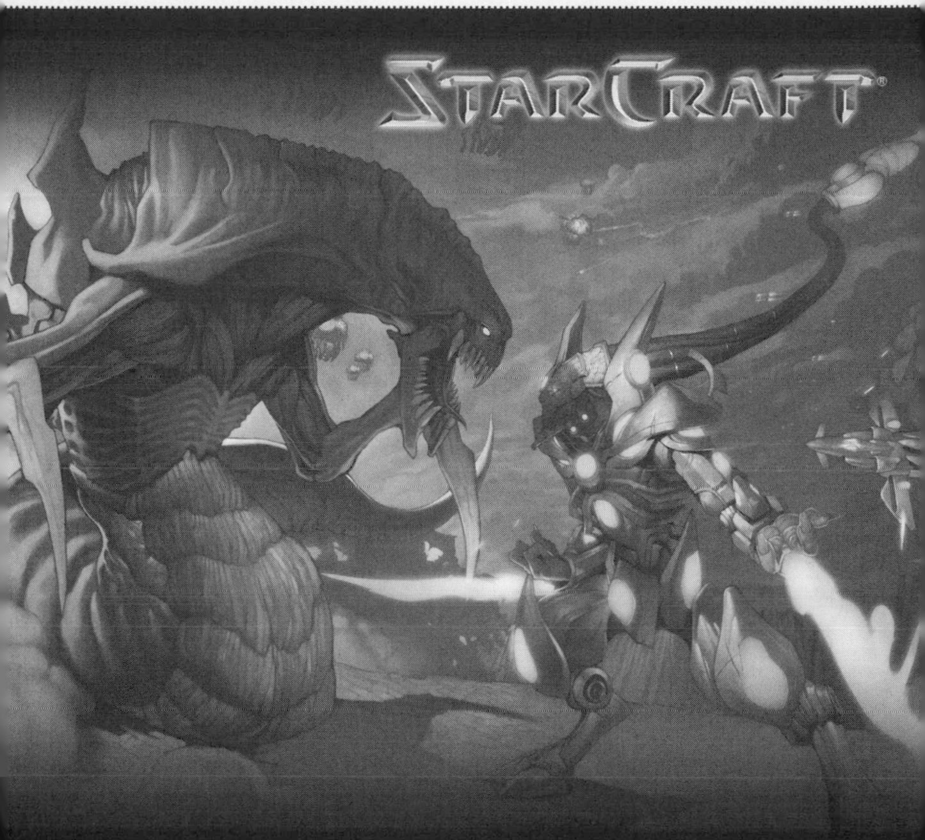
StarCraft®

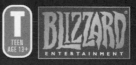

Actual Gameplay.

NO. I'D RATHER KILL RATS.

With millions of players online, World of Warcraft has made gaming
history — and now's it's never been easier to join the adventure.
Simply visit **www.warcraft.com**, download the FREE TRIAL and join
thousands of mighty heroes for ten days of bold online adventure.
A World Awaits...

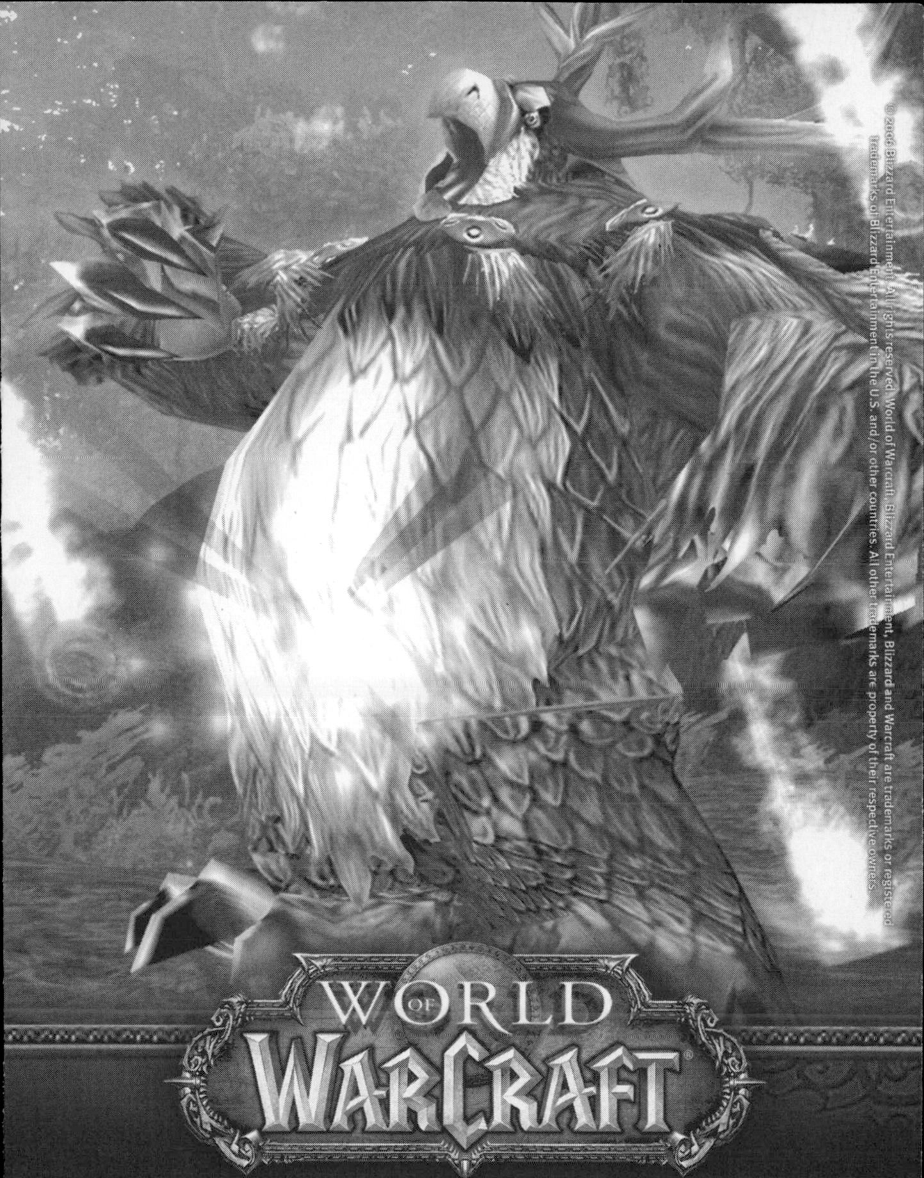
© 2006 Blizzard Entertainment. All rights reserved. World of Warcraft, Blizzard Entertainment, Blizzard and Warcraft are trademarks or registered trademarks of Blizzard Entertainment in the U.S. and/or other countries. All other trademarks are property of their respective owners.
WORLD OF WARCRAFT

EPIC BATTLES
IN THE PALM OF YOUR HAND

World of WarCraft
MINIATURES GAME

World of Warcraft® Collectible Miniatures Game

Premium miniatures with detailed paints designed by Studio McV

Standard and deluxe starter sets plus three-figure boosters

Innovative game play utilizing the unique detachable UBase

Coming Fall 2008!

For more information, visit

WoWMINIS.COM

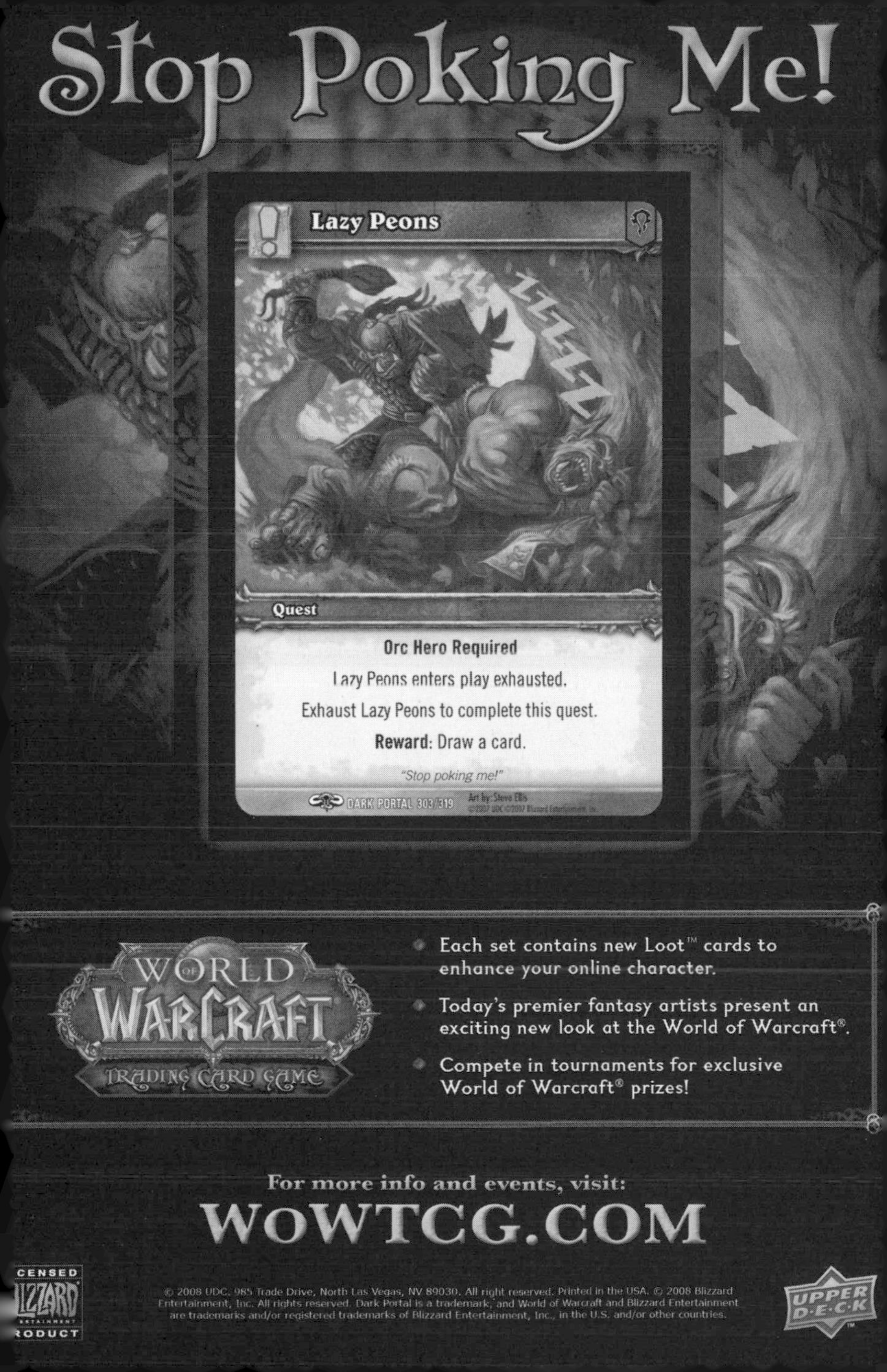
Stop Poking Me!
Lazy Peons
Quest
Orc Hero Required
Lazy Peons enters play exhausted.
Exhaust Lazy Peons to complete this quest.
Reward: Draw a card.
"Stop poking me!"
DARK PORTAL 303/319
Art by: Steve Ellis
WORLD OF WARCRAFT
TRADING CARD GAME
Each set contains new Loot™ cards to enhance your online character.
Today's premier fantasy artists present an exciting new look at the World of Warcraft®.
Compete in tournaments for exclusive World of Warcraft® prizes!
For more info and events, visit:
WoWTCG.COM
© 2008 UDC. 985 Trade Drive, North Las Vegas, NV 89030. All right reserved. Printed in the USA. © 2008 Blizzard Entertainment, Inc. All rights reserved. Dark Portal is a trademark, and World of Warcraft and Blizzard Entertainment are trademarks and/or registered trademarks of Blizzard Entertainment, Inc., in the U.S. and/or other countries.
UPPER DECK

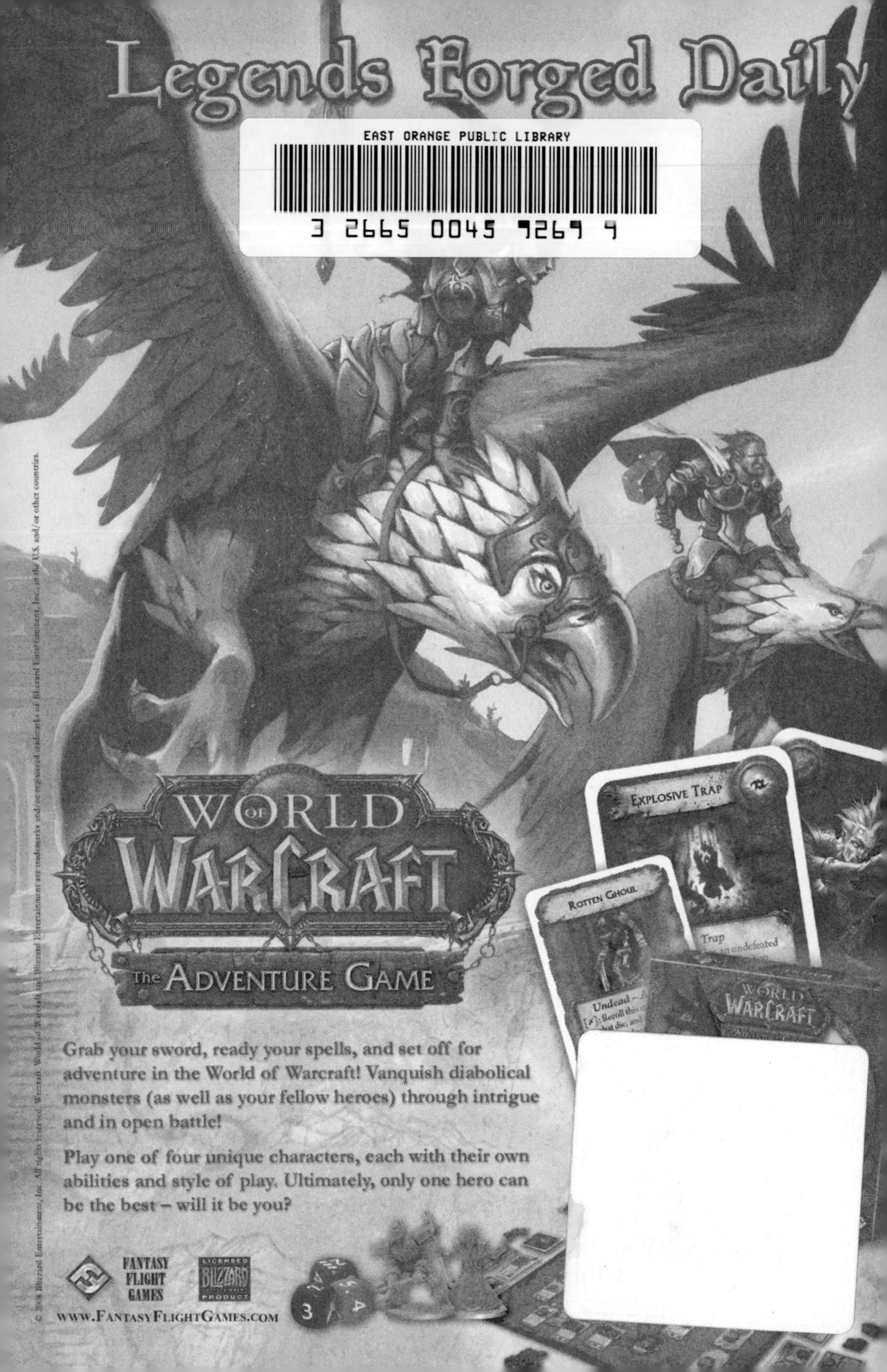
Legends Forged Daily
WORLD OF WARCRAFT
The ADVENTURE GAME
EXPLOSIVE TRAP
ROTTEN GHOUL
Grab your sword, ready your spells, and set off for adventure in the World of Warcraft! Vanquish diabolical monsters (as well as your fellow heroes) through intrigue and in open battle!
Play one of four unique characters, each with their own abilities and style of play. Ultimately, only one hero can be the best – will it be you?
FANTASY FLIGHT GAMES
LICENSED BLIZZARD PRODUCT
WWW.FANTASYFLIGHTGAMES.COM
© 2008 Blizzard Entertainment, Inc. All rights reserved. Warcraft, World of Warcraft and Blizzard Entertainment are trademarks and/or registered trademarks of Blizzard Entertainment, Inc., in the U.S. and/or other countries.